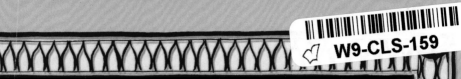

STEPHEN KING

THE DARK TOWER
~ THE GUNSLINGER ~

LAST SHOTS

THE DARK TOWER
~THE GUNSLINGER~

LAST SHOTS

CREATIVE DIRECTOR AND EXECUTIVE DIRECTOR
STEPHEN KING

PLOTTING AND CONSULTATION;
SCRIPT (SHEEMIE'S TALE)
ROBIN FURTH

SCRIPT (EVIL GROUND & SO FELL LORD PERTH)
PETER DAVID

ARTIST
RICHARD ISANOVE

WITH COLORIST
DEAN WHITE (EVIL GROUND #1 PAGE 1-7; #2 PAGE 20)

LETTERING
VC'S JOE SABINO

PRODUCTION
IDETTE WINECOOR

COVER ART
RICHARD ISANOVE

DARK TOWER: THE GUNSLINGER — LAST SHOTS. Contains material originally published in magazine form as DARK TOWER: THE GUNSLINGER — SHEEMIE'S TALE #1-2, DARK TOWER
GUNSLINGER — EVIL GROUND #1-2 and DARK TOWER: THE GUNSLINGER — SO FELL LORD PERTH #1. Second printing 2014. ISBN# 978-0-7851-4941-5. Published by MARVEL WORLD
INC., a subsidiary of MARVEL ENTERTAINMENT, LLC. OFFICE OF PUBLICATION: 135 West 50th Street, New York, NY 10020. Copyright © 2013 Stephen King. All rights reserved. All char
featured in this issue and the distinctive names and likenesses thereof, and all related indicia are trademarks of Stephen King. No similarity between any of the names, characters, person
or institutions in this magazine with those of any living or dead person or institution is intended, and any such similarity which may exist is purely coincidental. Marvel and its logos are T
Marvel Characters, Inc. **Printed in Canada.** ALAN FINE, EVP - Office of the President, Marvel Worldwide, Inc. and EVP & CMO Marvel Characters B.V.; DAN BUCKLEY, Publisher & President
Animation & Digital Divisions; JOE QUESADA, Chief Creative Officer; TOM BREVOORT, SVP of Publishing; DAVID BOGART, SVP of Operations & Procurement, Publishing; C.B. CEBULSKI,
Creator & Content Development; DAVID GABRIEL, SVP Print, Sales & Marketing; JIM O'KEEFE, VP of Operations & Logistics; DAN CARR, Executive Director of Publishing Technology; SUSAN C
Editorial Operations Manager; ALEX MORALES, Publishing Operations Manager; STAN LEE, Chairman Emeritus. For information regarding advertising in Marvel Comics or on Marvel.com,
contact Niza Disla, Director of Marvel Partnerships, at ndisla@marvel.com. For Marvel subscription inquiries, please call 800-217-9158. **Manufactured between 1/29/2014 and 3/3/2**
SOLISCO PRINTERS, SCOTT, QC, CANADA.

1 0 9 8 7 6 5 4 3 2

ASSISTANT EDITORS
ELLIE PYLE & JON MOISAN

CONSULTING EDITOR
RALPH MACCHIO

EDITORS
SANA AMANAT & BILL ROSEMANN

COLLECTION EDITOR
MARK D. BEAZLEY

ASSOCIATE MANAGING EDITOR
ALEX STARBUCK

EDITOR, SPECIAL PROJECTS
JENNIFER GRÜNWALD

SENIOR EDITOR, SPECIAL PROJECTS
JEFF YOUNGQUIST

SVP PRINT, SALES & MARKETING
DAVID GABRIEL

BOOK DESIGN
PATRICK McGRATH

EDITOR IN CHIEF
AXEL ALONSO

CHIEF CREATIVE OFFICER
JOE QUESADA

PUBLISHER
DAN BUCKLEY

SPECIAL THANKS TO
MATHIEU ISANOVE

SPECIAL THANKS TO
CHUCK VERRILL, MARSHA DEFILIPPO, BARBARA ANN McINTYRE, BRIAN STARK,
JIM NAUSEDAS, JIM McCANN, ARUNE SINGH, JEFF SUTER, JOHN BARBER, LAUREN
SANKOVITCH, MIKE HORWITZ, CHARLIE BECKERMAN, CHRIS ELIOPOULOS &
RUWAN JAYATILLEKE

"In a world that has moved on"…So did Stephen King succinctly describe Mid-World. And now, the creative staff of the DARK TOWER series itself moves on to other projects with the stellar completion of this series of one-shot stories. The journey from inception to completion has been long and truly satisfying. Rarely has a project so neatly crystallized. And rarely have I been privileged to travel with such a splendid ka-tet for so long.

Robin Furth's unparalleled grasp of the subject matter allowed her to confidently lead us through the multiverse of the Dark Tower. Peter David's sublime scripting gave voice to the many characters who populate Mid-World and environs. The visual iconography was pioneered by Jae Lee and Richard Isanove. Jae was not an artist to be tied down long on any single project, but his desire to explore the graphic possibilities of this realm kept him with us through the initial arcs. A variety of pencilers too numerous to mention ably succeeded Jae Lee, each putting their own distinctive stamp on King's magnum opus. I thank them all for their contributions. Richard Isanove, who has so powerfully illustrated these recent one-shots, has been the artistic backbone of the series since issue one, lo those many years ago. His limitless palette and formidable draftsmanship gave Mid-World an awesome, otherworldly quality that always distinguished the series from anything else being published.

Those who stepped in to oversee the project along the way deserve mention, including Sana Amanat and currently the redoubtable Bill Rosemann. They are the people behind the curtain who make the entire enterprise run smoothly. Farther back behind the figurative curtain is Stephen King's main man Chuck Verrill, who scrutinized each and every issue before it went to press, always making salient suggestions and corrections. His eagle eyes were invaluable. Of course, none of this would even exist were it not for one of the great imaginations of our time: Stephen King. And were it not for the legions of constant readers, this series would have ceased publication early on.

For me, having been involved in this wonderful take on the Dark Tower since the initial meeting with Stephen, Chuck, publisher Dan Buckley and then editor in chief Joe Quesada, its ending here is both happy and bittersweet. It's happy because we accomplished what we set out to do: Draw you in to this incredible mythology on a monthly basis as imaginatively as we knew how. And it's bittersweet because the ka-tet who brought it all to you is now breaking up. Still, the hope endures that Marvel will again revisit this extraordinary literary landscape. If and when we do, we'll gather again to pursue the Man in Black across the trackless waste of that endless desert.

Ralph Macc
July 11th, 20

ell, here it is: the End of the Road. I'm 1,549 pages older and, constant (or casional) reader, it is now time to bid you adieu.

e lived and breathed Mid-world for the past eight years and it's been azingly fun. Sure, stress and insomnia have shaved a few years off my e and pushed to the limit the patience of my wife and kids. Despite Ralph acchio's yoda-like wisdom, I've driven editors to the edge of insanity holding on to each page until I was satisfied with it. I've made friends, enated others, knowing all the while how lucky I was to be allowed to play in ephen King's Dark Tower sandbox. Freaking Stephen King, man! I still can't lieve it! "They taste like lady fingers," "Fornit Some Fornus." I wish I could st go tell my 20-year-old self what's up ahead!

ere are more Dark Tower stories to tell but, thanks to Robin, Peter, Jae, an, Luke, Michael, Laurence, Alex and Dean, we can look back at this body of rk with pride and without regrets. We done good, I think.

en the time came to draw the final cover, Bill (Rosemann) and I thought it'd cool to do a symbolic image. A still life showing the props I used throughout e years could be a nice way to wrap things up. I took some photos, did some etches, but, in the end, we decided to go for an action shot of young Arthur stay closer to the specific content of this issue. So, as a nostalgic wink, I'd e to share with you this little display of memorabilia. I hope you dig it.

w we part, dear reader, and I want to thank you for coming along for the e.

e-thee-well,
hard Isanove

"I'd already helped them to snap one Beam and I was cutting centuries off their work on Shardik's Beam. And when Shardik's Beam snaps, lady and gentlemen, Gan's can only last a little while. And when Gan's Beam also snaps, the Dark Tower will fall, creation will end, and the very Eye of Existence will turn blind."

The Dark Tower, 296

STEPHEN KING

THE DARK TOWER
~THE GUNSLINGER~

SHEEMIE'S TALE

CHAPTER ONE

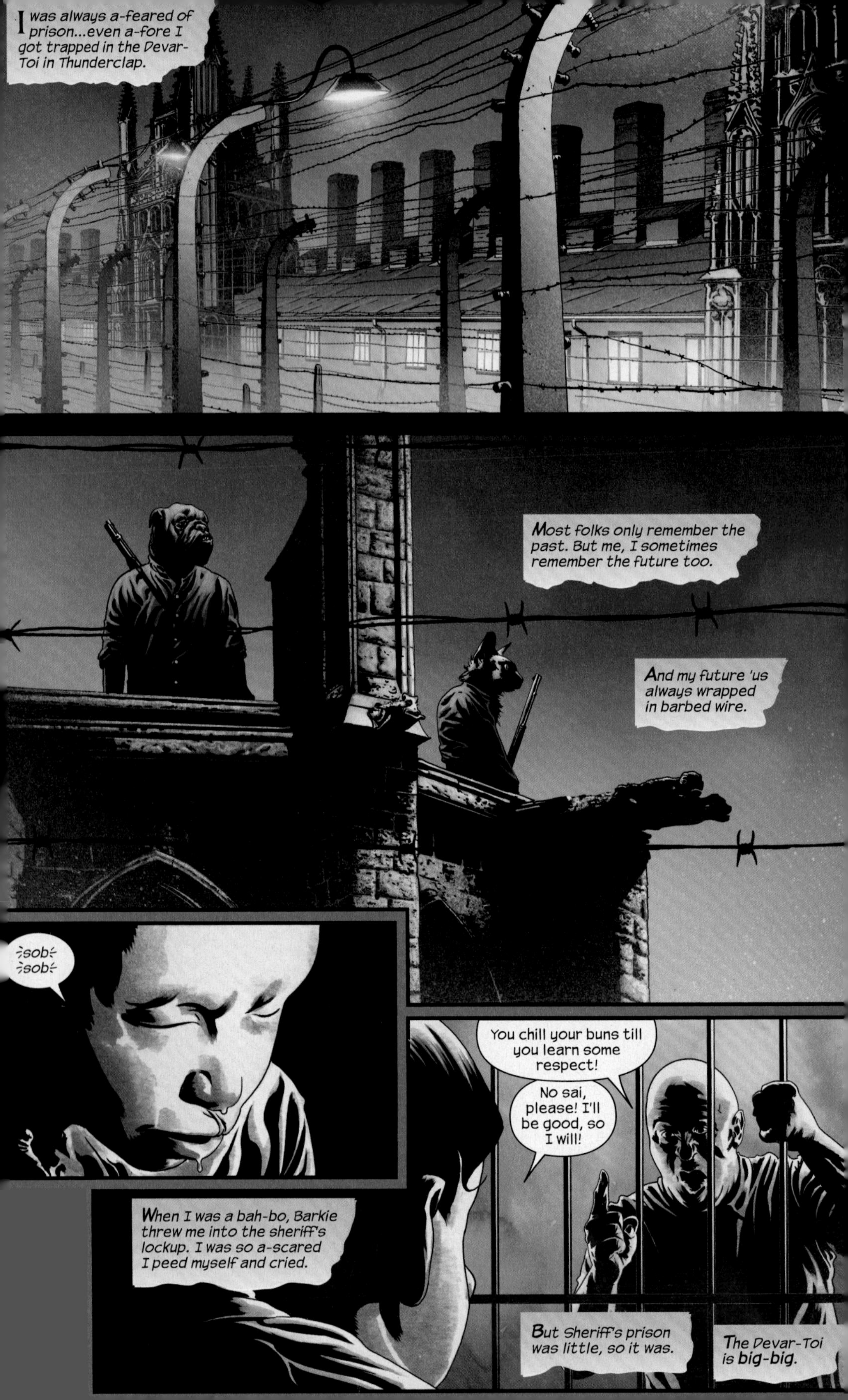
I was always a-feared of prison...even a-fore I got trapped in the Devar-Toi in Thunderclap.
Most folks only remember the past. But me, I sometimes remember the future too.
And my future 'us always wrapped in barbed wire.
sob sob
You chill your buns till you learn some respect!
No sai, please! I'll be good, so I will!
When I was a bah-bo, Barkie threw me into the sheriff's lockup. I was so a-scared I peed myself and cried.
But Sheriff's prison was little, so it was.
The Devar-Toi is big-big.

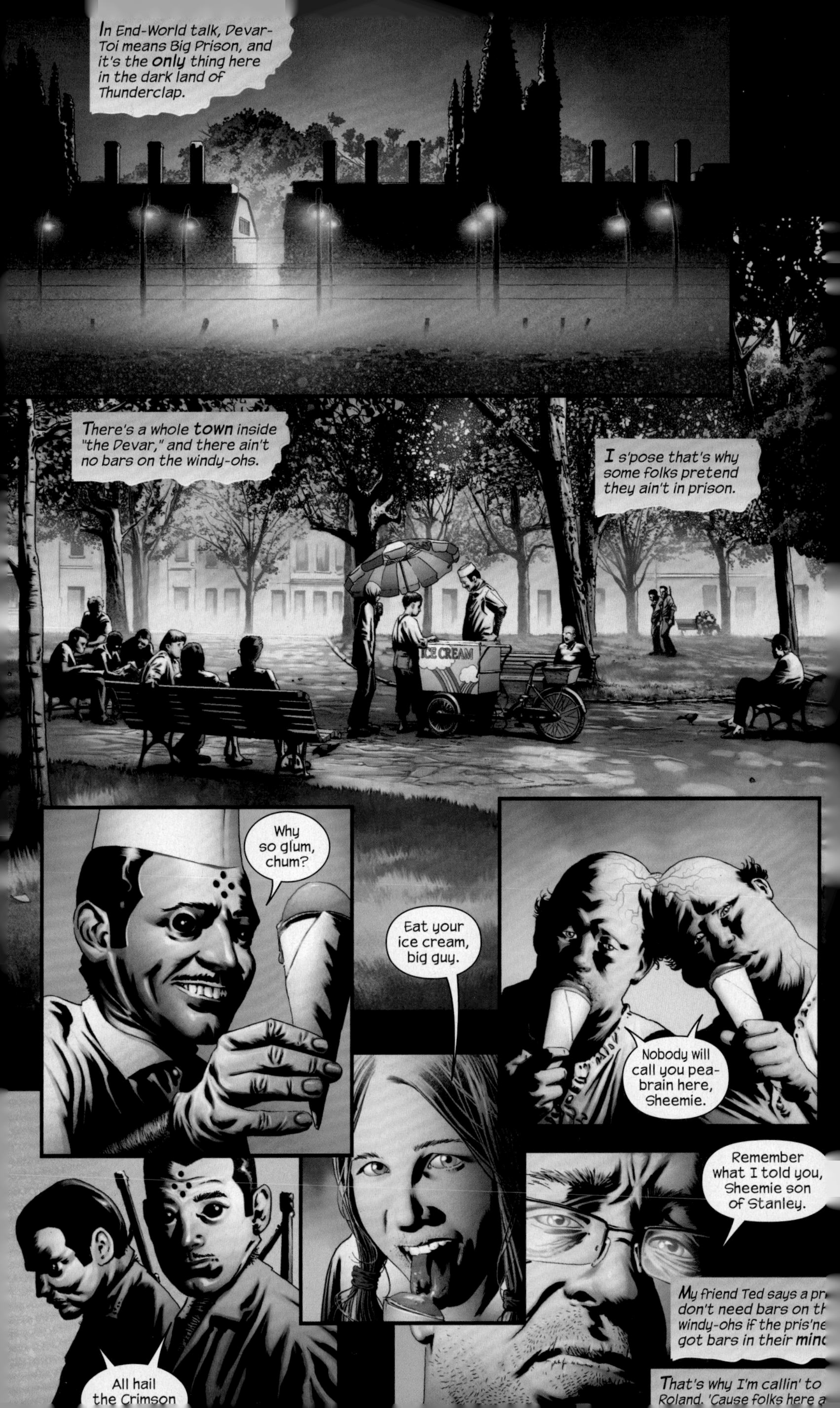

In End-World talk, Devar-Toi means Big Prison, and it's the only thing here in the dark land of Thunderclap.
There's a whole town inside "the Devar," and there ain't no bars on the windy-ohs.
I s'pose that's why some folks pretend they ain't in prison.
ICE CREAM
Why so glum, chum?
Eat your ice cream, big guy.
Nobody will call you pea-brain here, Sheemie.
Remember what I told you, Sheemie son of Stanley.
My friend Ted says a pr
don't need bars on th
windy-ohs if the pris'ne
got bars in their min
That's why I'm callin' to
Roland. 'Cause folks here a
All hail
the Crimson

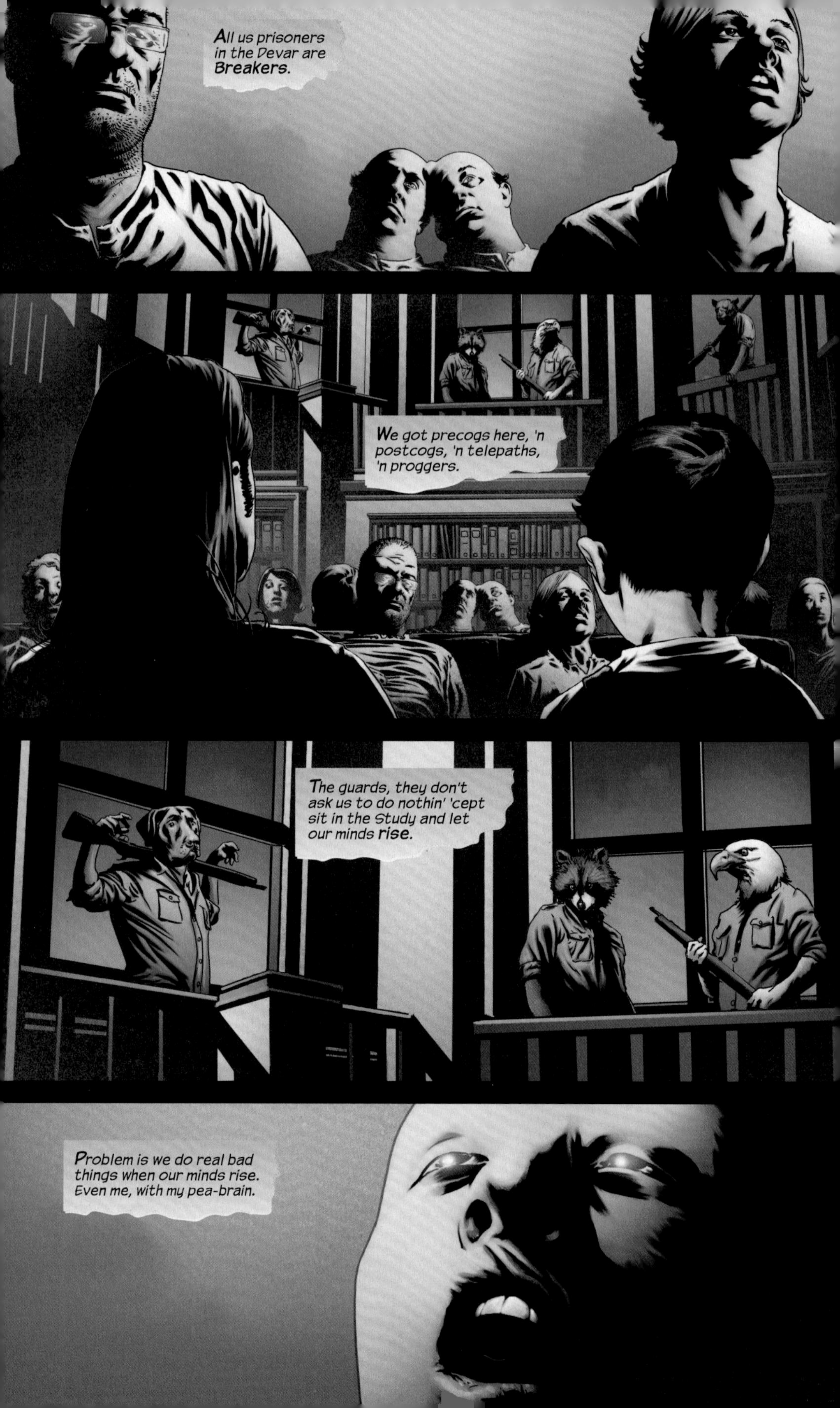
All us prisoners in the Devar are Breakers.
We got precogs here, 'n postcogs, 'n telepaths, 'n proggers.
The guards, they don't ask us to do nothin' 'cept sit in the Study and let our minds rise.
Problem is we do real bad things when our minds rise. Even me, with my pea-brain.

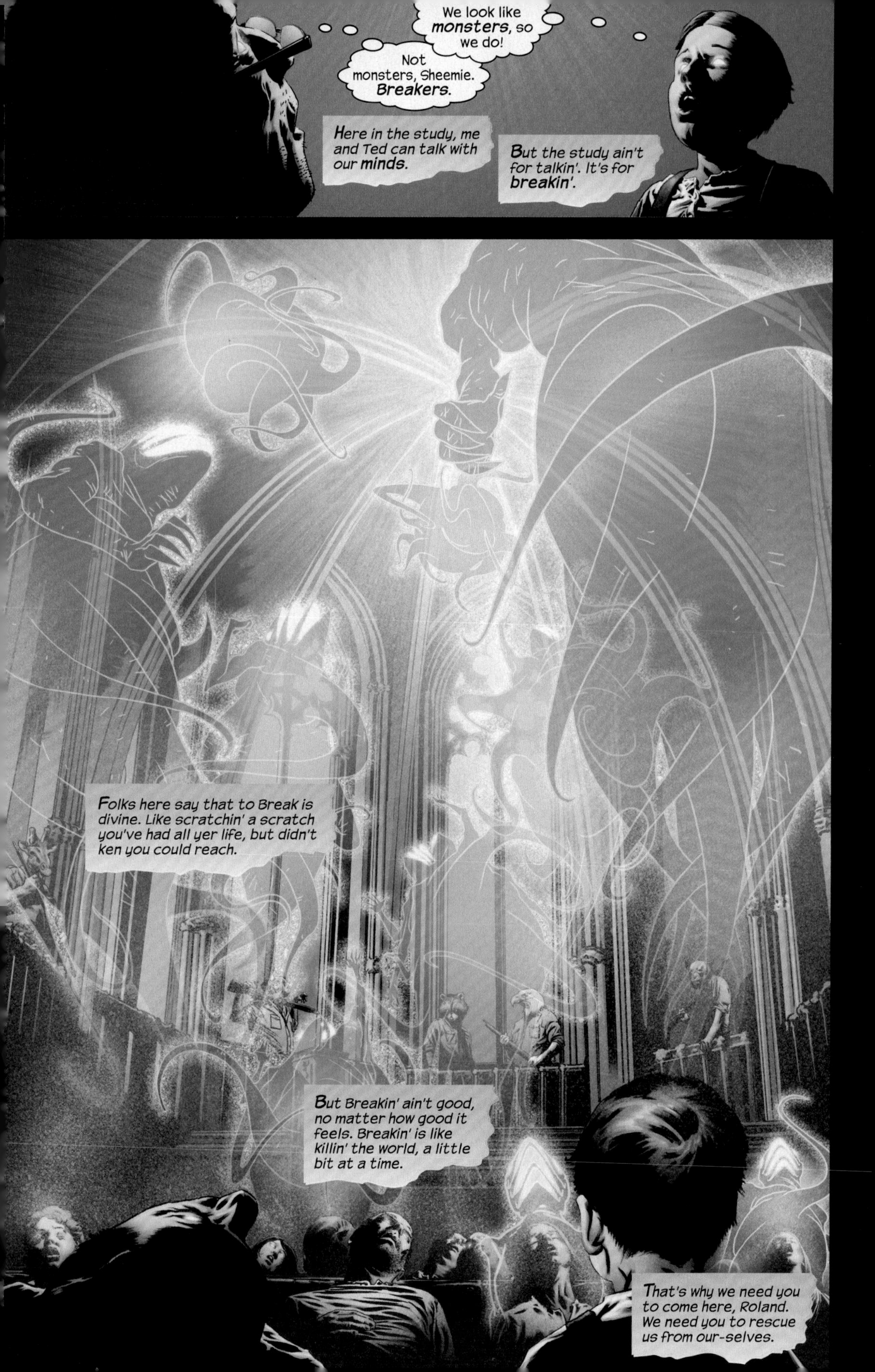
We look like monsters, so we do!
Not monsters, Sheemie. Breakers.
Here in the study, me and Ted can talk with our minds.
But the study ain't for talkin'. It's for breakin'.
Folks here say that to Break is divine. Like scratchin' a scratch you've had all yer life, but didn't ken you could reach.
But Breakin' ain't good, no matter how good it feels. Breakin' is like killin' the world, a little bit at a time.
That's why we need you to come here, Roland. We need you to rescue us from our-selves.

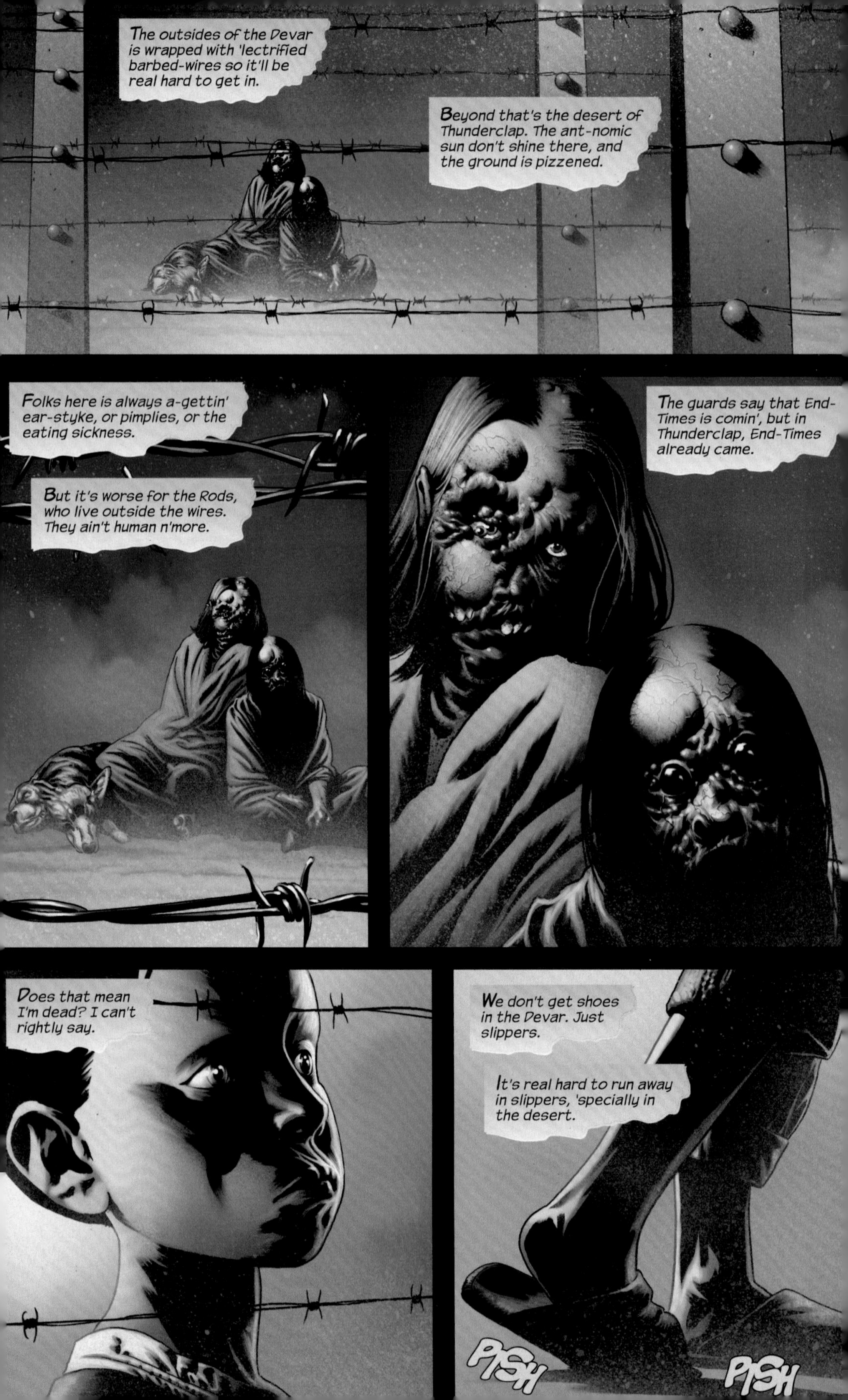
The outsides of the Devar is wrapped with 'lectrified barbed-wires so it'll be real hard to get in.
Beyond that's the desert of Thunderclap. The ant-nomic sun don't shine there, and the ground is pizzened.
Folks here is always a-gettin' ear-styke, or pimplies, or the eating sickness.
But it's worse for the Rods, who live outside the wires. They ain't human n'more.
The guards say that End-Times is comin', but in Thunderclap, End-Times already came.
Does that mean I'm dead? I can't rightly say.
We don't get shoes in the Devar. Just slippers.
It's real hard to run away in slippers, 'specially in the desert.
PISH
PISH

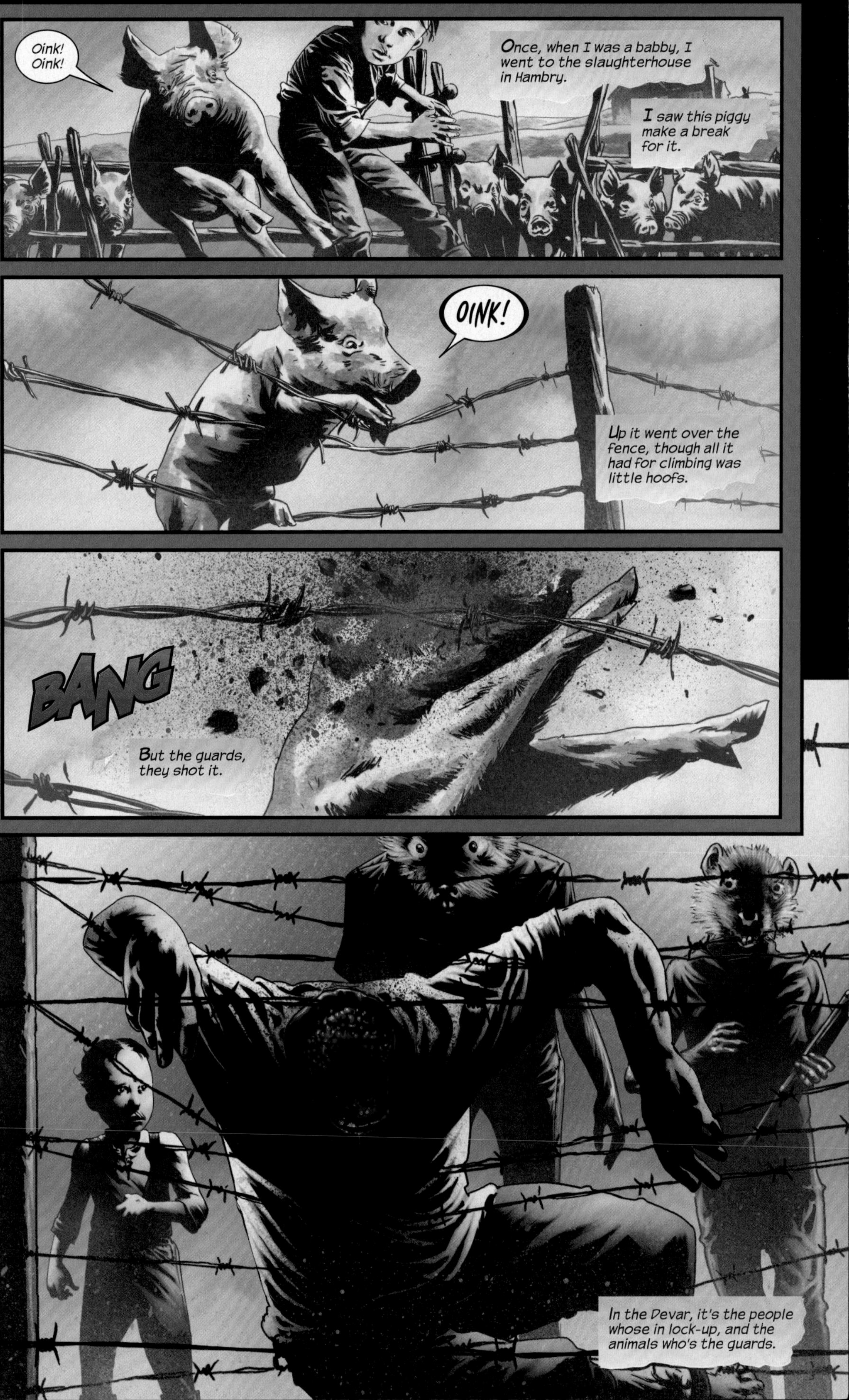
Oink! Oink!
Once, when I was a babby, I went to the slaughterhouse in Hambry.
I saw this piggy make a break for it.
OINK!
Up it went over the fence, though all it had for climbing was little hoofs.
BANG
But the guards, they shot it.
In the Devar, it's the people whose in lock-up, and the animals who's the guards.

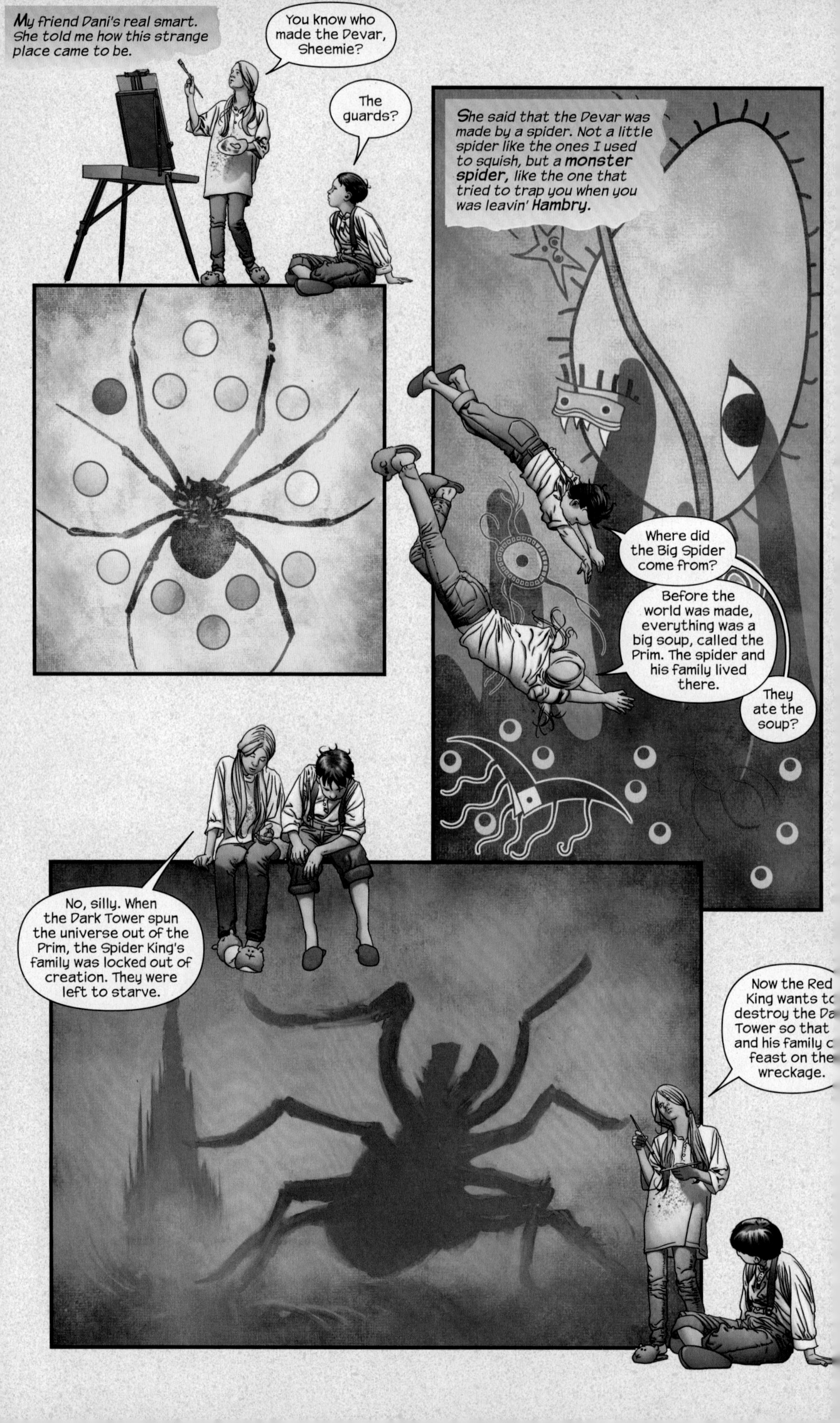
My friend Dani's real smart. She told me how this strange place came to be.
You know who made the Devar, Sheemie?
The guards?
She said that the Devar was made by a spider. Not a little spider like the ones I used to squish, but a **monster spider,** like the one that tried to trap you when you was leavin' **Hambry.**
Where did the Big Spider come from?
Before the world was made, everything was a big soup, called the Prim. The spider and his family lived there.
They ate the soup?
No, silly. When the Dark Tower spun the universe out of the Prim, the Spider King's family was locked out of creation. They were left to starve.
Now the Red King wants to destroy the Da Tower so that and his family c feast on the wreckage.

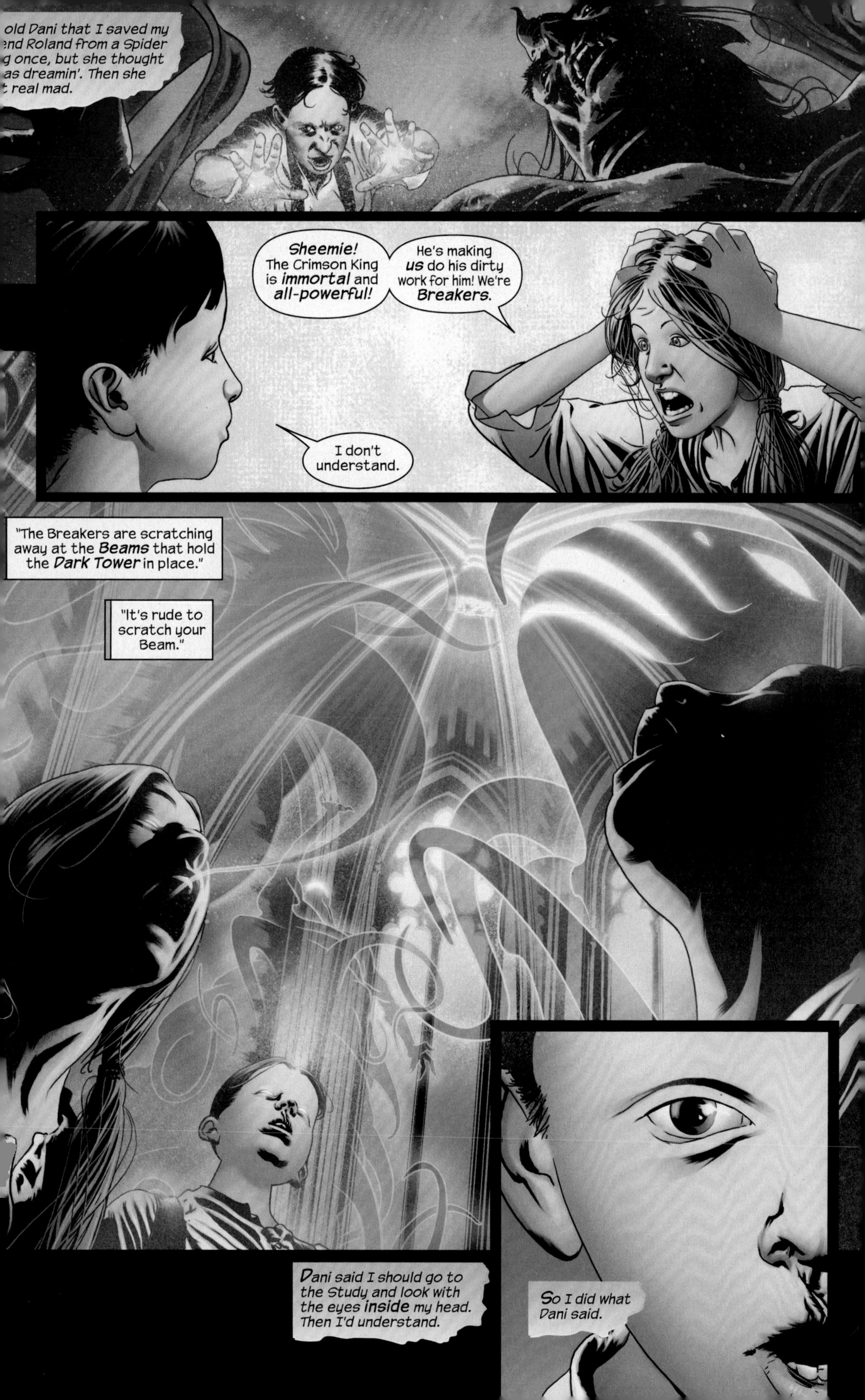

old Dani that I saved my
end Roland from a Spider
g once, but she thought
as dreamin'. Then she
t real mad.
Sheemie! The Crimson King is immortal and all-powerful!
He's making us do his dirty work for him! We're Breakers.
I don't understand.
"The Breakers are scratching away at the Beams that hold the Dark Tower in place."
"It's rude to scratch your Beam."
Dani said I should go to the Study and look with the eyes inside my head. Then I'd understand.
So I did what Dani said.

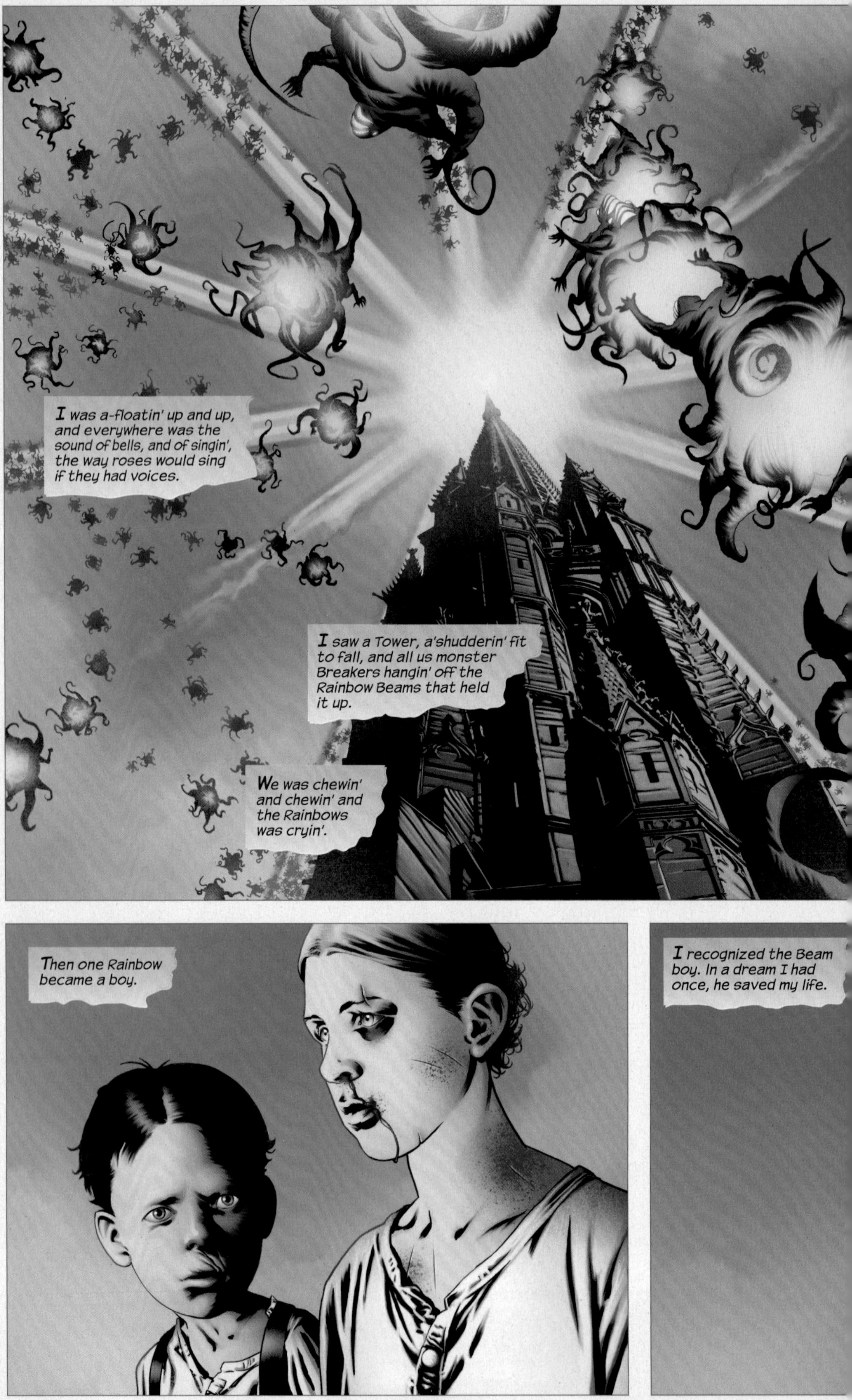
I was a-floatin' up and up, and everywhere was the sound of bells, and of singin', the way roses would sing if they had voices.
I saw a Tower, a'shudderin' fit to fall, and all us monster Breakers hangin' off the Rainbow Beams that held it up.
We was chewin' and chewin' and the Rainbows was cryin'.
Then one Rainbow became a boy.
I recognized the Beam boy. In a dream I had once, he saved my life.

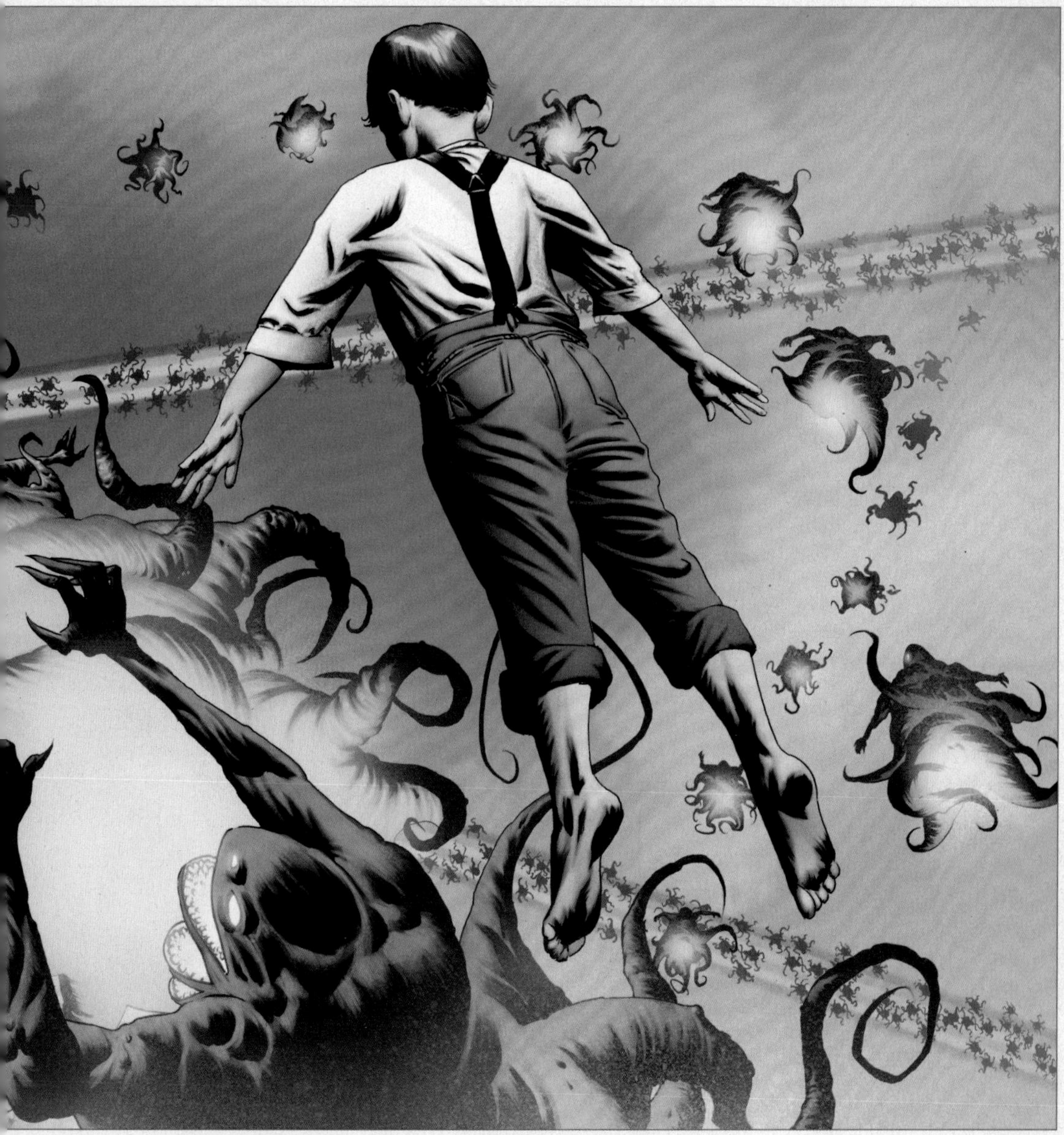

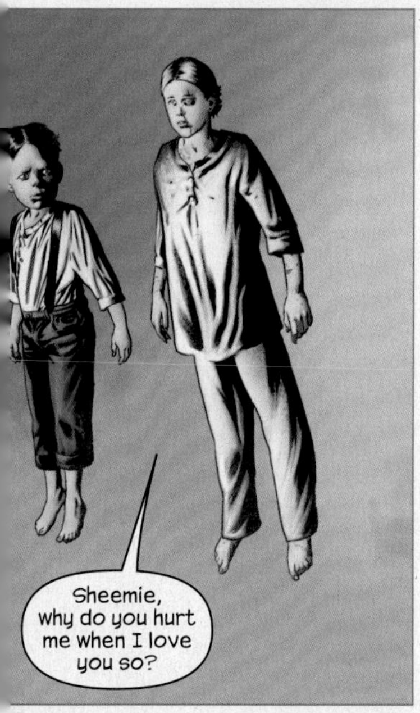
Sheemie, why do you hurt me when I love you so?

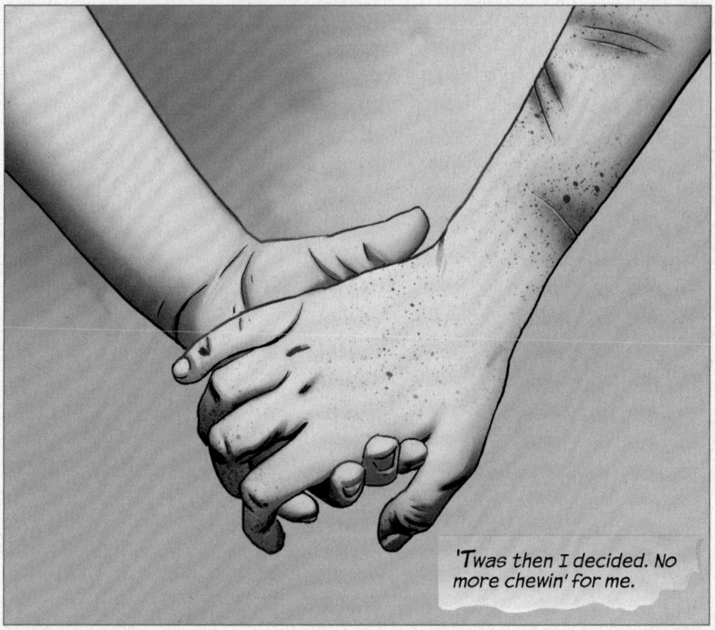
'Twas then I decided. No more chewin' for me.

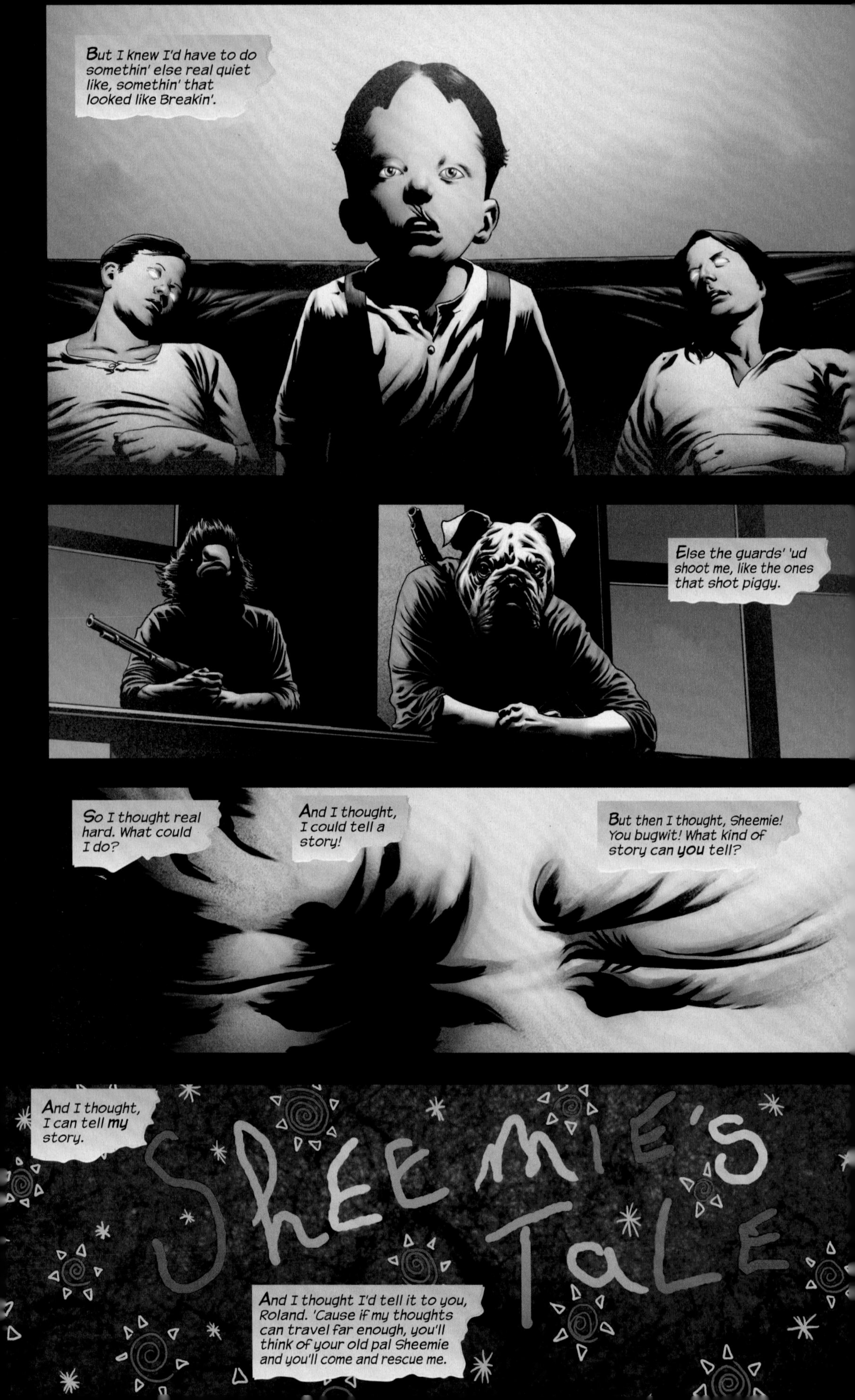
But I knew I'd have to do somethin' else real quiet like, somethin' that looked like Breakin'.
Else the guards' 'ud shoot me, like the ones that shot piggy.
So I thought real hard. What could I do?
And I thought, I could tell a story!
But then I thought, Sheemie! You bugwit! What kind of story can **you** tell?
And I thought, I can tell **my** story.
SHEEMIE'S TALE
And I thought I'd tell it to you, Roland. 'Cause if my thoughts can travel far enough, you'll think of your old pal Sheemie and you'll come and rescue me.

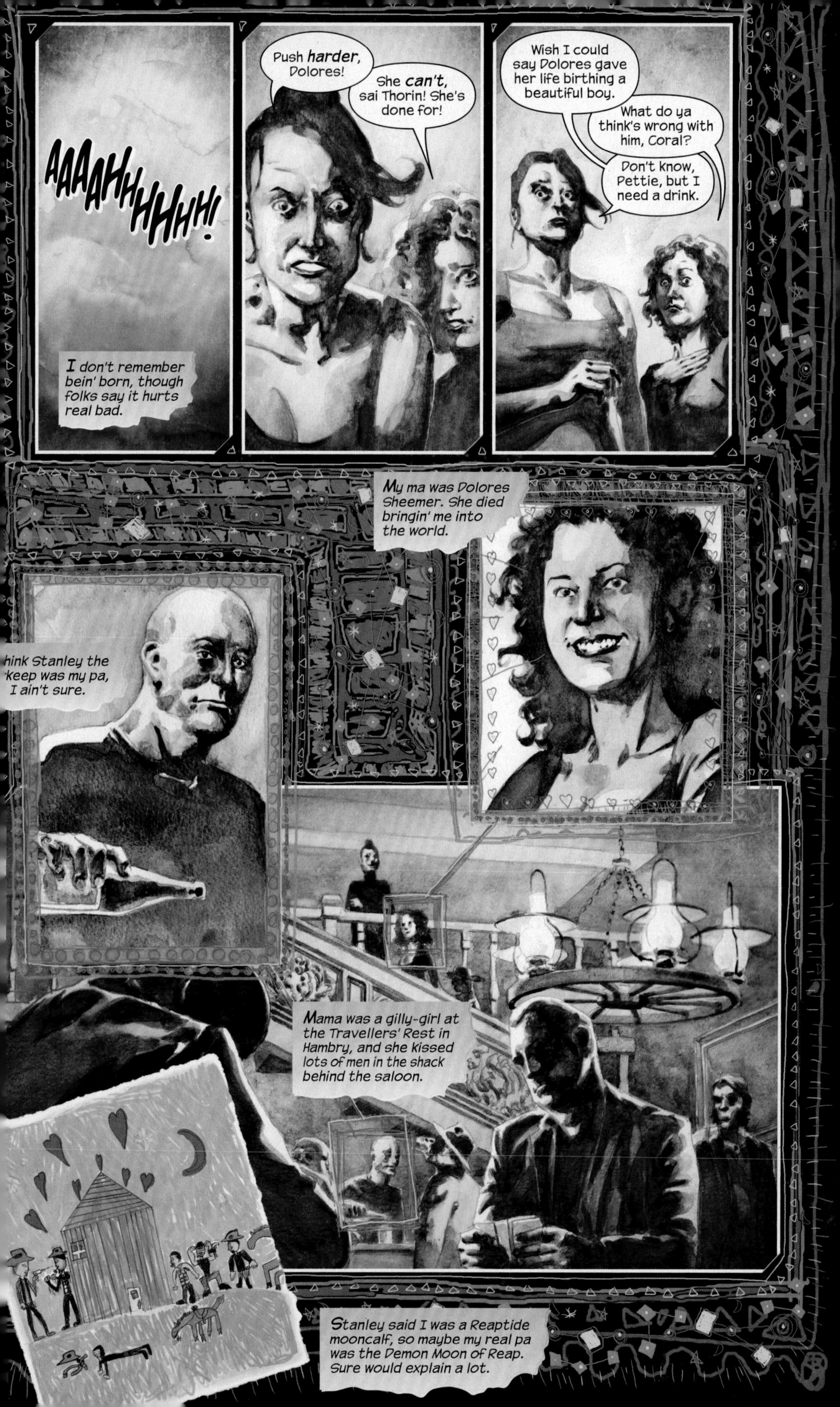
AAAAHHHHH!
I don't remember bein' born, though folks say it hurts real bad.
Push harder, Dolores!
She can't, sai Thorin! She's done for!
Wish I could say Dolores gave her life birthing a beautiful boy.
What do ya think's wrong with him, Coral?
Don't know, Pettie, but I need a drink.
My ma was Dolores Sheemer. She died bringin' me into the world.
hink Stanley the
keep was my pa,
I ain't sure.
Mama was a gilly-girl at the Travellers' Rest in Hambry, and she kissed lots of men in the shack behind the saloon.
Stanley said I was a Reaptide mooncalf, so maybe my real pa was the Demon Moon of Reap. Sure would explain a lot.

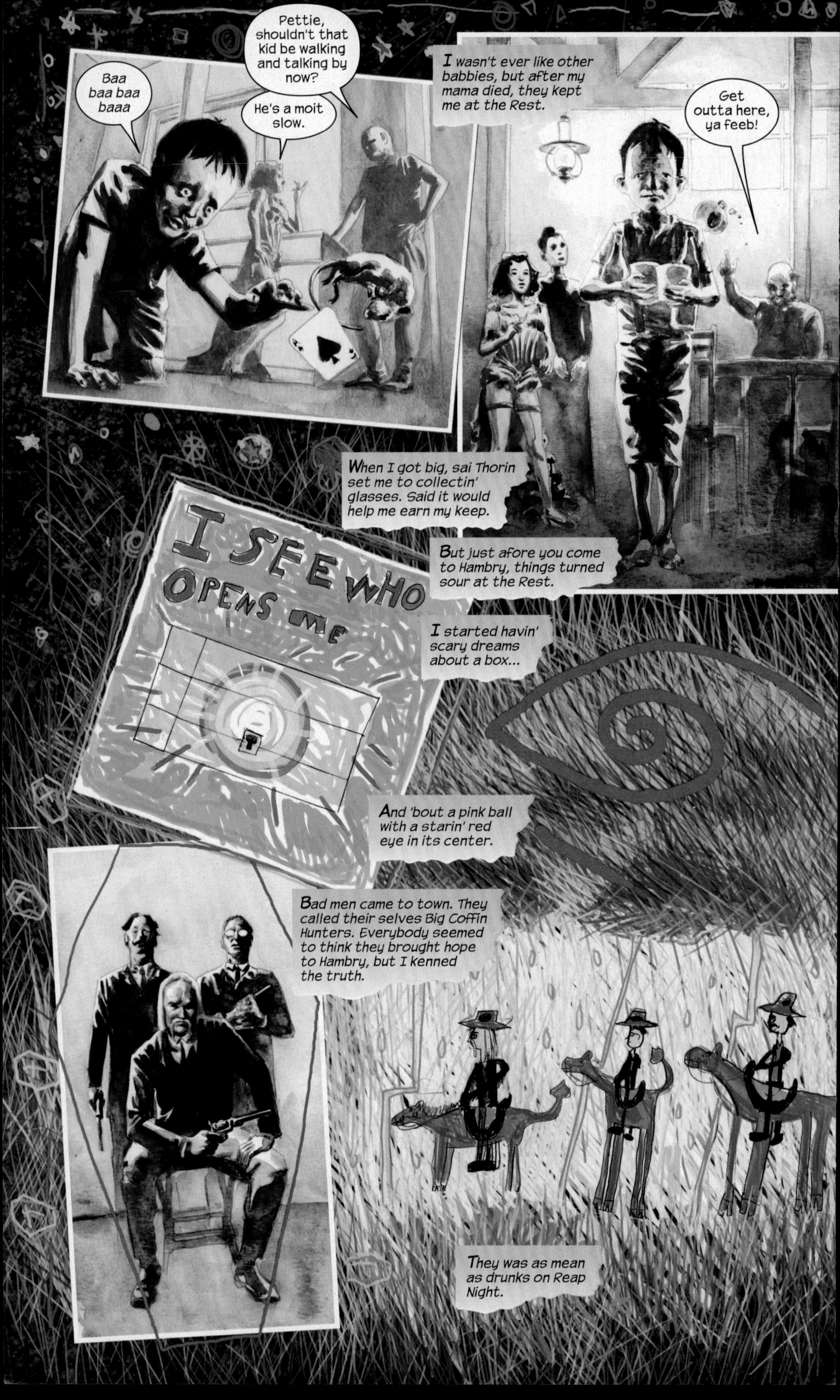
Baa baa baa baaa
Pettie, shouldn't that kid be walking and talking by now?
He's a moit slow.
I wasn't ever like other babbies, but after my mama died, they kept me at the Rest.
Get outta here, ya feeb!
When I got big, sai Thorin set me to collectin' glasses. Said it would help me earn my keep.
But just afore you come to Hambry, things turned sour at the Rest.
I SEE WHO OPENS ME
I started havin' scary dreams about a box...
And 'bout a pink ball with a starin' red eye in its center.
Bad men came to town. They called their selves Big Coffin Hunters. Everybody seemed to think they brought hope to Hambry, but I kenned the truth.
They was as mean as drunks on Reap Night.

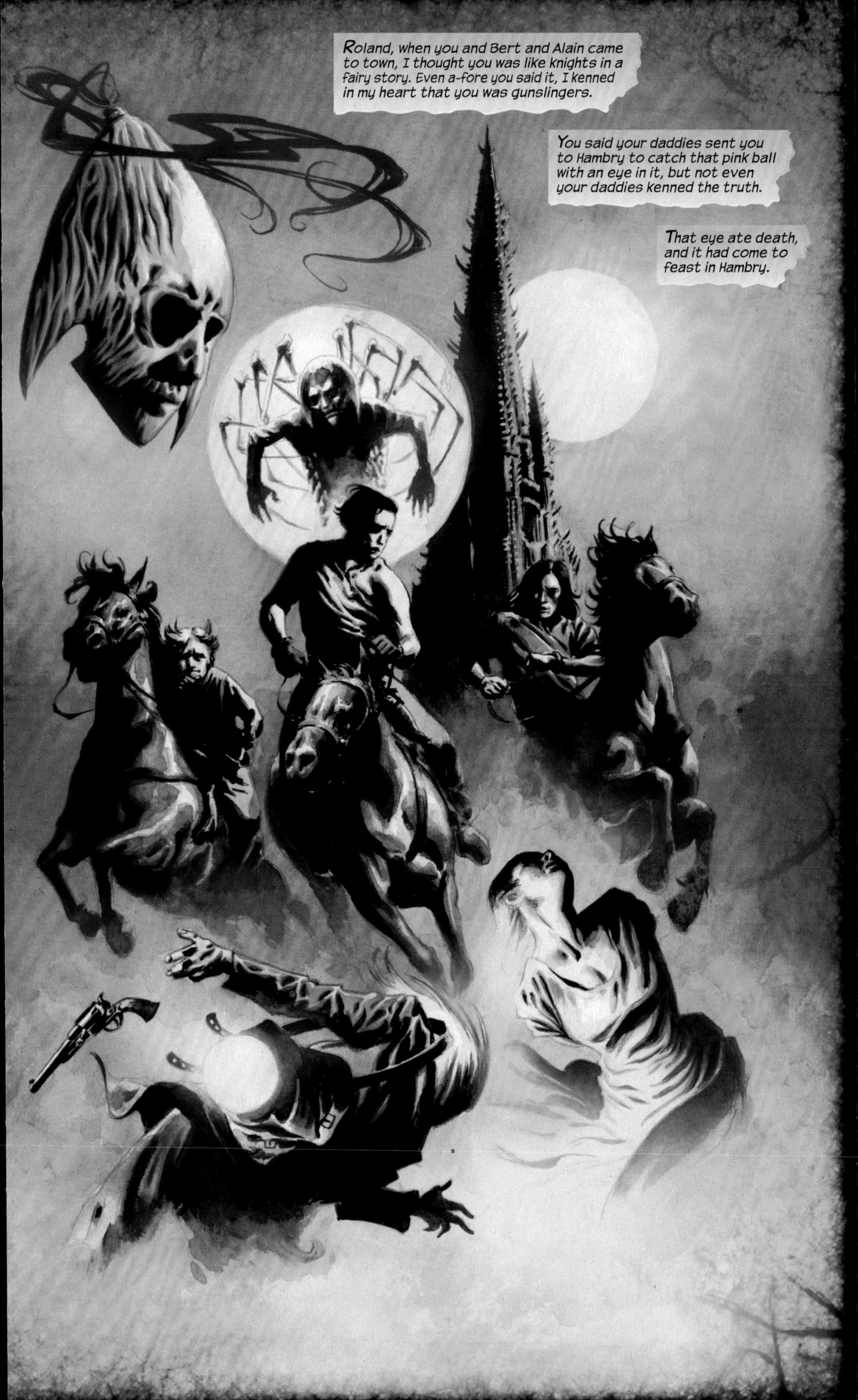
Roland, when you and Bert and Alain came to town, I thought you was like knights in a fairy story. Even a-fore you said it, I kenned in my heart that you was gunslingers.
You said your daddies sent you to Hambry to catch that pink ball with an eye in it, but not even your daddies kenned the truth.
That eye ate death, and it had come to feast in Hambry.

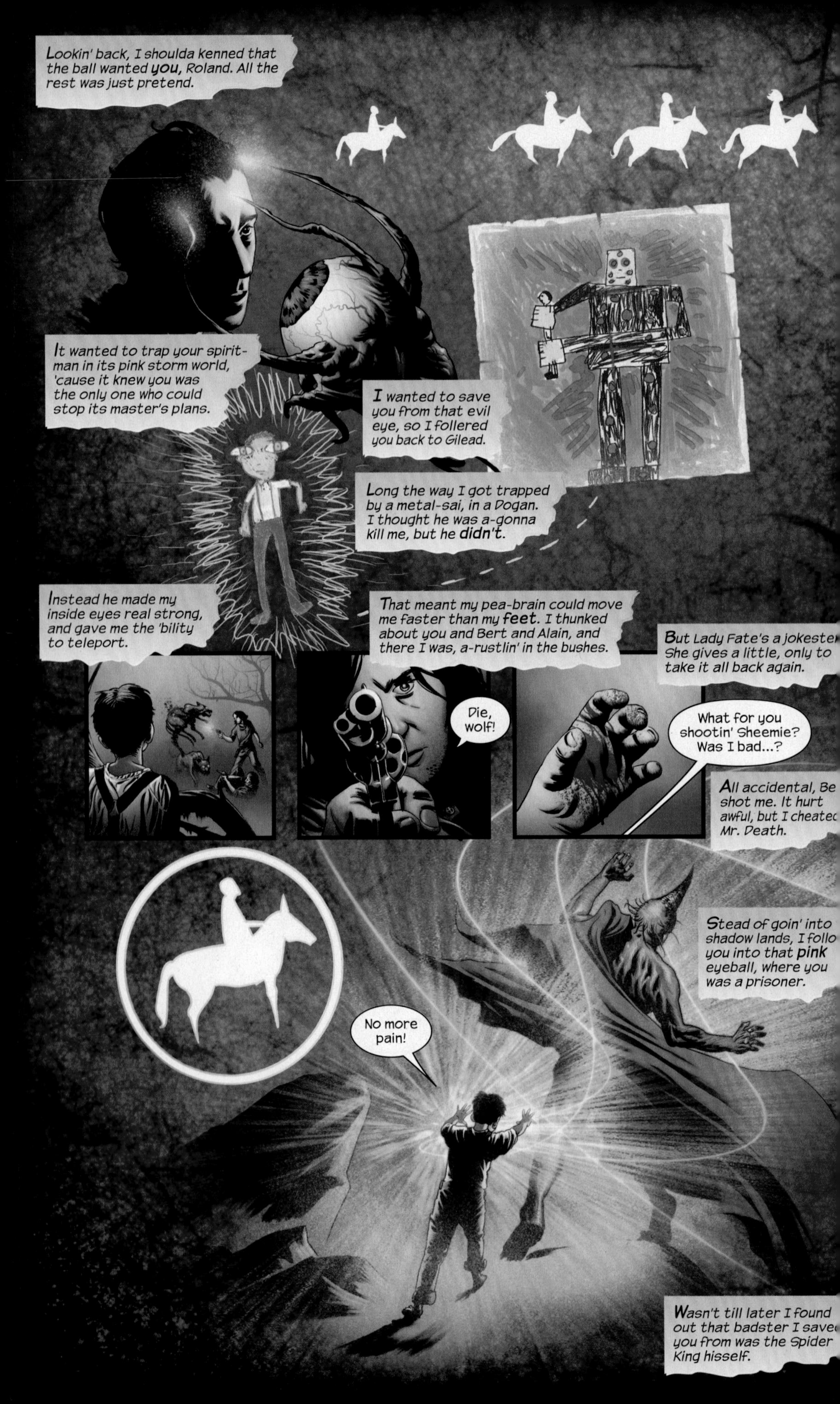
Lookin' back, I shoulda kenned that the ball wanted you, Roland. All the rest was just pretend.
It wanted to trap your spirit-man in its pink storm world, 'cause it knew you was the only one who could stop its master's plans.
I wanted to save you from that evil eye, so I follered you back to Gilead.
Long the way I got trapped by a metal-sai, in a Dogan. I thought he was a-gonna kill me, but he didn't.
Instead he made my inside eyes real strong, and gave me the 'bility to teleport.
That meant my pea-brain could move me faster than my feet. I thunked about you and Bert and Alain, and there I was, a-rustlin' in the bushes.
Die, wolf!
But Lady Fate's a jokeste She gives a little, only to take it all back again.
What for you shootin' Sheemie? Was I bad...?
All accidental, Be shot me. It hurt awful, but I cheatec Mr. Death.
Stead of goin' into shadow lands, I follo you into that pink eyeball, where you was a prisoner.
No more pain!
Wasn't till later I found out that badster I save you from was the Spider King hisself.

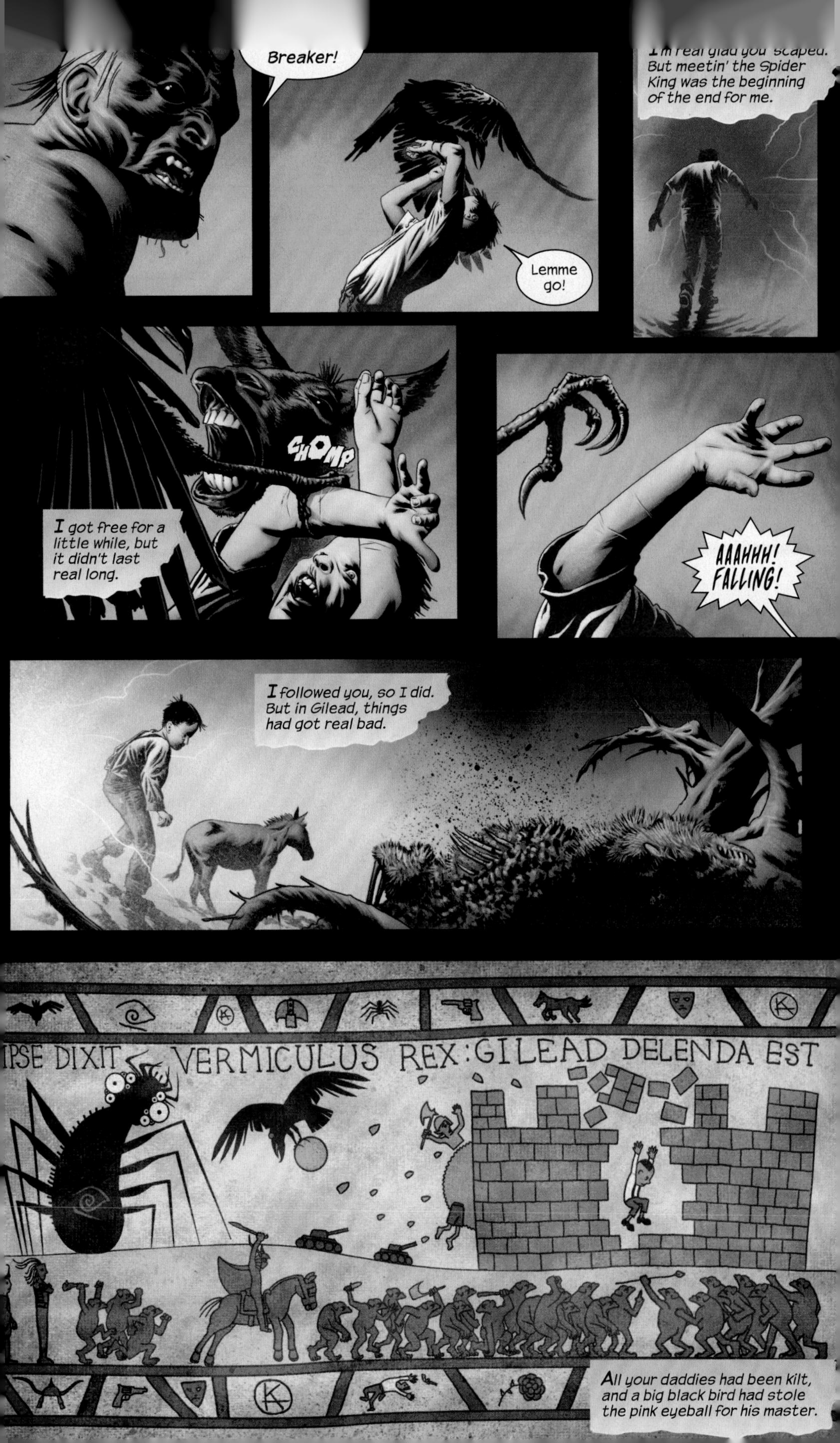

Breaker!
Lemme go!
I'm real glad you 'scaped. But meetin' the Spider King was the beginning of the end for me.
CHOMP
I got free for a little while, but it didn't last real long.
AAAHHH! FALLING!
I followed you, so I did. But in Gilead, things had got real bad.
IPSE DIXIT VERMICULUS REX: GILEAD DELENDA EST
All your daddies had been kilt, and a big black bird had stole the pink eyeball for his master.

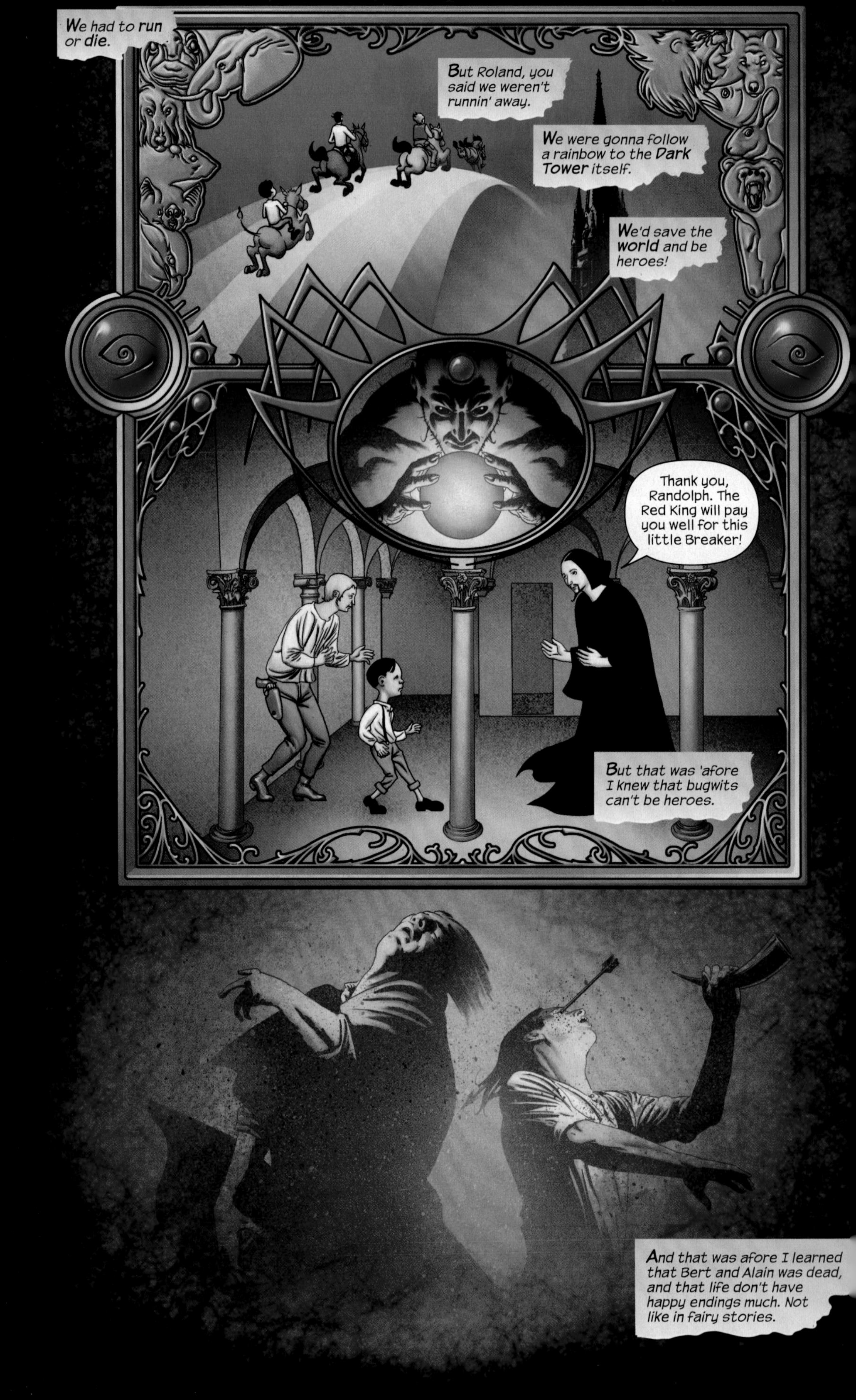

We had to run or die.
But Roland, you said we weren't runnin' away.
We were gonna follow a rainbow to the Dark Tower itself.
We'd save the world and be heroes!
Thank you, Randolph. The Red King will pay you well for this little Breaker!
But that was 'afore I knew that bugwits can't be heroes.
And that was afore I learned that Bert and Alain was dead, and that life don't have happy endings much. Not like in fairy stories.

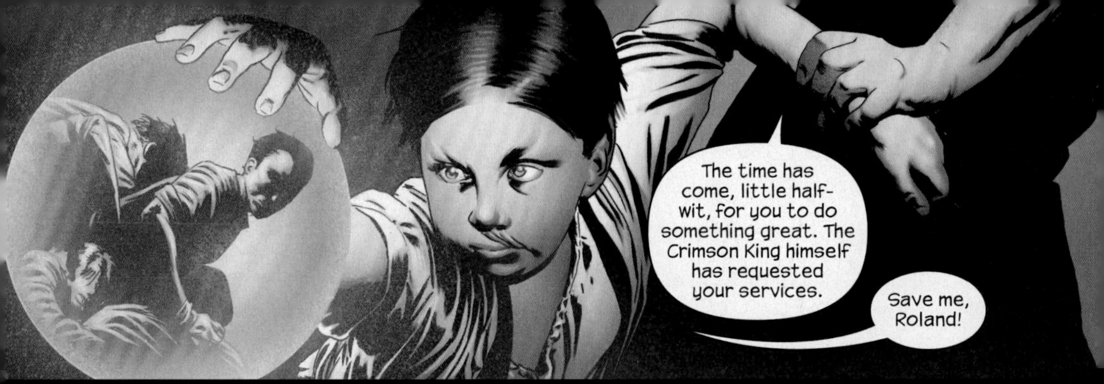
The time has come, little half-wit, for you to do something great. The Crimson King himself has requested your services.
Save me, Roland!

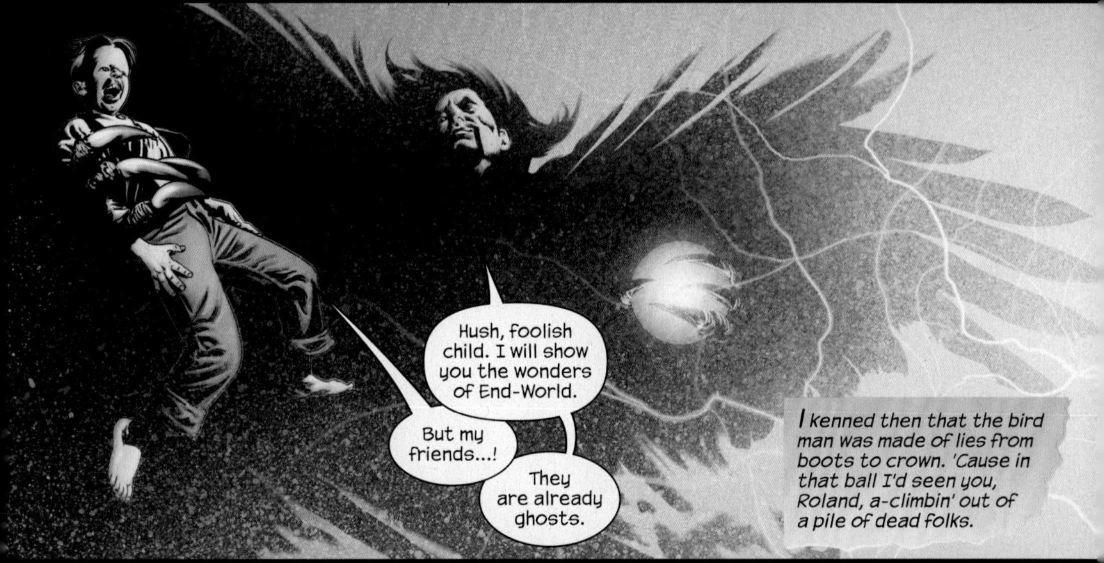
Hush, foolish child. I will show you the wonders of End-World.
But my friends...!
They are already ghosts.
I kenned then that the bird man was made of lies from boots to crown. 'Cause in that ball I'd seen you, Roland, a-climbin' out of a pile of dead folks.

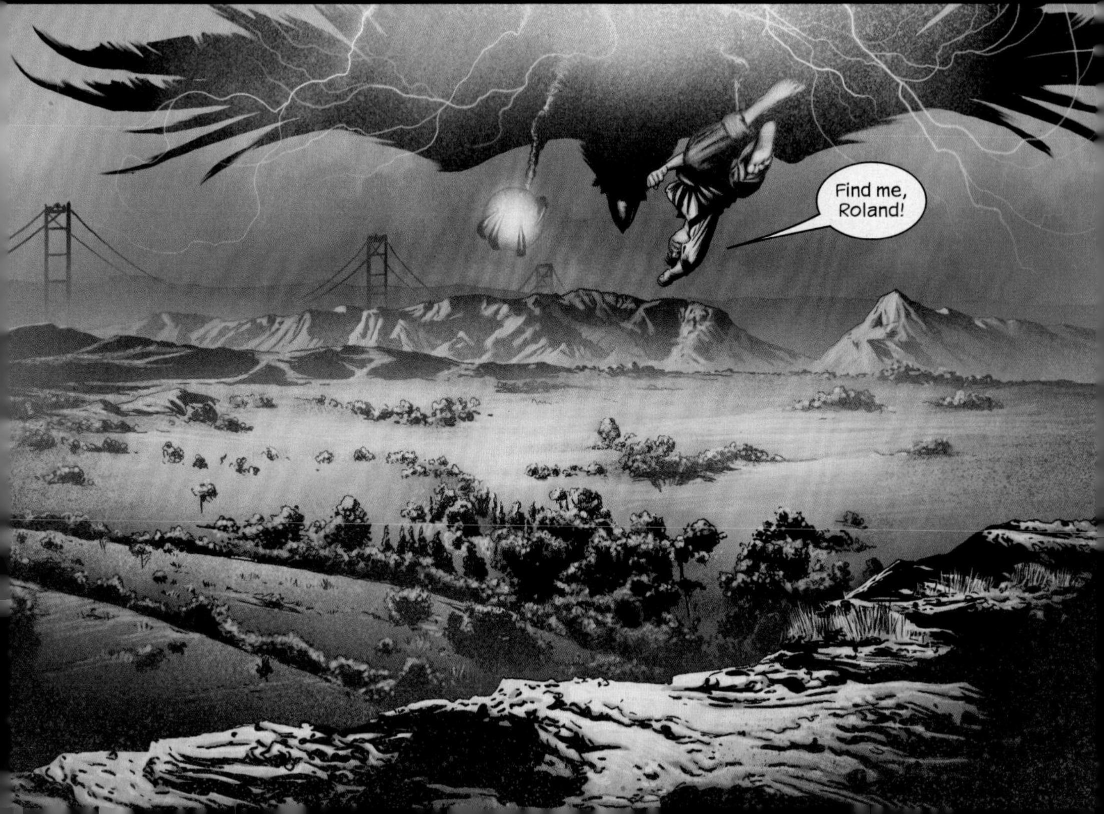
Find me, Roland!

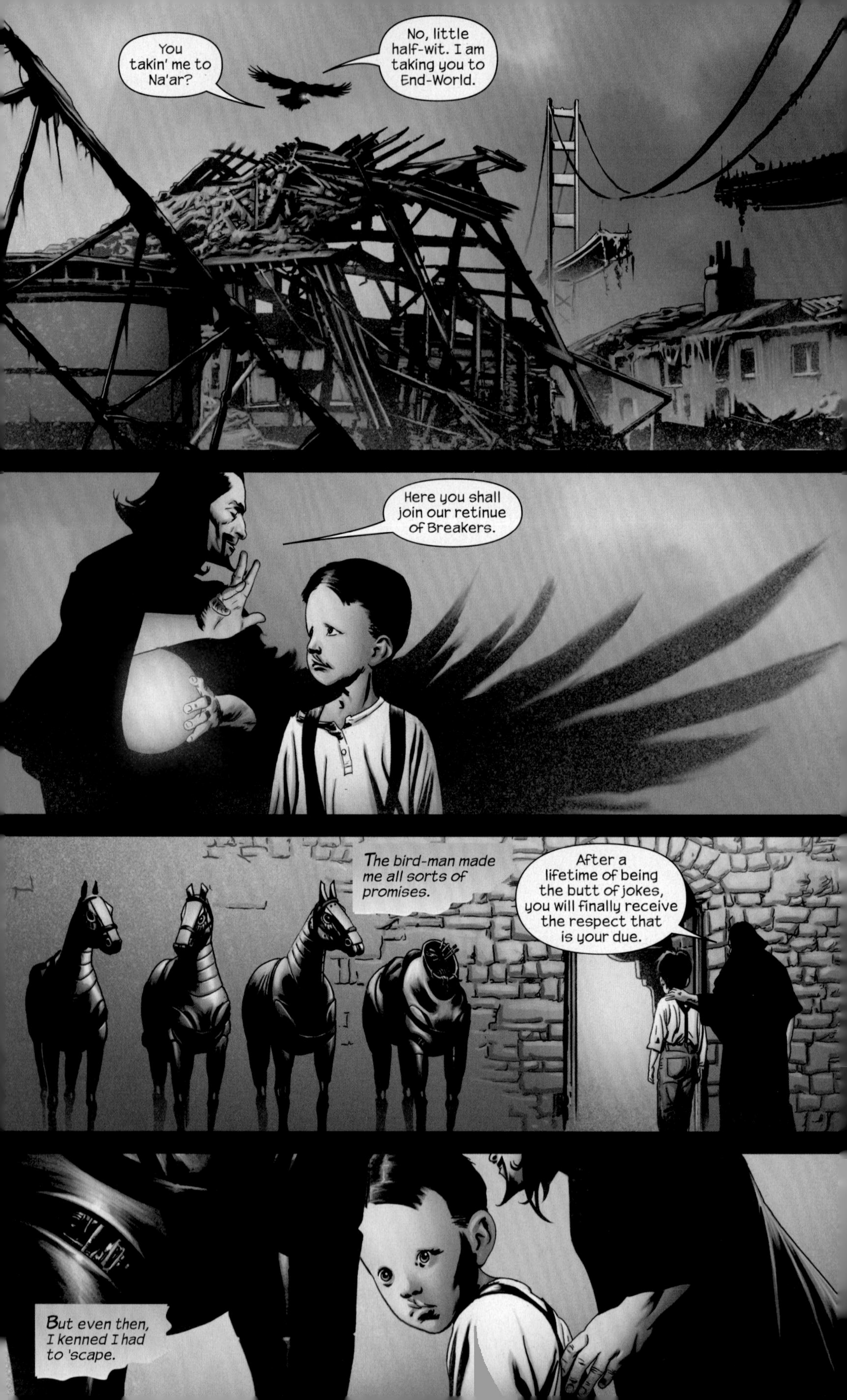

You takin' me to Na'ar?
No, little half-wit. I am taking you to End-World.
Here you shall join our retinue of Breakers.
The bird-man made me all sorts of promises.
After a lifetime of being the butt of jokes, you will finally receive the respect that is your due.
But even then, I kenned I had to 'scape.

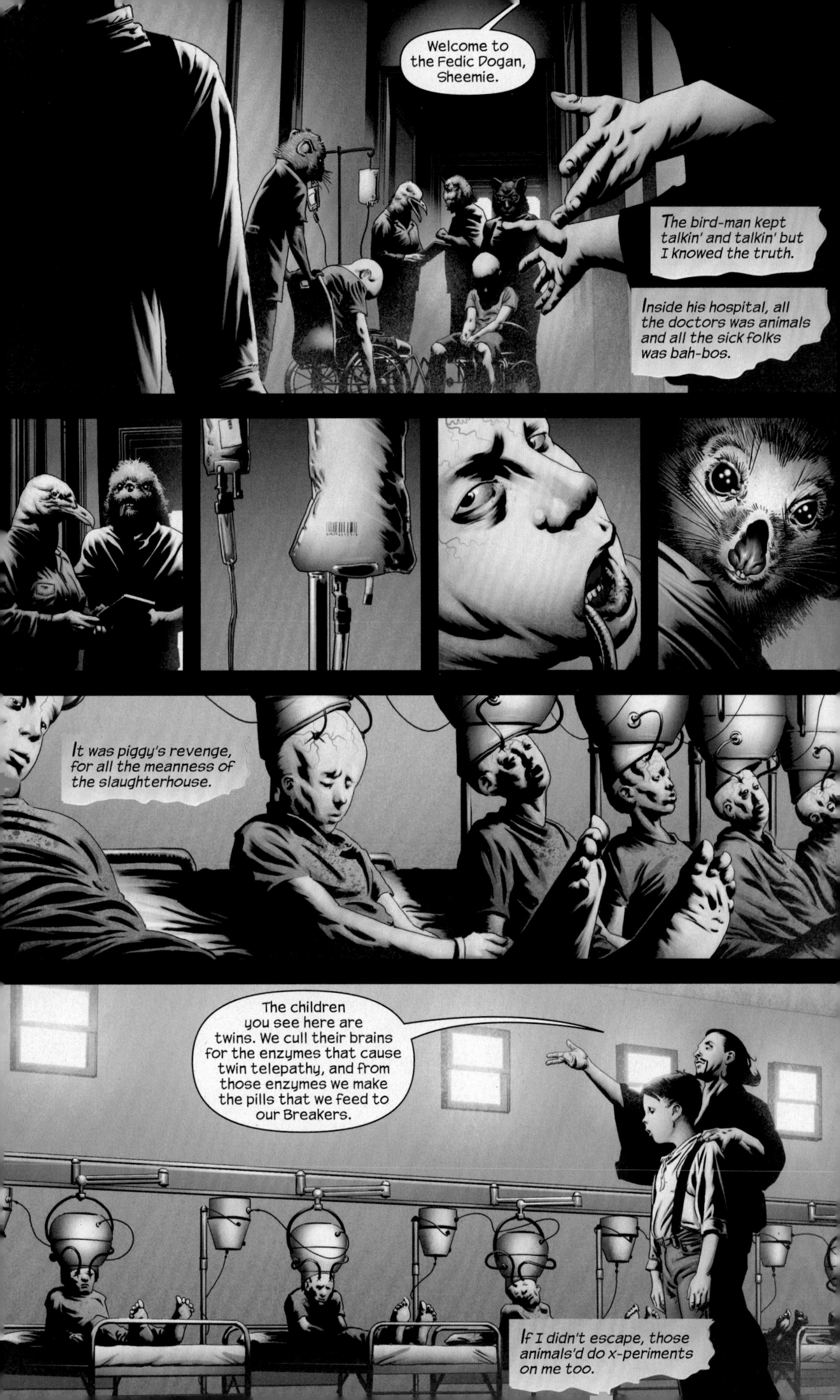
Welcome to the Fedic Dogan, Sheemie.
The bird-man kept talkin' and talkin' but I knowed the truth.
Inside his hospital, all the doctors was animals and all the sick folks was bah-bos.
It was piggy's revenge, for all the meanness of the slaughterhouse.
The children you see here are twins. We cull their brains for the enzymes that cause twin telepathy, and from those enzymes we make the pills that we feed to our Breakers.
If I didn't escape, those animals'd do x-periments on me too.

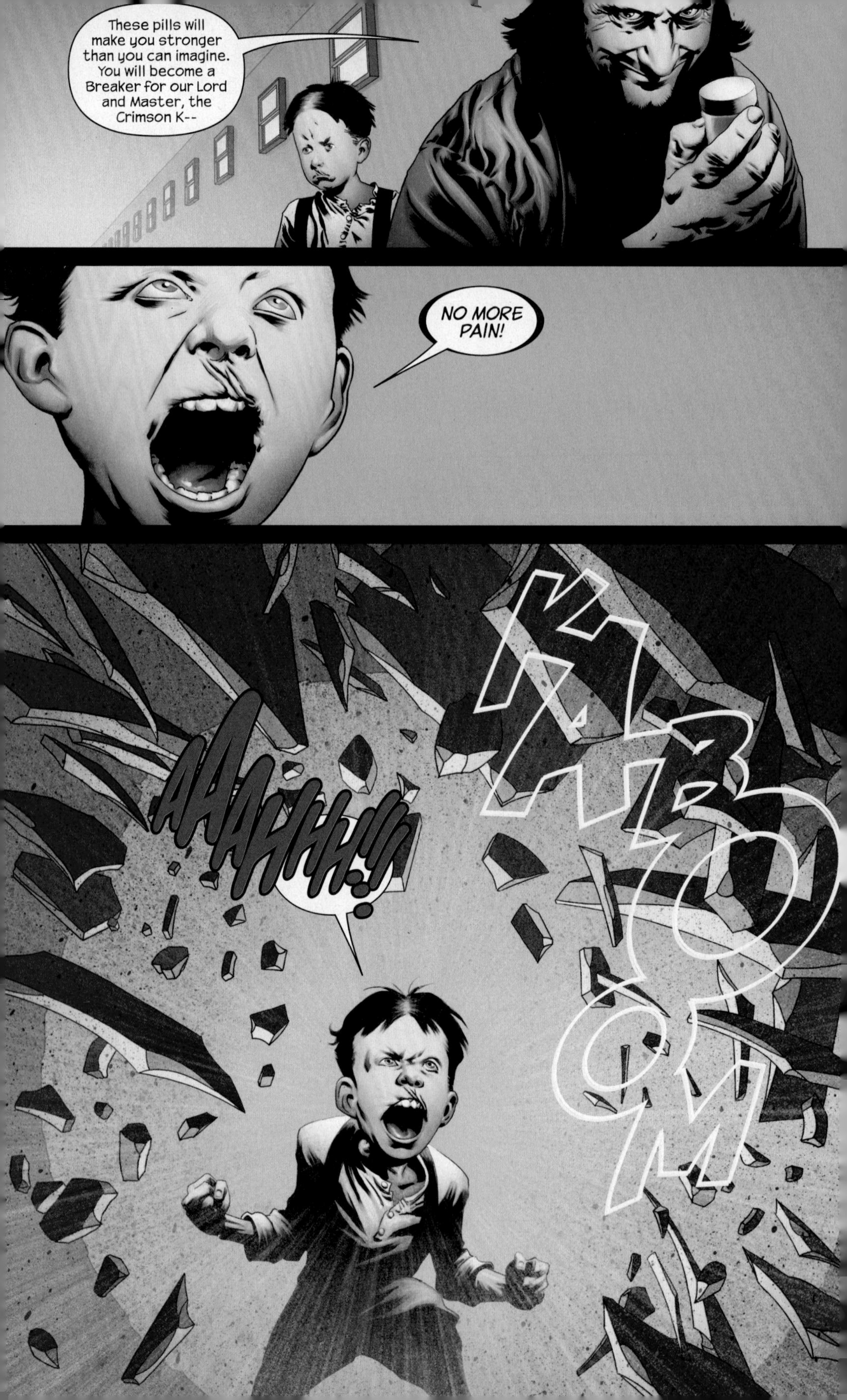
These pills will make you stronger than you can imagine. You will become a Breaker for our Lord and Master, the Crimson K--
NO MORE PAIN!
AAAHHH!!!
KABOOM

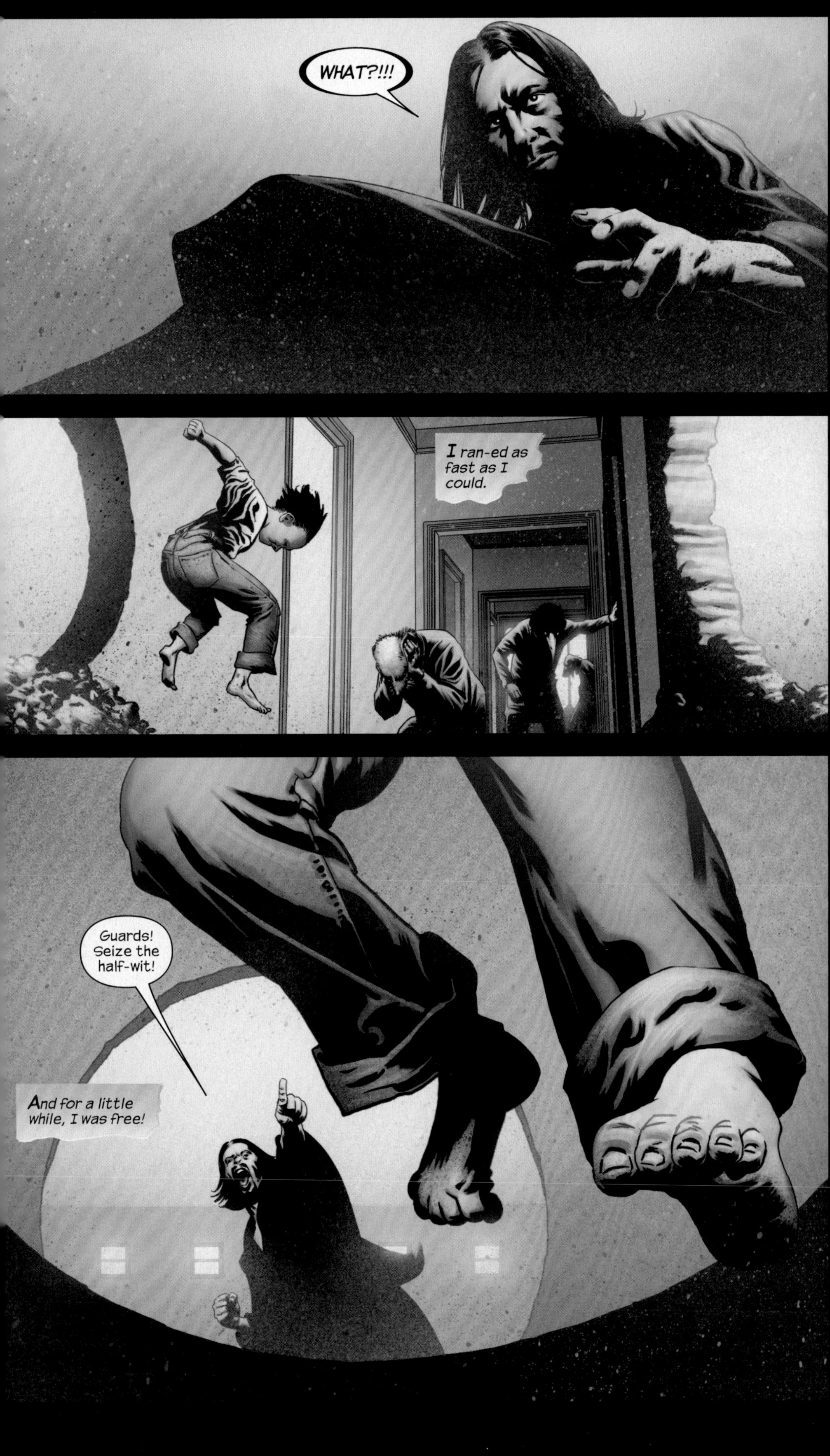
WHAT?!!!
I ran-ed as fast as I could.
Guards! Seize the half-wit!
And for a little while, I was free!

STEPHEN KING

THE DARK TOWER
~ THE GUNSLINGER ~

SHEEMIE'S TALE

CHAPTER TWO

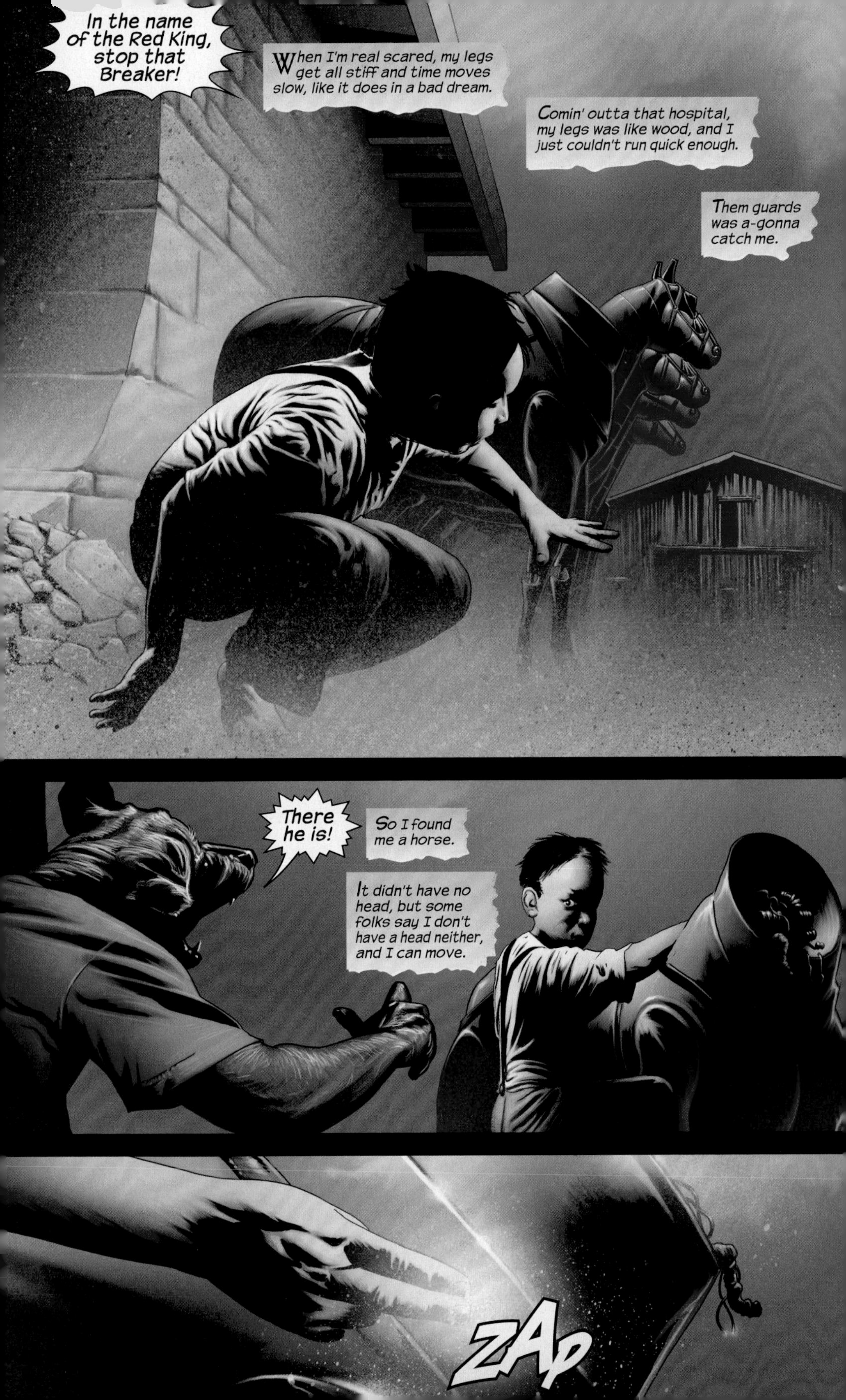
In the name of the Red King, stop that Breaker!
When I'm real scared, my legs get all stiff and time moves slow, like it does in a bad dream.
Comin' outta that hospital, my legs was like wood, and I just couldn't run quick enough.
Them guards was a-gonna catch me.
There he is!
So I found me a horse.
It didn't have no head, but some folks say I don't have a head neither, and I can move.
ZAP

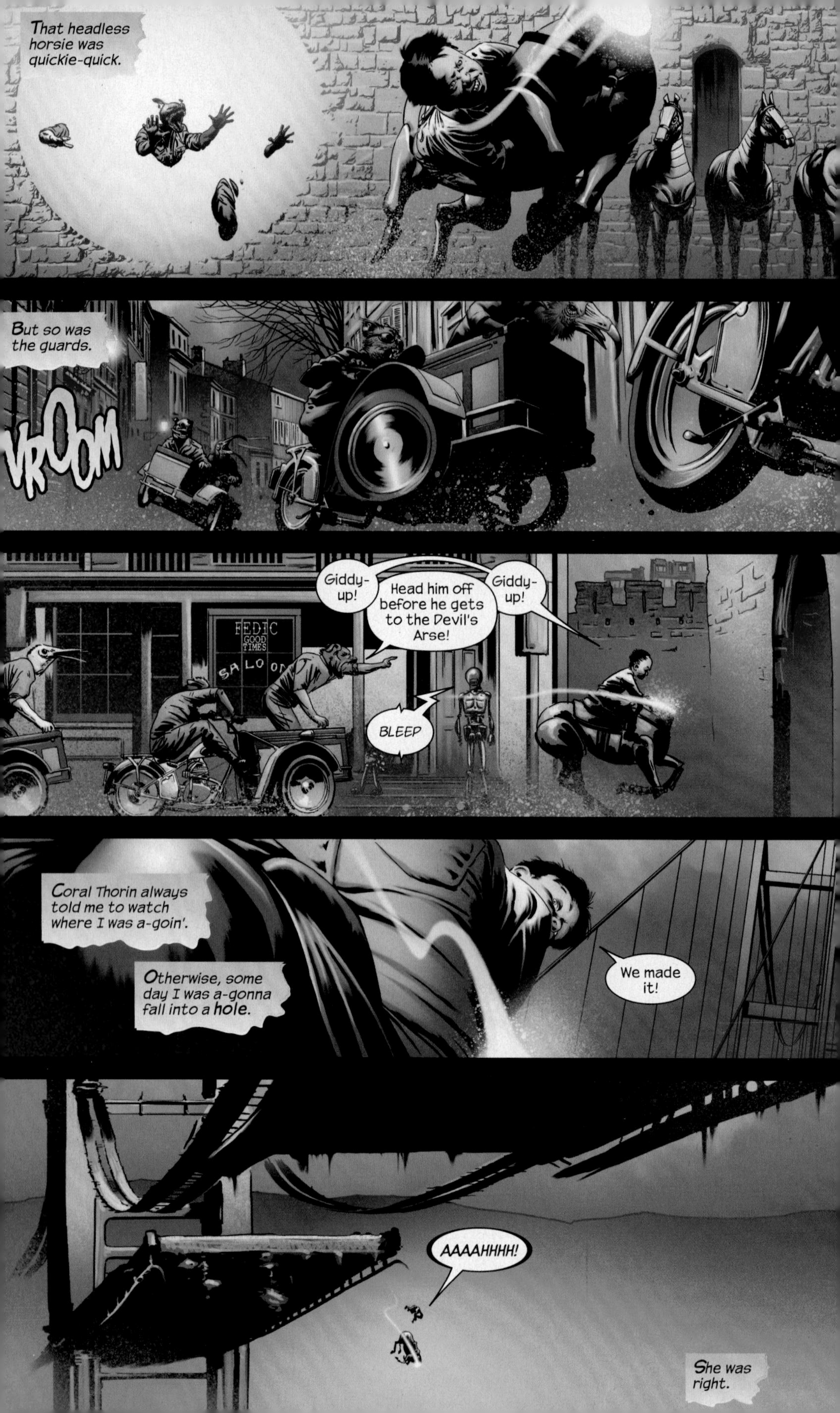
That headless horsie was quickie-quick.
But so was the guards.
VROOM
Giddy-up!
Head him off before he gets to the Devil's Arse!
Giddy-up!
FEDIC GOOD TIMES SALOON
BLEEP
Coral Thorin always told me to watch where I was a-goin'.
Otherwise, some day I was a-gonna fall into a hole.
We made it!
AAAAHHHH!
She was right.

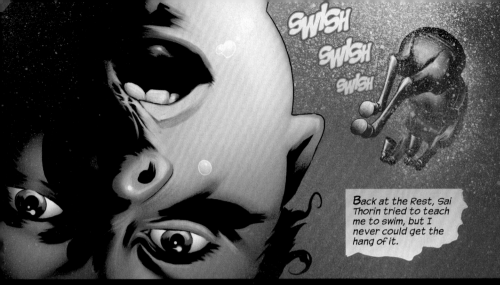

SWISH
SWISH
SWISH

Back at the Rest, Sai Thorin tried to teach me to swim, but I never could get the hang of it.

I always sunk like a stone, so I did.

But even as my breath bubbled out of my body, I felt somethin' a-snakin' into my **mind**.

Welcome, Sheemie, son of Stanley.

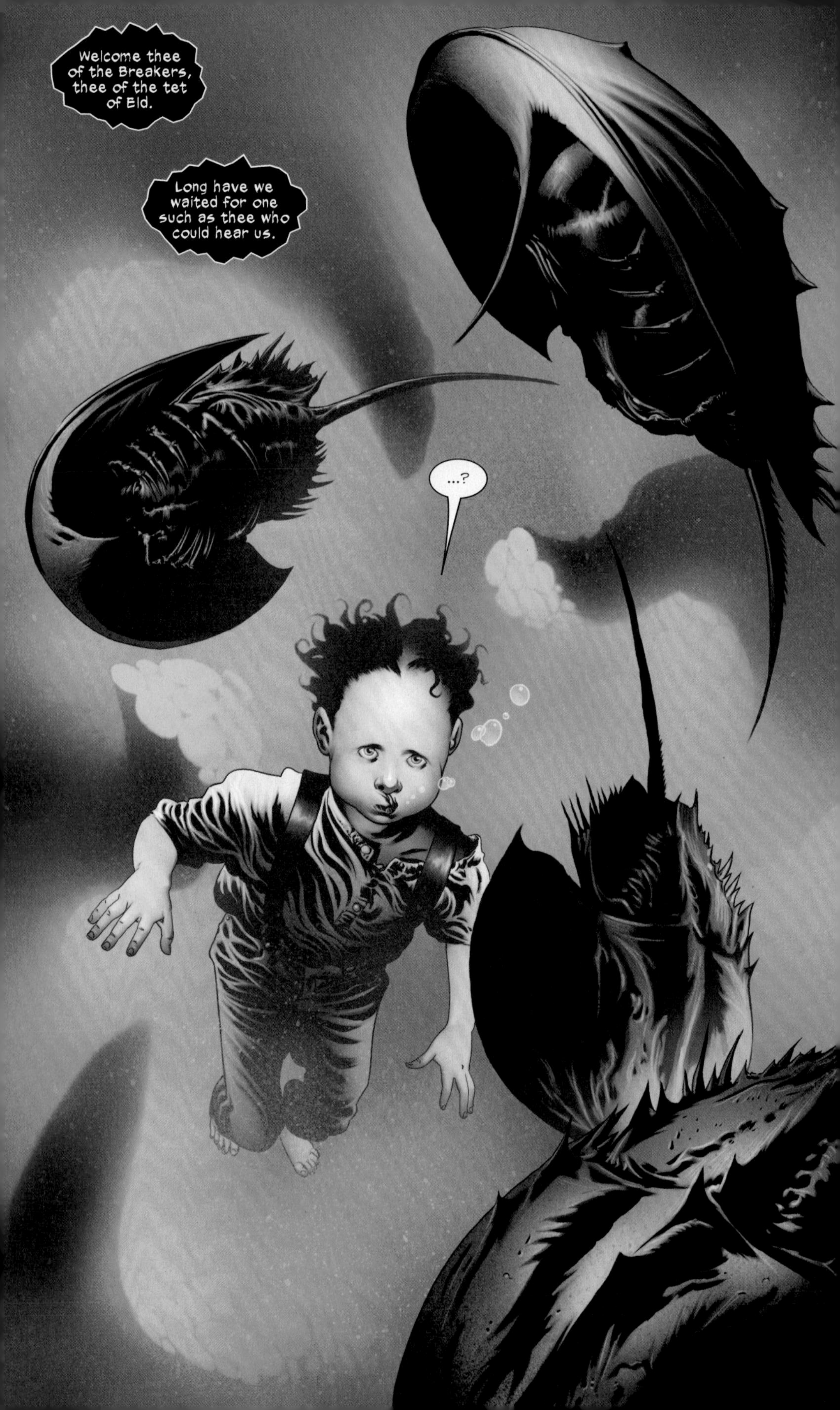
Welcome thee of the Breakers, thee of the tet of Eld.
Long have we waited for one such as thee who could hear us.
...?

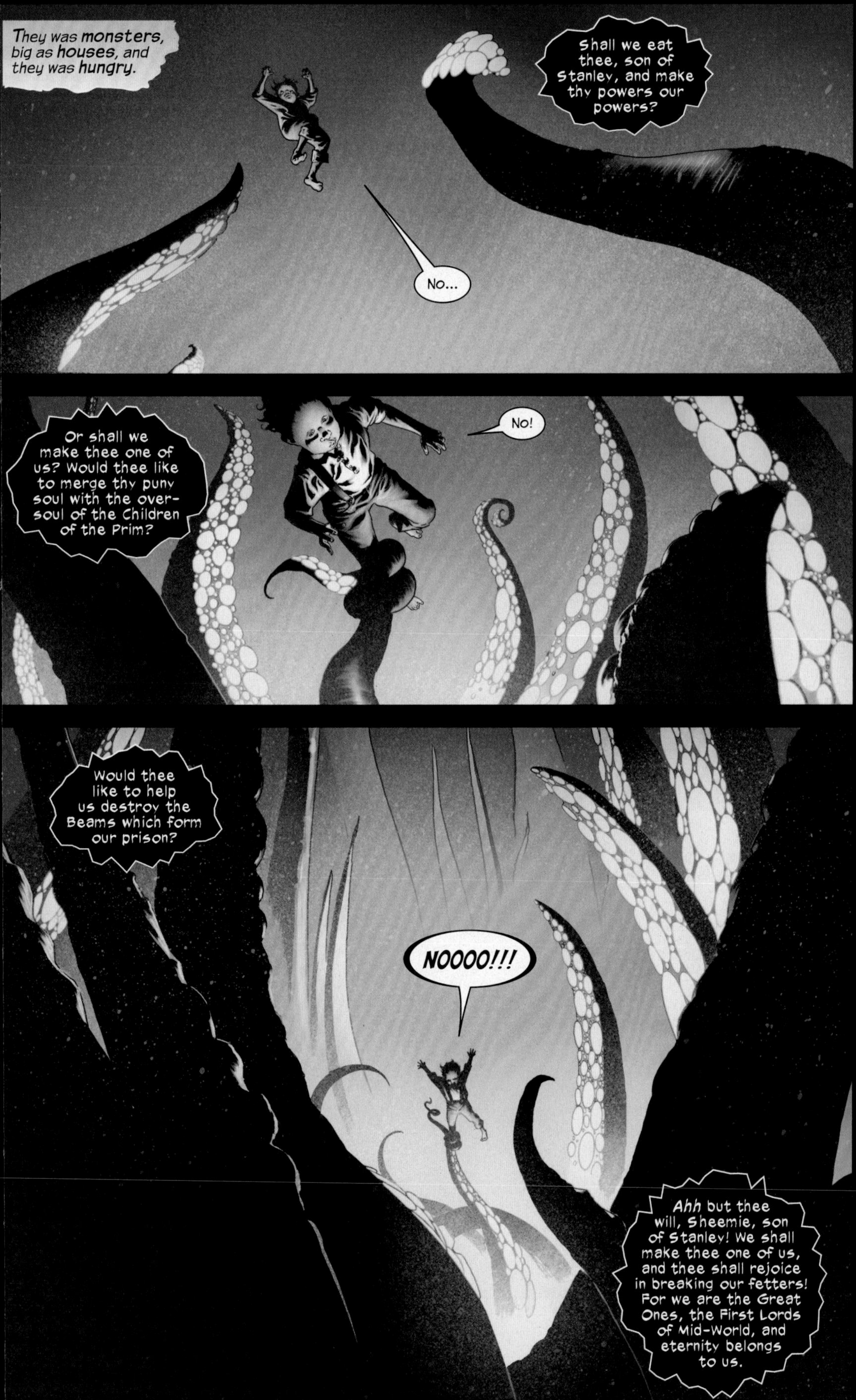
They was monsters, big as houses, and they was hungry.
Shall we eat thee, son of Stanley, and make thy powers our powers?
No...
Or shall we make thee one of us? Would thee like to merge thy puny soul with the over-soul of the Children of the Prim?
No!
Would thee like to help us destroy the Beams which form our prison?
NOOOO!!!
Ahh but thee will, Sheemie, son of Stanley! We shall make thee one of us, and thee shall rejoice in breaking our fetters! For we are the Great Ones, the First Lords of Mid-World, and eternity belongs to us.

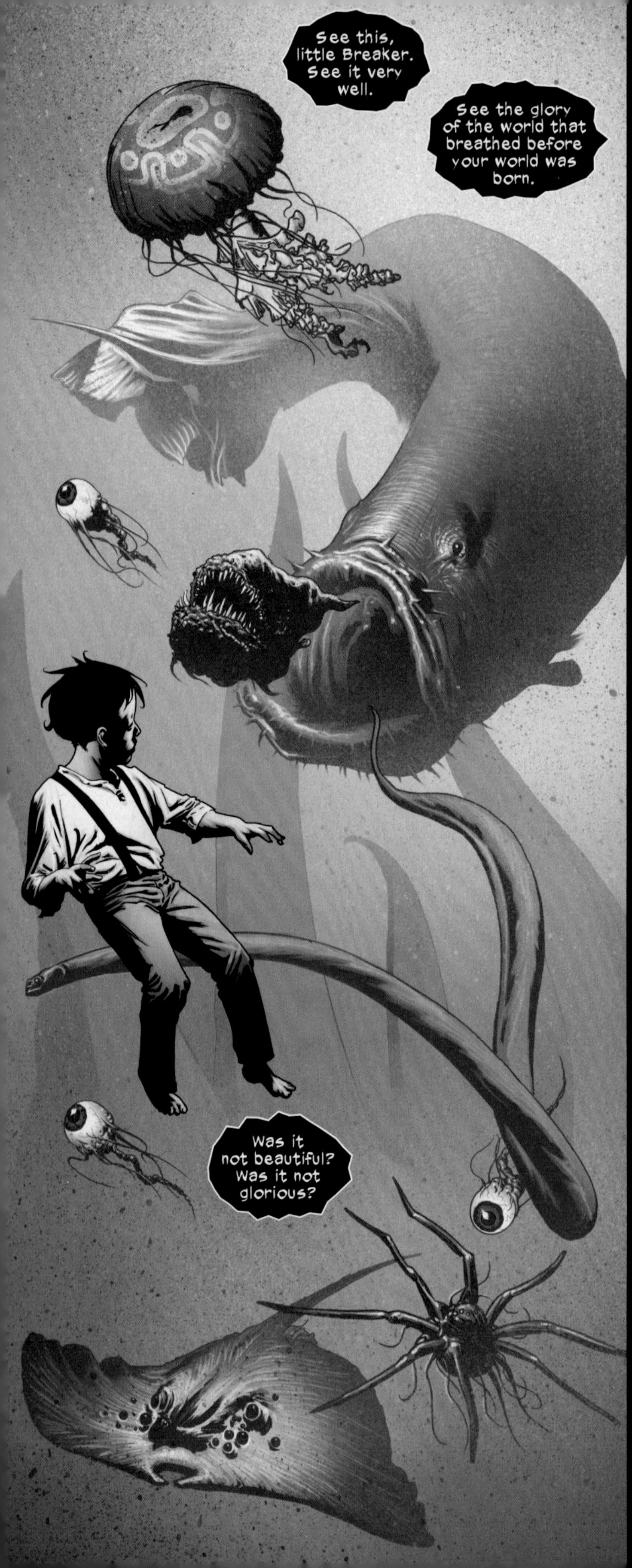
See this, little Breaker. See it very well.
See the glory of the world that breathed before your world was born.
Was it not beautiful? Was it not glorious?
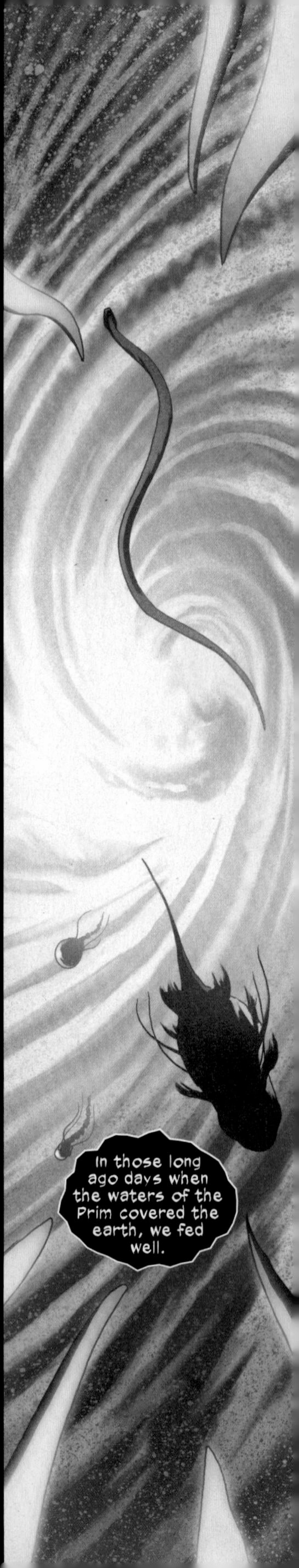
In those long ago days when the waters of the Prim covered the earth, we fed well.

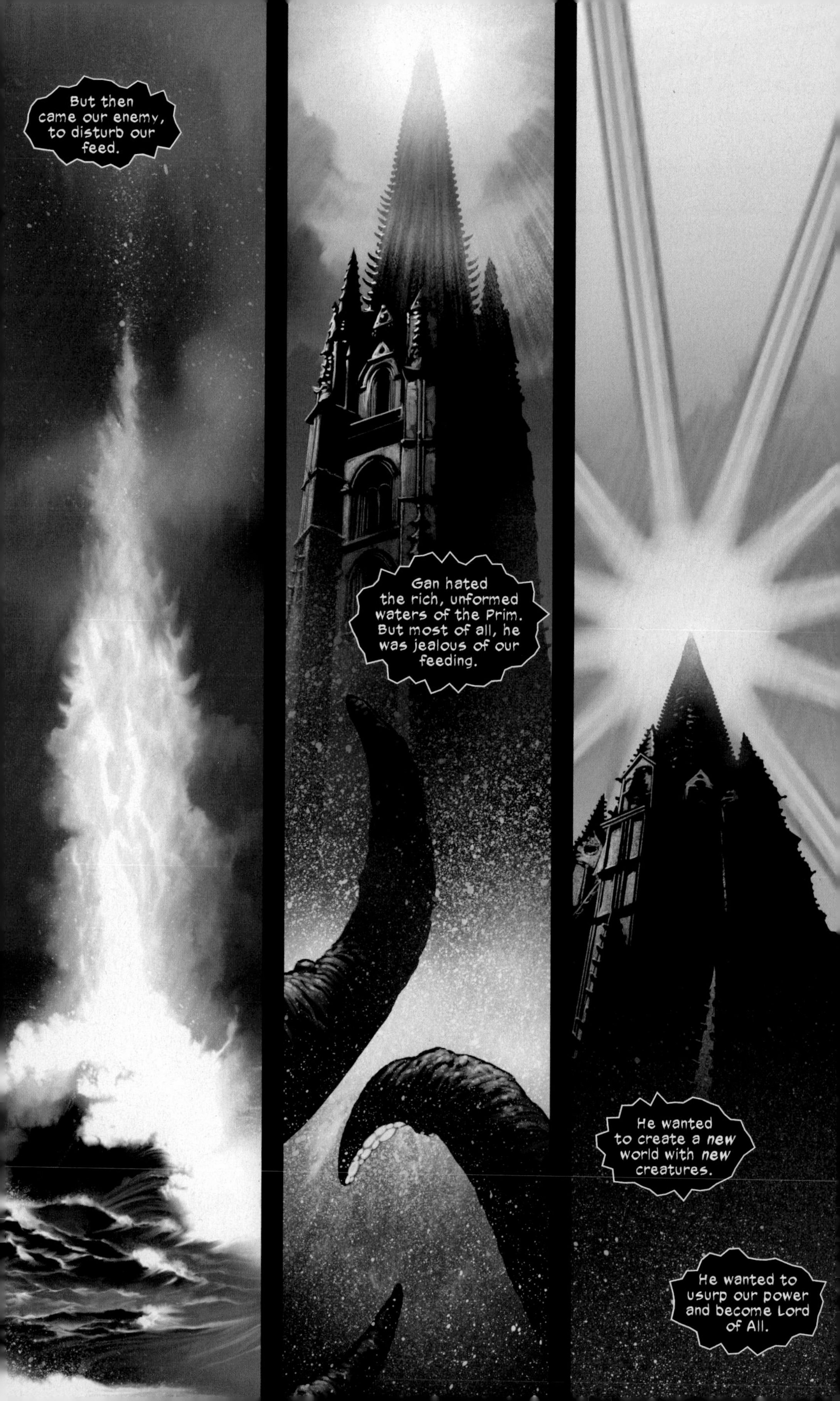
But then came our enemy, to disturb our feed.
Gan hated the rich, unformed waters of the Prim. But most of all, he was jealous of our feeding.
He wanted to create a *new* world with *new* creatures.
He wanted to usurp our power and become Lord of All.

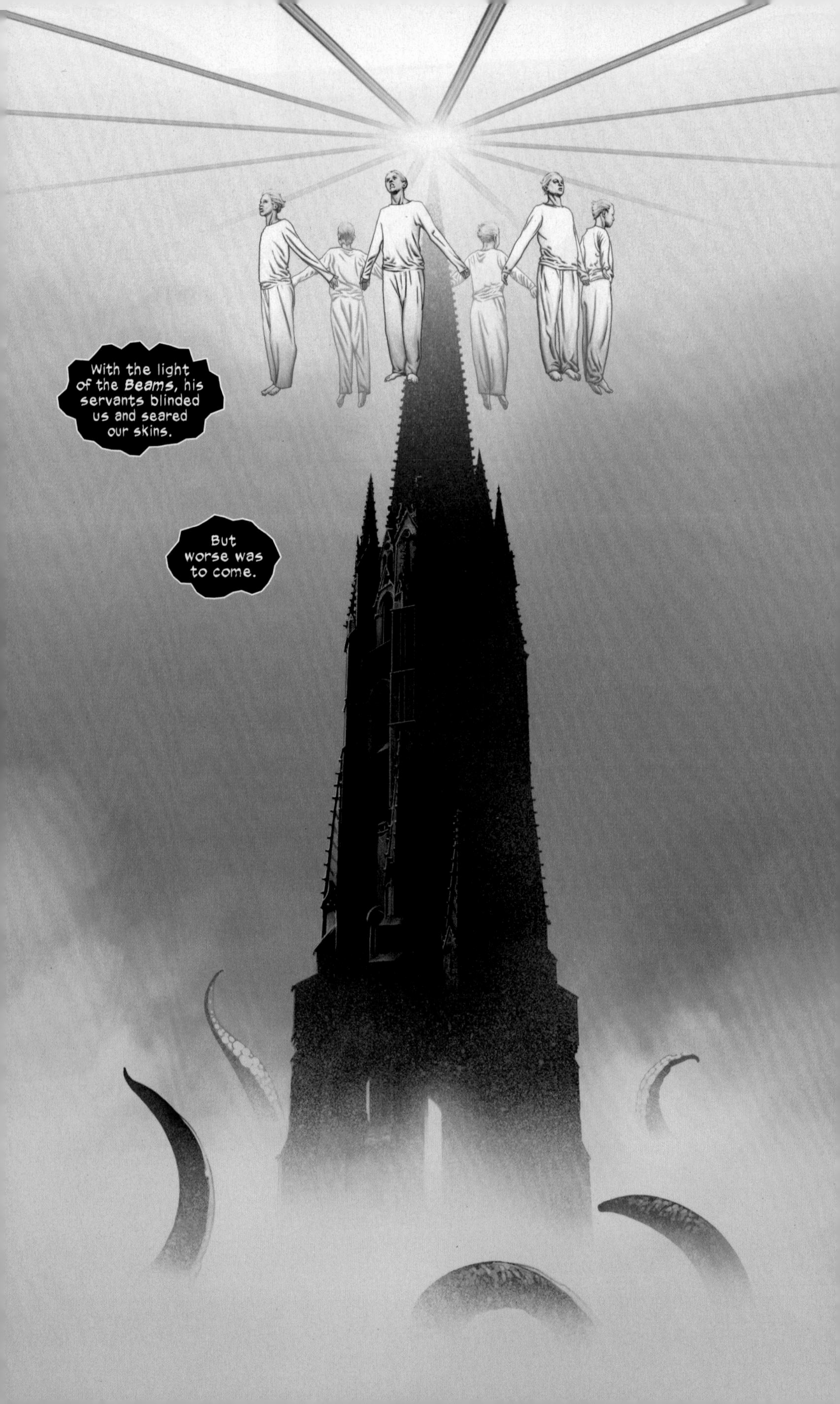
With the light of the *Beams*, his servants blinded us and seared our skins.
But worse was to come.

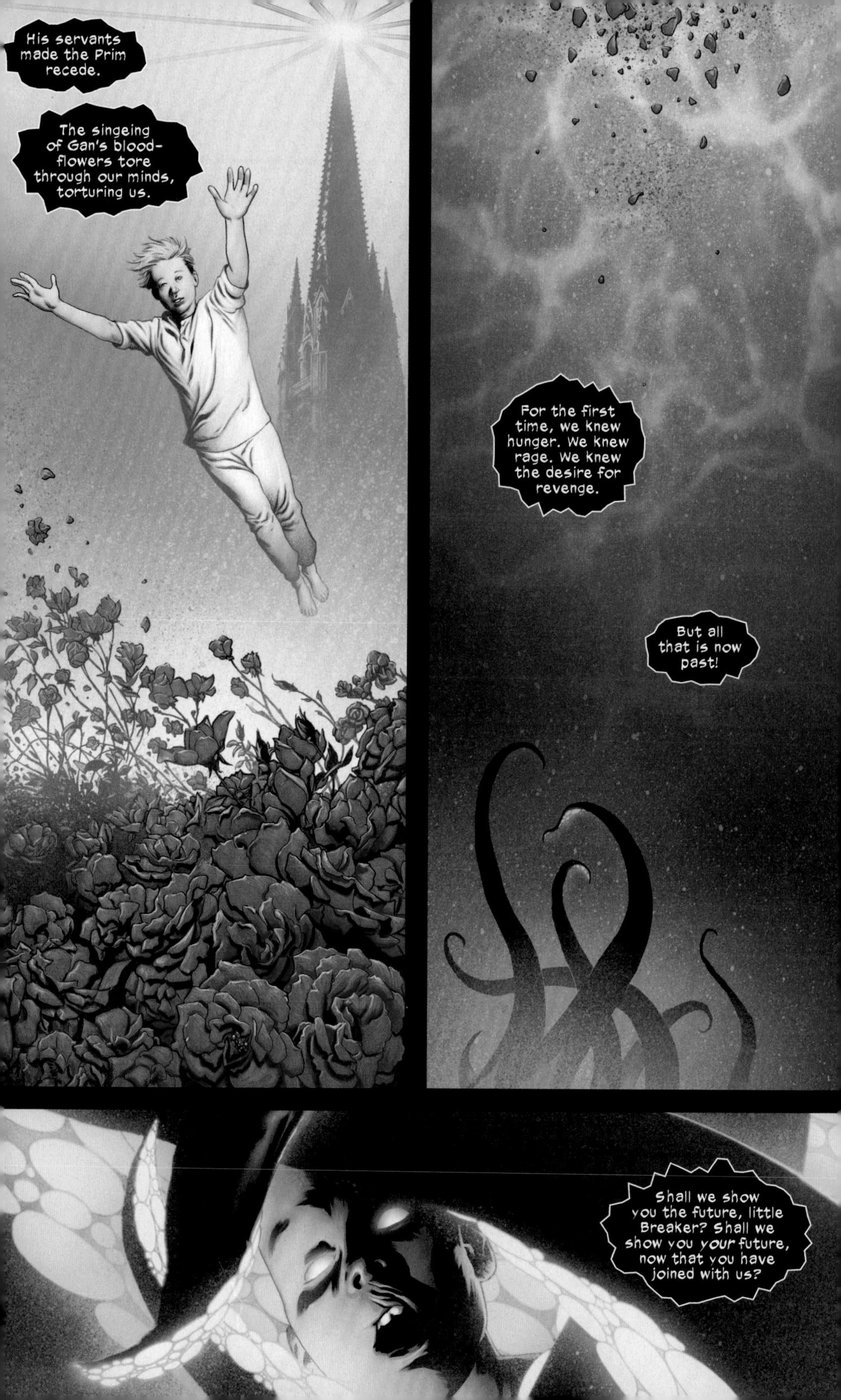
His servants made the Prim recede.
The singeing of Gan's blood-flowers tore through our minds, torturing us.
For the first time, we knew hunger. We knew rage. We knew the desire for revenge.
But all that is now past!
Shall we show you the future, little Breaker? Shall we show you *your* future, now that you have joined with us?

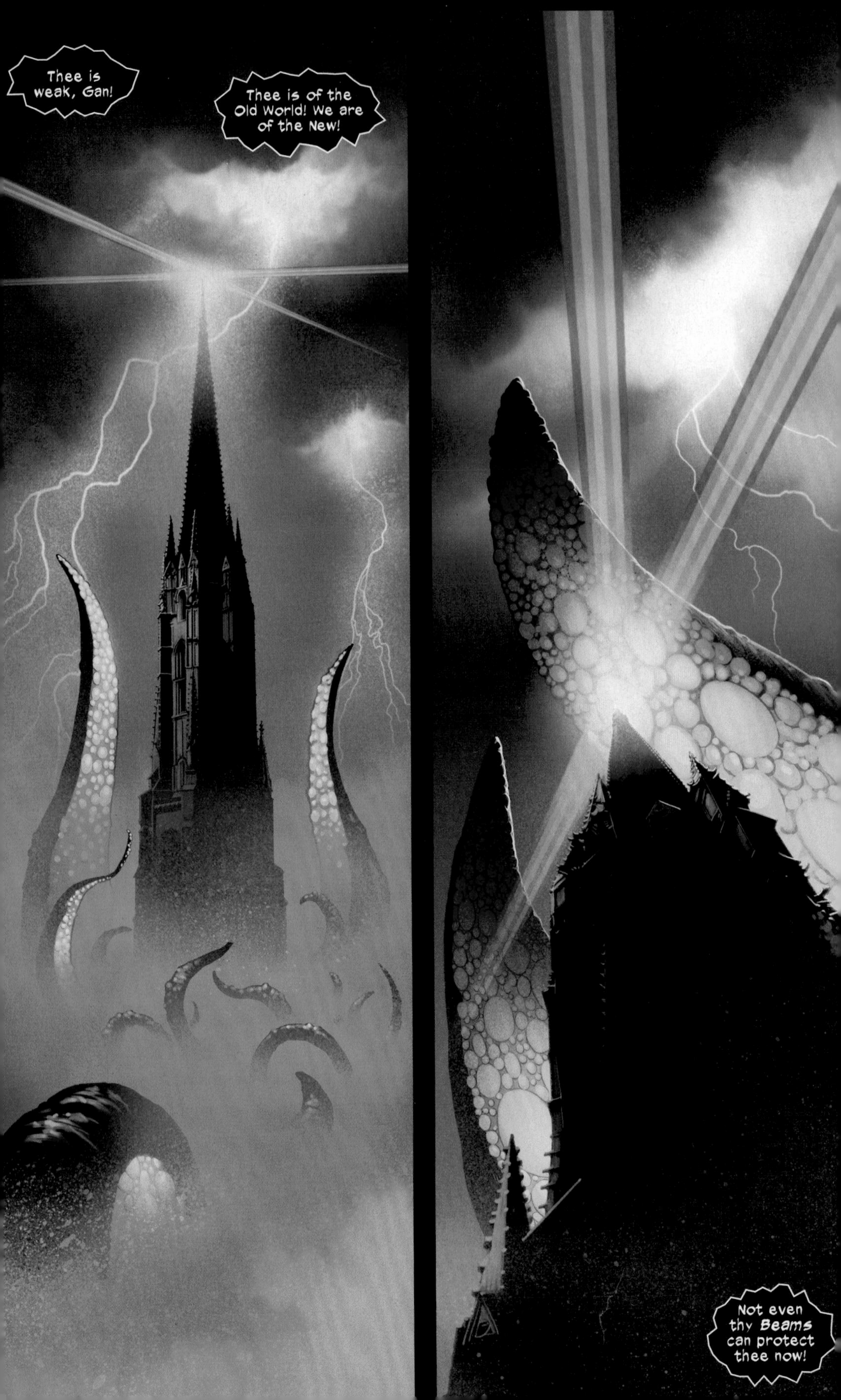
Thee is weak, Gan!
Thee is of the Old World! We are of the New!
Not even thy *Beams* can protect thee now!

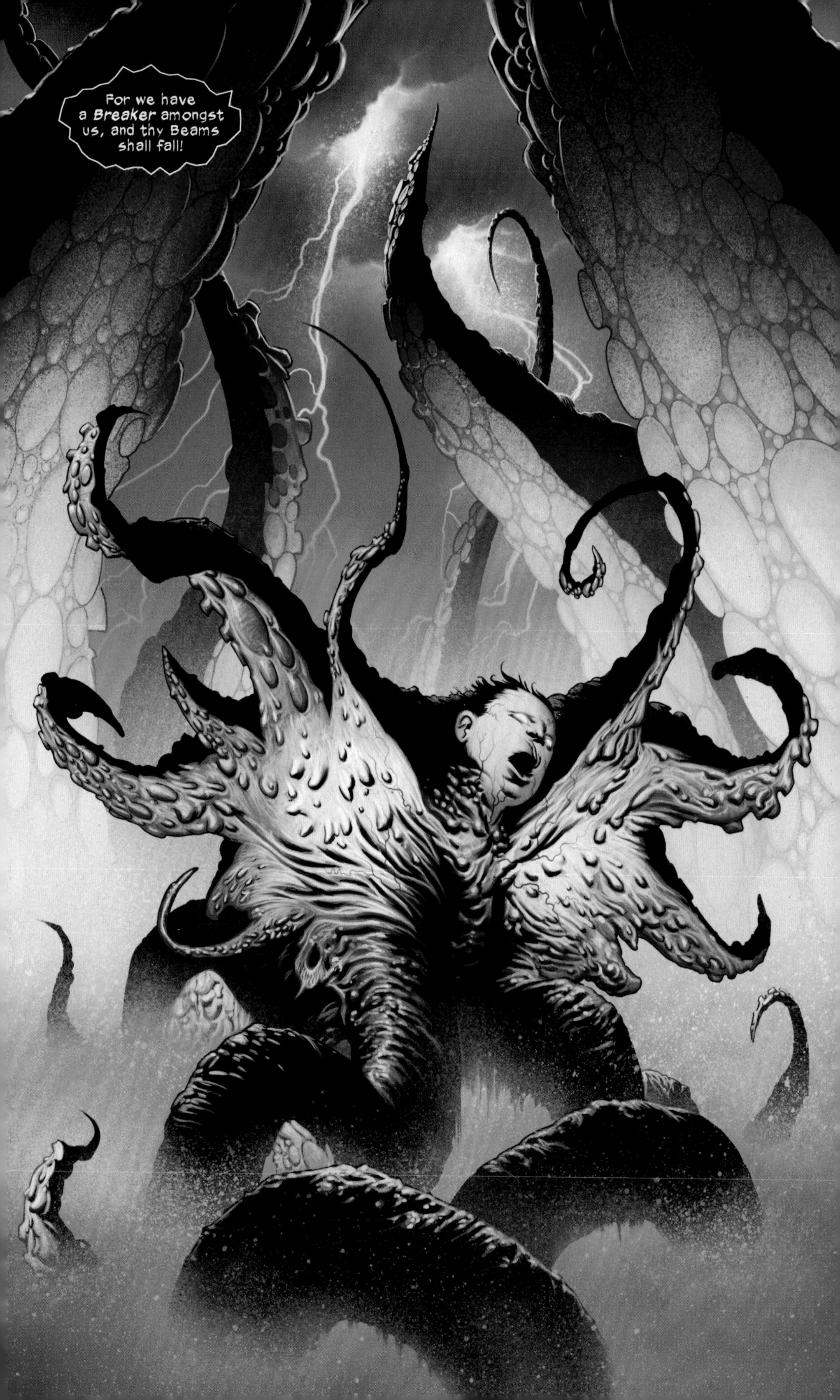
For we have a Breaker amongst us, and thy Beams shall fall!

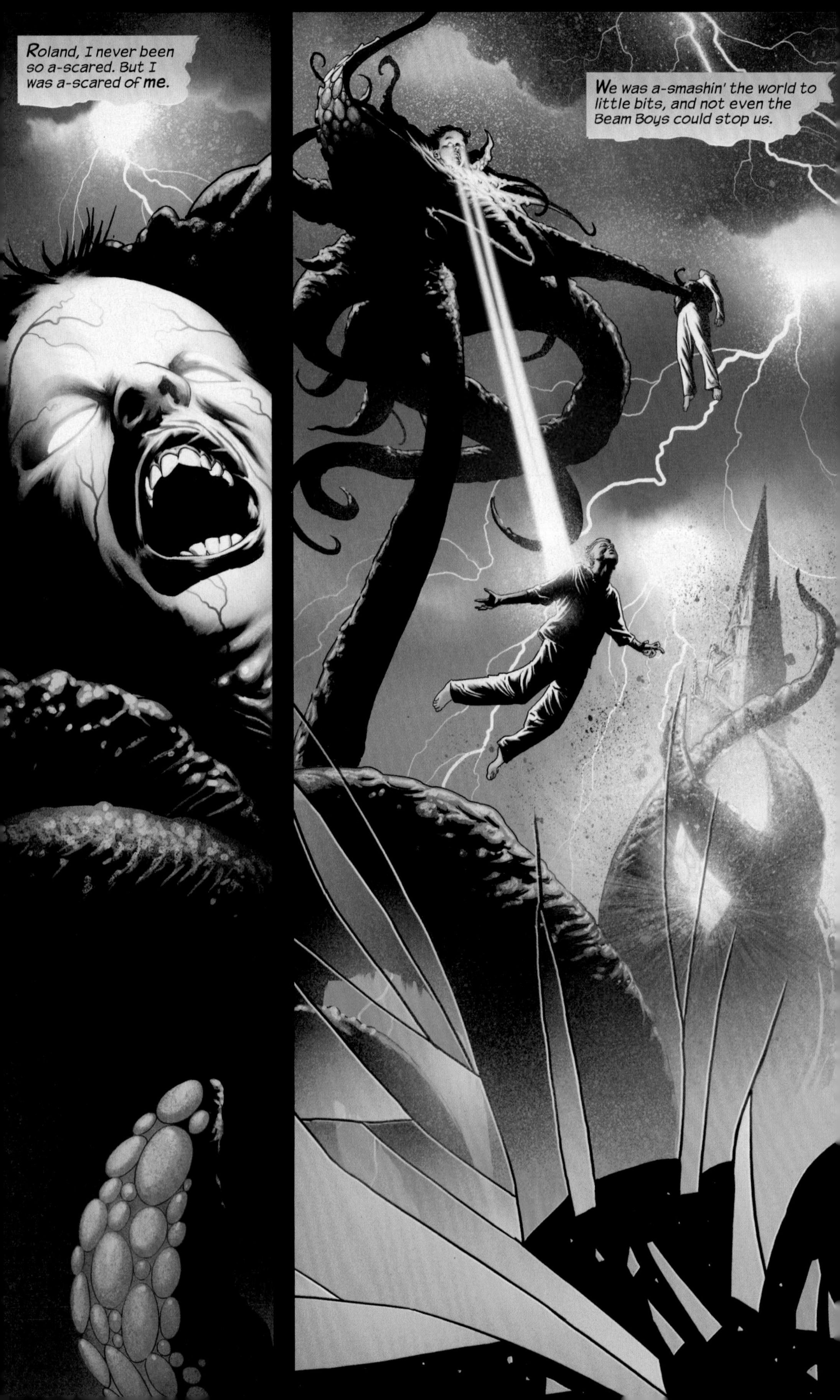
Roland, I never been so a-scared. But I was a-scared of me.
We was a-smashin' the world to little bits, and not even the Beam Boys could stop us.

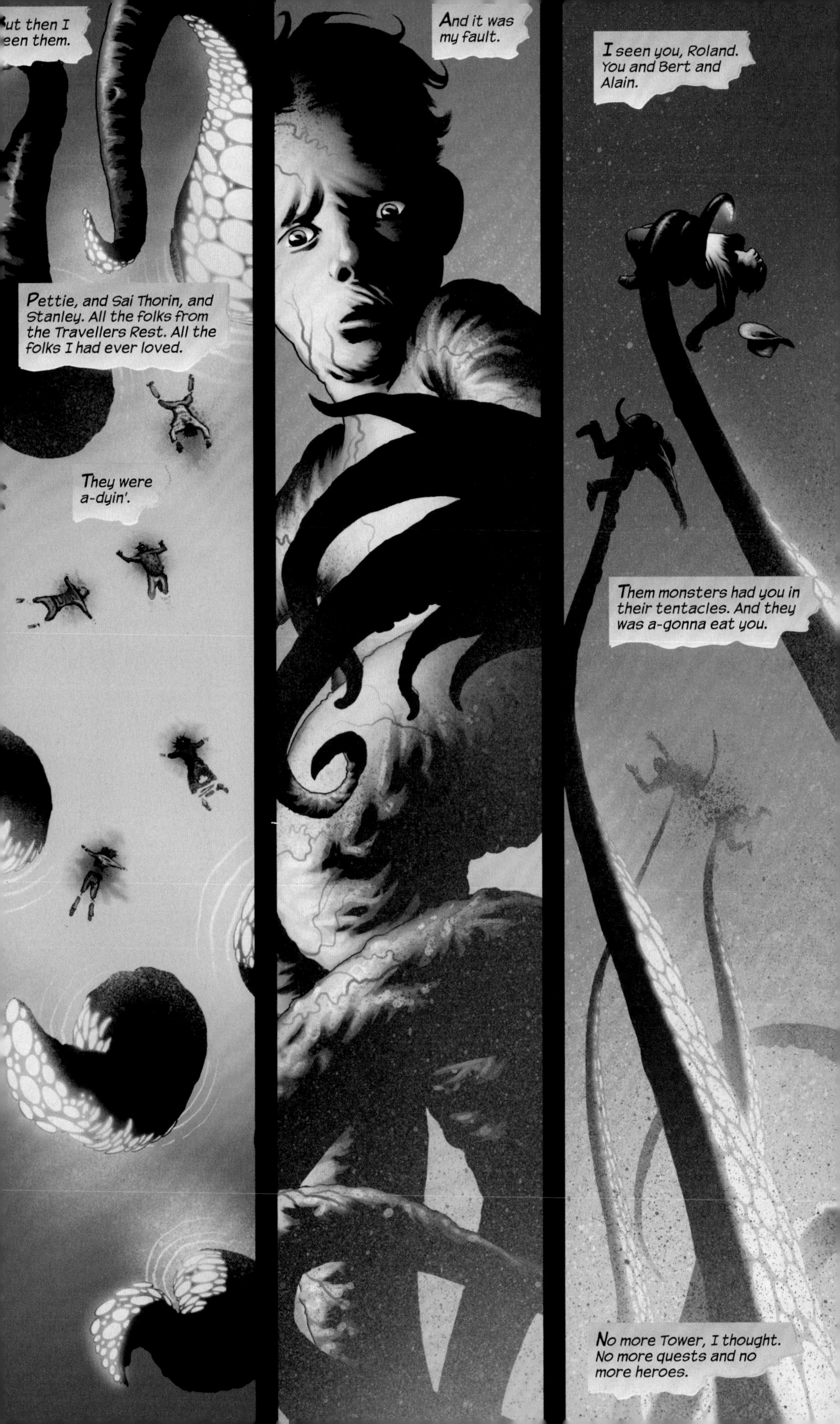

ut then I
een them.
Pettie, and Sai Thorin, and Stanley. All the folks from the Travellers Rest. All the folks I had ever loved.
They were a-dyin'.
And it was my fault.
I seen you, Roland. You and Bert and Alain.
Them monsters had you in their tentacles. And they was a-gonna eat you.
No more Tower, I thought. No more quests and no more heroes.

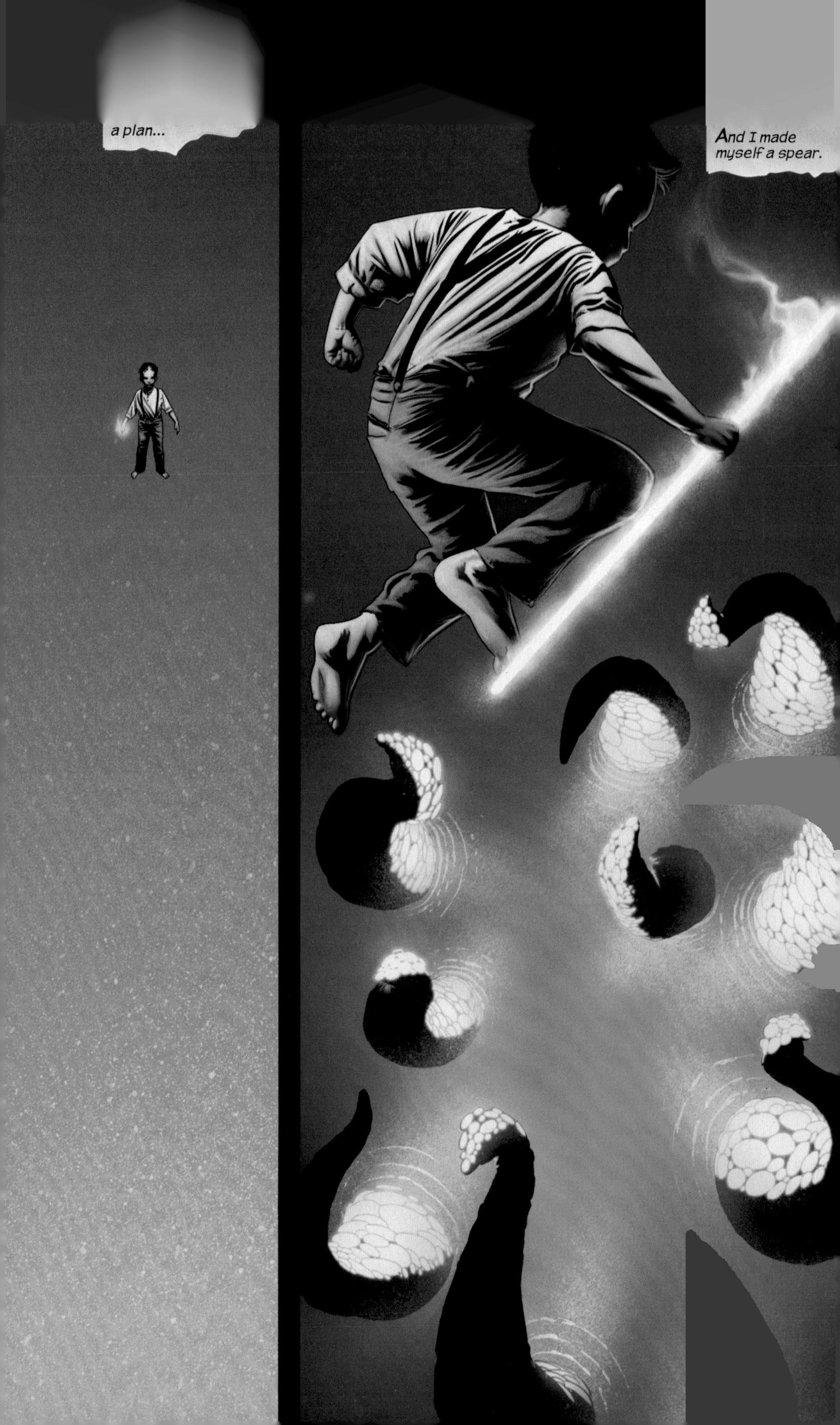
a plan...
And I made myself a spear.

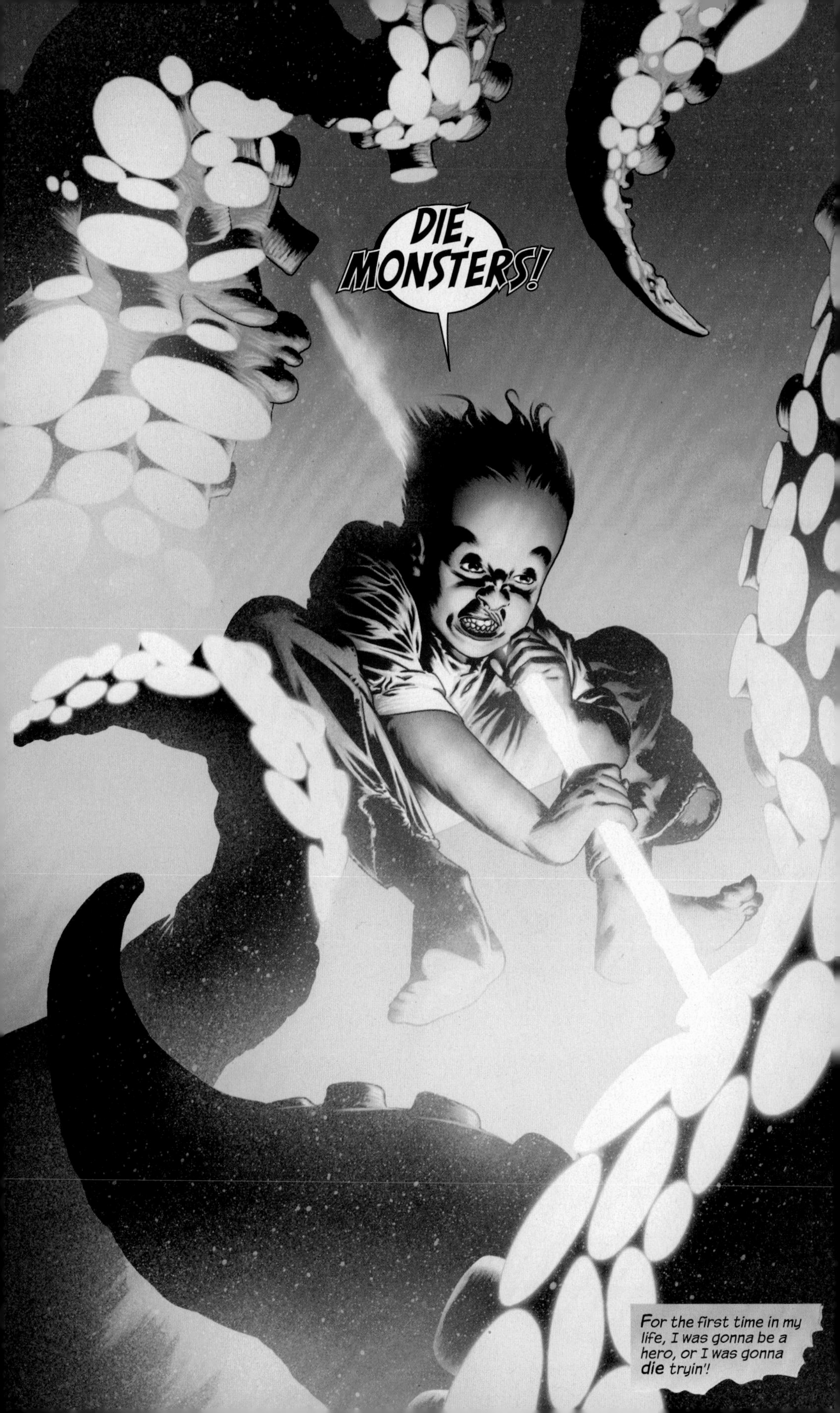
DIE, MONSTERS!
For the first time in my life, I was gonna be a hero, or I was gonna die tryin'!

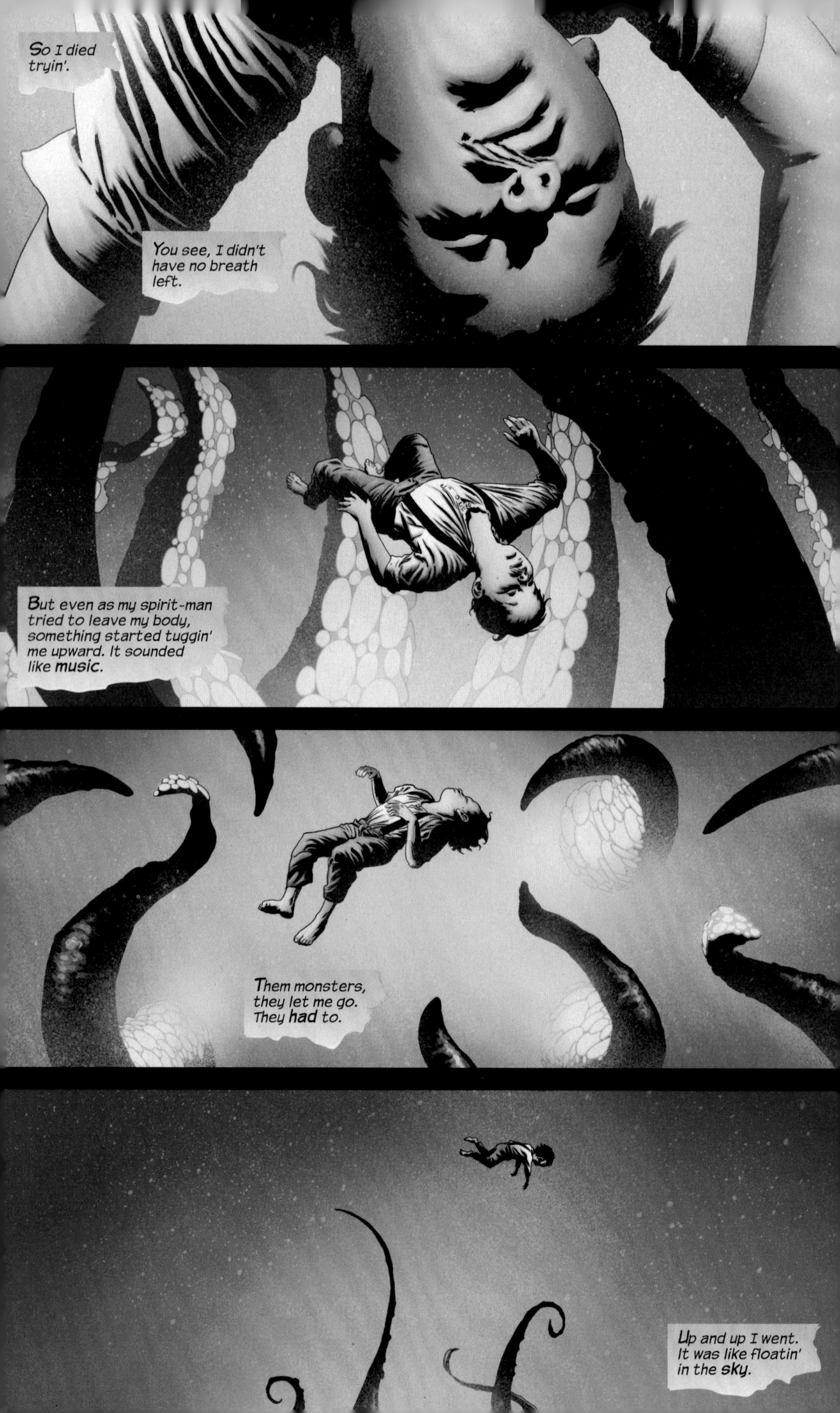
So I died tryin'.
You see, I didn't have no breath left.
But even as my spirit-man tried to leave my body, something started tuggin' me upward. It sounded like **music**.
Them monsters, they let me go. They **had** to.
Up and up I went. It was like floatin' in the **sky**.

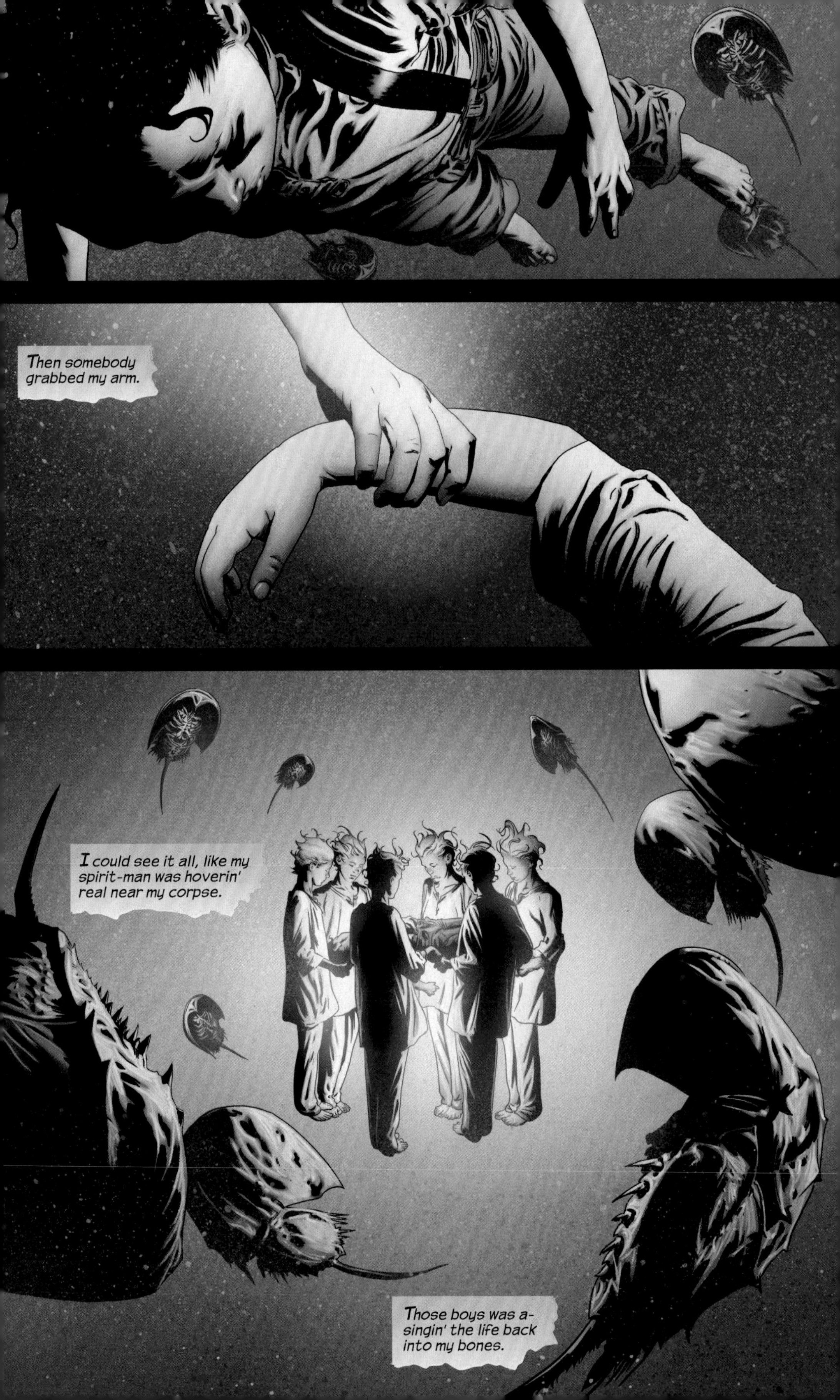

Then somebody grabbed my arm.
I could see it all, like my spirit-man was hoverin' real near my corpse.
Those boys was a-singin' the life back into my bones.

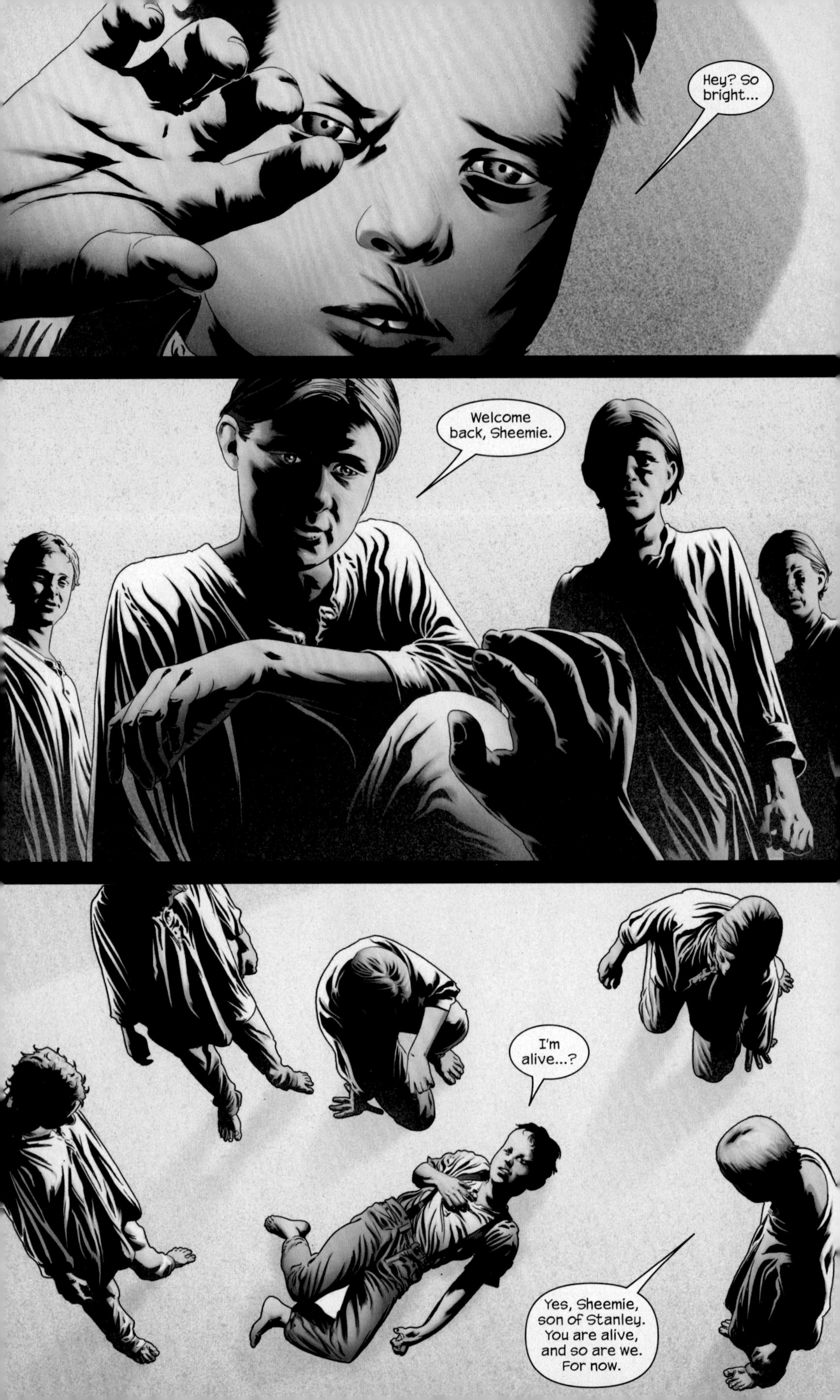

Hey? So bright...
Welcome back, Sheemie.
I'm alive...?
Yes, Sheemie, son of Stanley. You are alive, and so are we. For now.

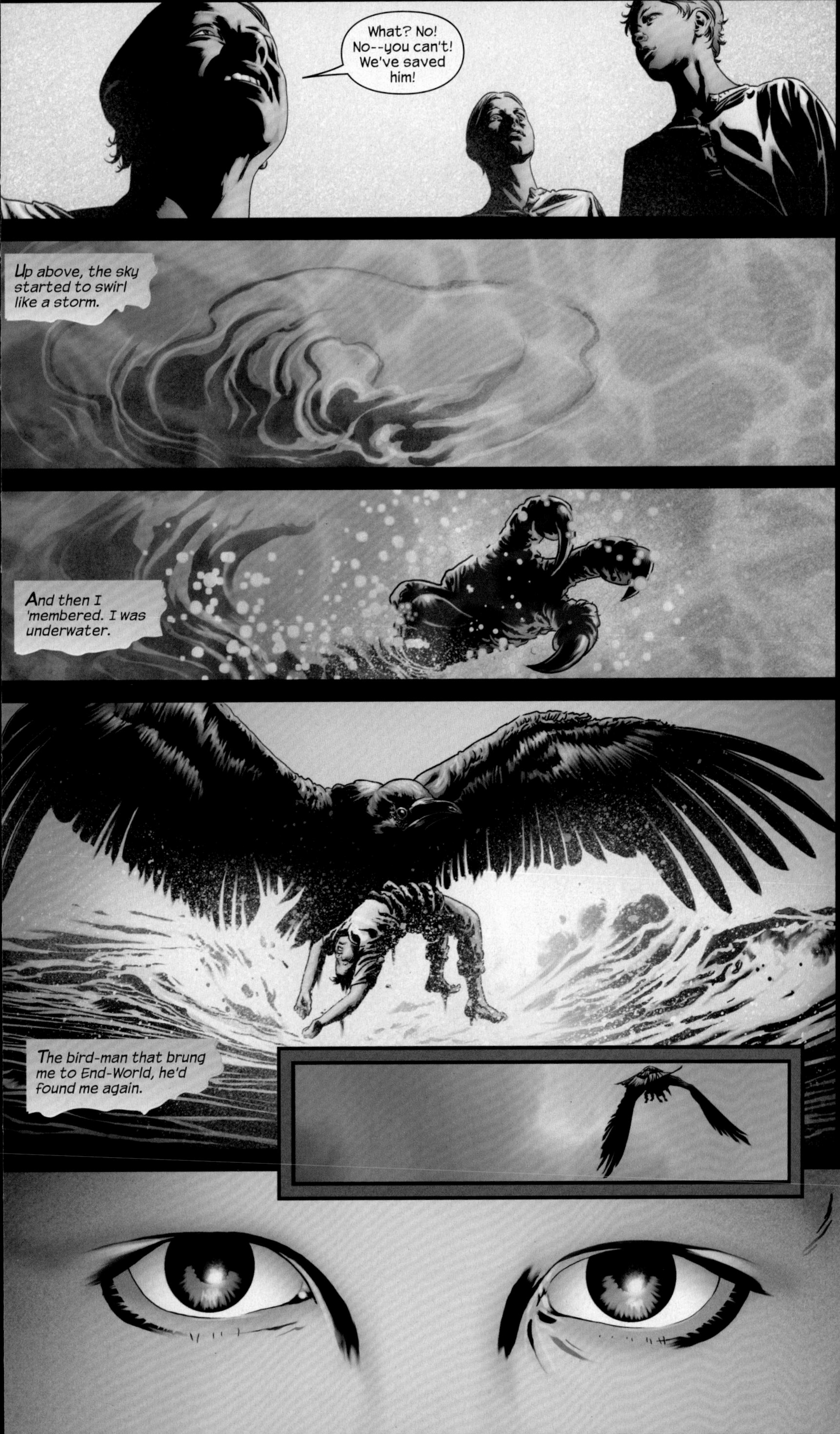
What? No! No--you can't! We've saved him!
Up above, the sky started to swirl like a storm.
And then I 'membered. I was underwater.
The bird-man that brung me to End-World, he'd found me again.

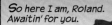

So here I am, Roland. Awaitin' for you.

I'm a-doin' my best to protect the Beam Boys, 'cause they're the weak ones now.

But I'm only small, and my brain's not all that big neither.

We need you.

Real soon.

You won't forget about your old pal, Sheemie.

Will you?

THE END

"He knows it's a dream . . . and yet he can't escape it. Always look for the back door, Cort used to tell them, but if there's a back door in this dream, Roland cannot find it."

WOLVES OF THE CALLA, 169

STEPHEN KING

THE DARK TOWER

~ THE GUNSLINGER ~

EVIL GROUND

CHAPTER ONE

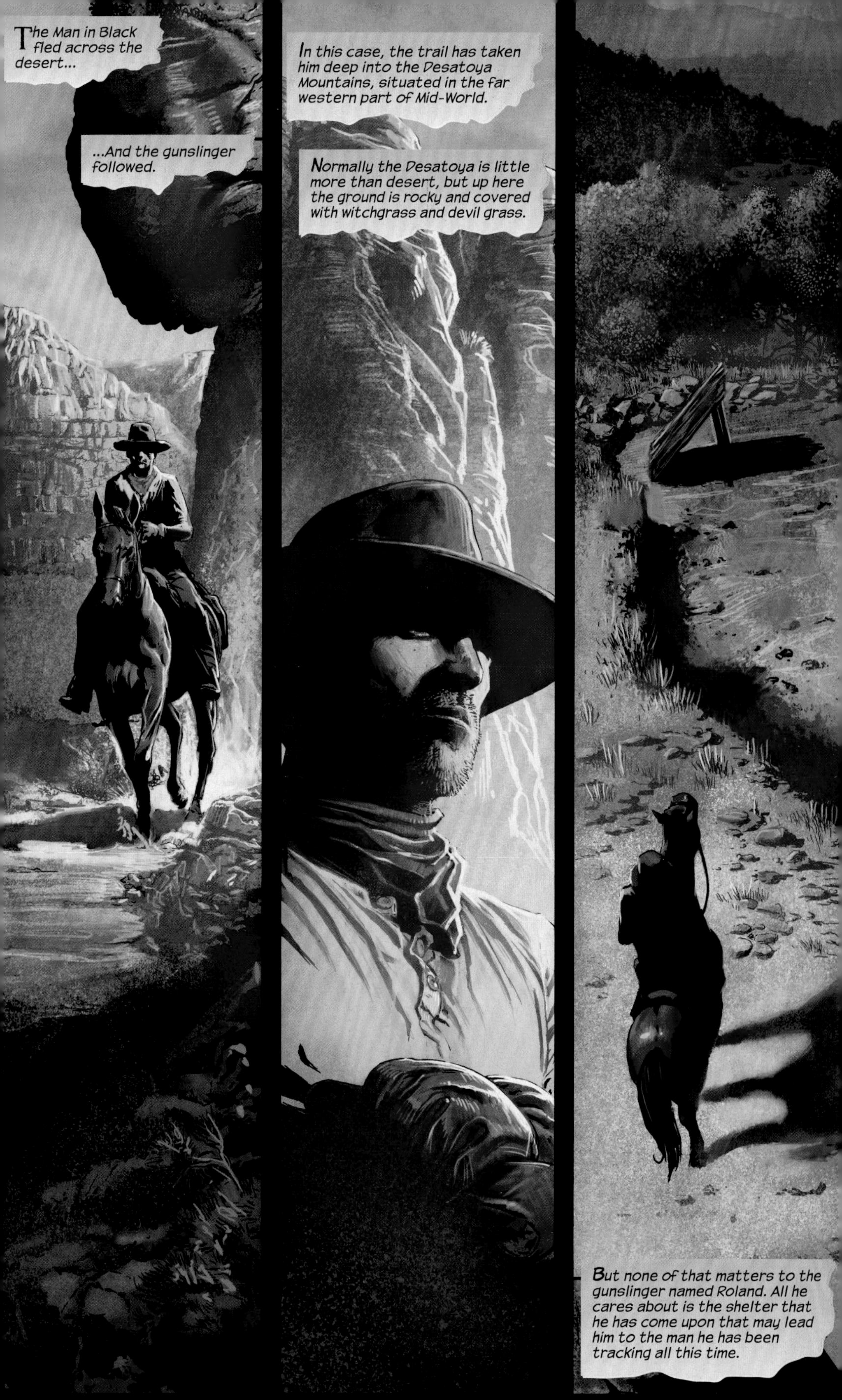
The Man in Black fled across the desert...
...And the gunslinger followed.
In this case, the trail has taken him deep into the Desatoya Mountains, situated in the far western part of Mid-World.
Normally the Desatoya is little more than desert, but up here the ground is rocky and covered with witchgrass and devil grass.
But none of that matters to the gunslinger named Roland. All he cares about is the shelter that he has come upon that may lead him to the man he has been tracking all this time.

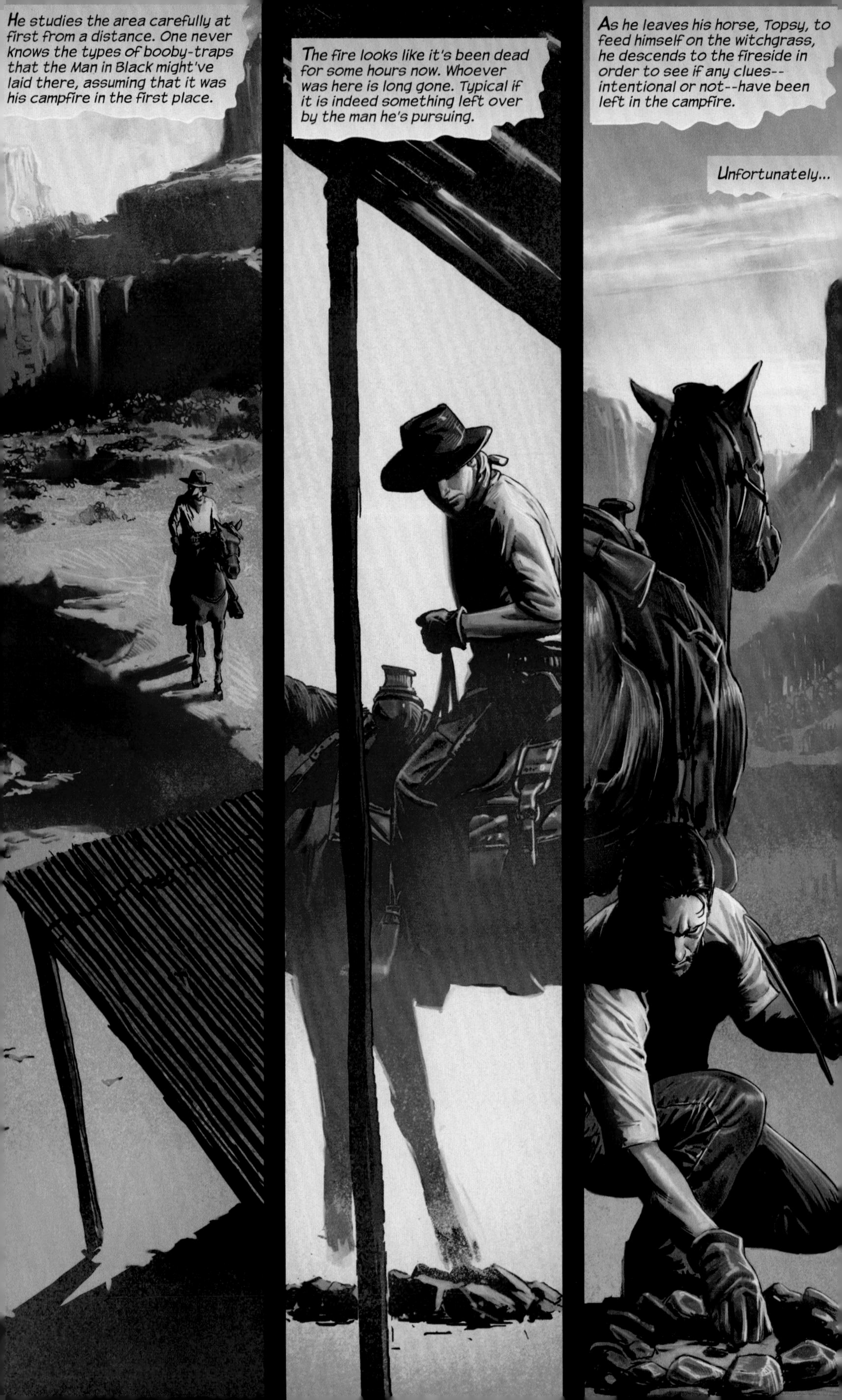
He studies the area carefully at first from a distance. One never knows the types of booby-traps that the Man in Black might've laid there, assuming that it was his campfire in the first place.
The fire looks like it's been dead for some hours now. Whoever was here is long gone. Typical if it is indeed something left over by the man he's pursuing.
As he leaves his horse, Topsy, to feed himself on the witchgrass, he descends to the fireside in order to see if any clues--intentional or not--have been left in the campfire.
Unfortunately...

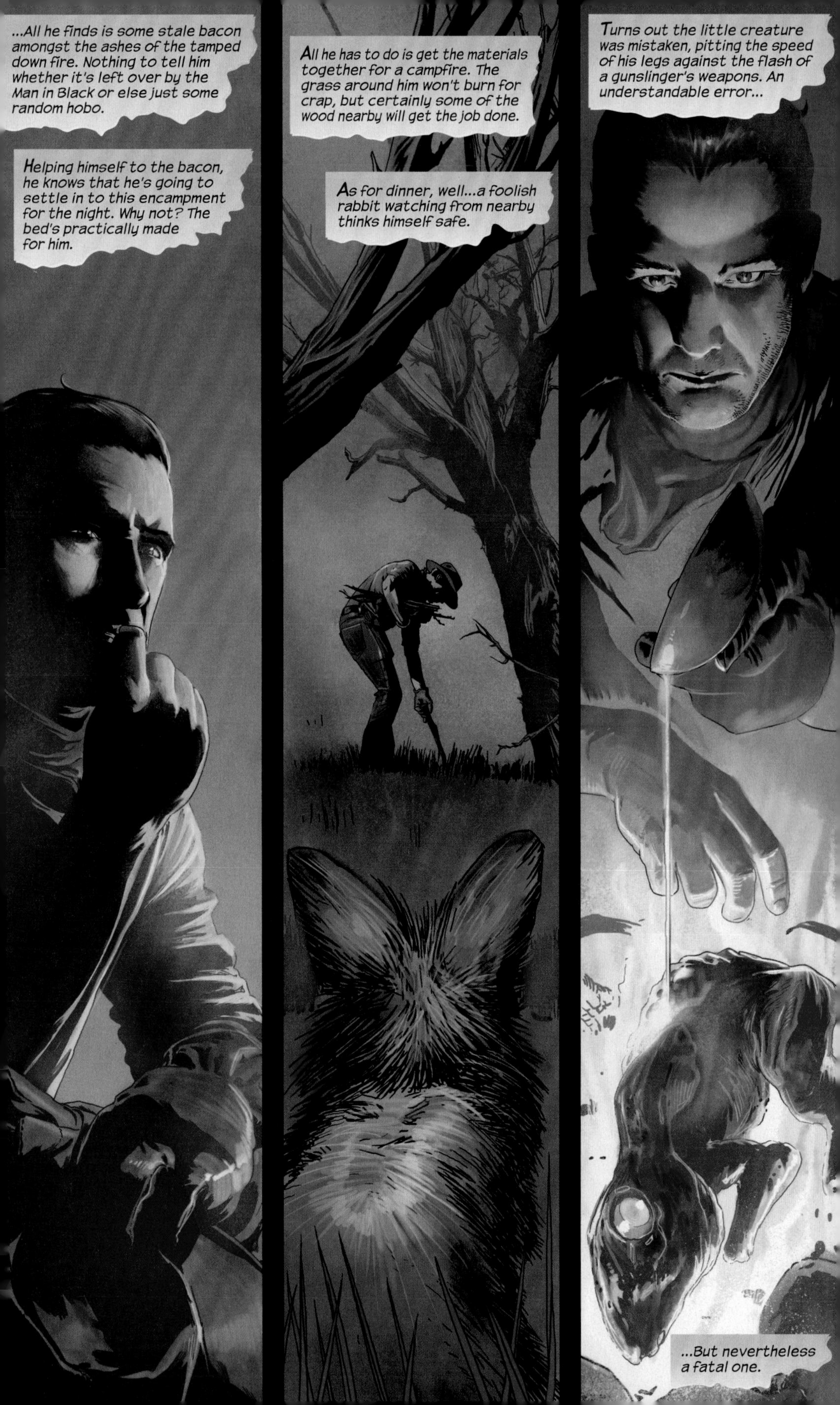

...All he finds is some stale bacon amongst the ashes of the tamped down fire. Nothing to tell him whether it's left over by the Man in Black or else just some random hobo.
Helping himself to the bacon, he knows that he's going to settle in to this encampment for the night. Why not? The bed's practically made for him.
All he has to do is get the materials together for a campfire. The grass around him won't burn for crap, but certainly some of the wood nearby will get the job done.
As for dinner, well...a foolish rabbit watching from nearby thinks himself safe.
Turns out the little creature was mistaken, pitting the speed of his legs against the flash of a gunslinger's weapons. An understandable error...
...But nevertheless a fatal one.

"Spark-a-dark, where's my sire? Will I lay me?

"Will I stay me? Bless this camp with fire."

This is the poem that Roland mutters to himself as he sets the campfire blazing. They're the first words he said aloud in two days, and they bring welcome recollections of many other campfires and days of greater innocence.

Now he sleeps, the words of his poem long forgotten. Instead his mind is fraught with bad dreams, likely courtesy of the devil grass upon which he is currently stretched out.

Topsy, tied up nearby, whinnies loudly, trying to rouse him from his slumber so that he can see the potential menace lurking close. But it will take a lot more than a frantic horse to rouse him to wakefulness.

And so, as Roland continues in his trapped slumber, close to the campfire something is sucking discarded rabbit bones.

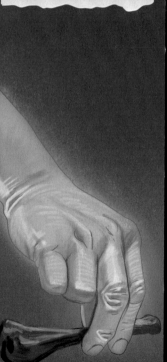

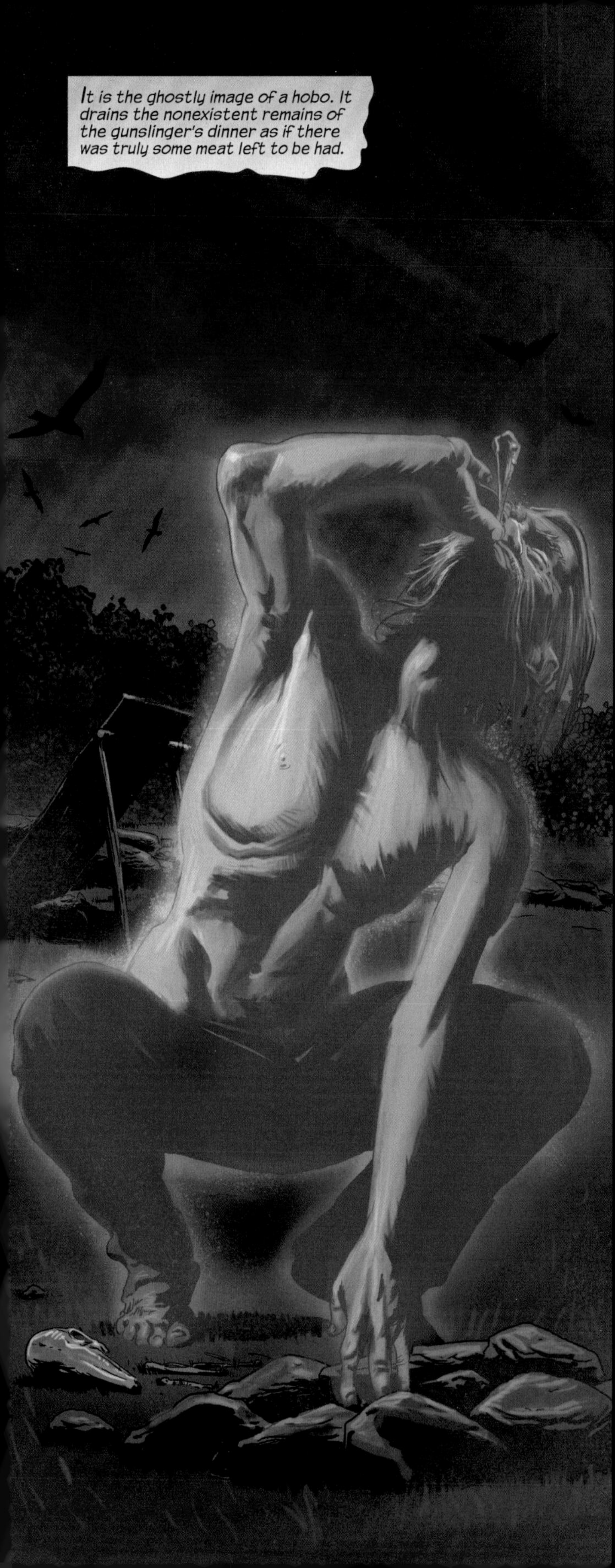
It is the ghostly image of a hobo. It drains the nonexistent remains of the gunslinger's dinner as if there was truly some meat left to be had.

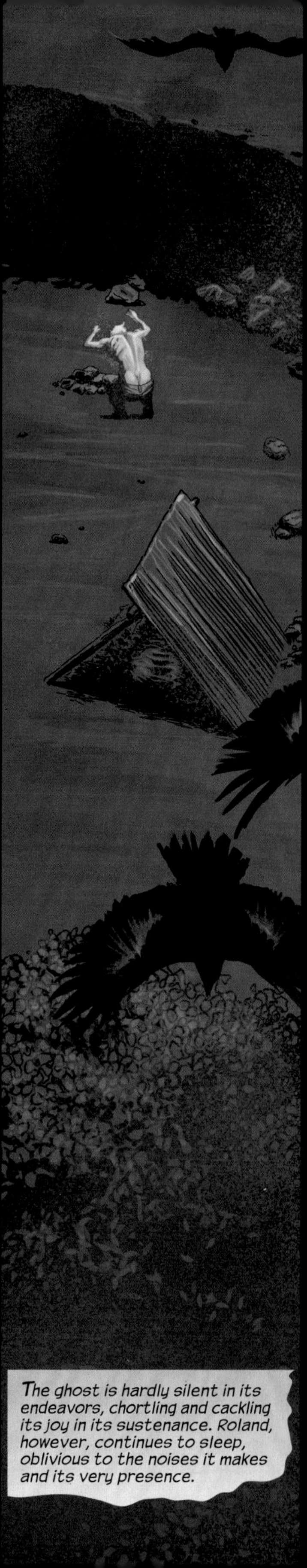
The ghost is hardly silent in its endeavors, chortling and cackling its joy in its sustenance. Roland, however, continues to sleep, oblivious to the noises it makes and its very presence.

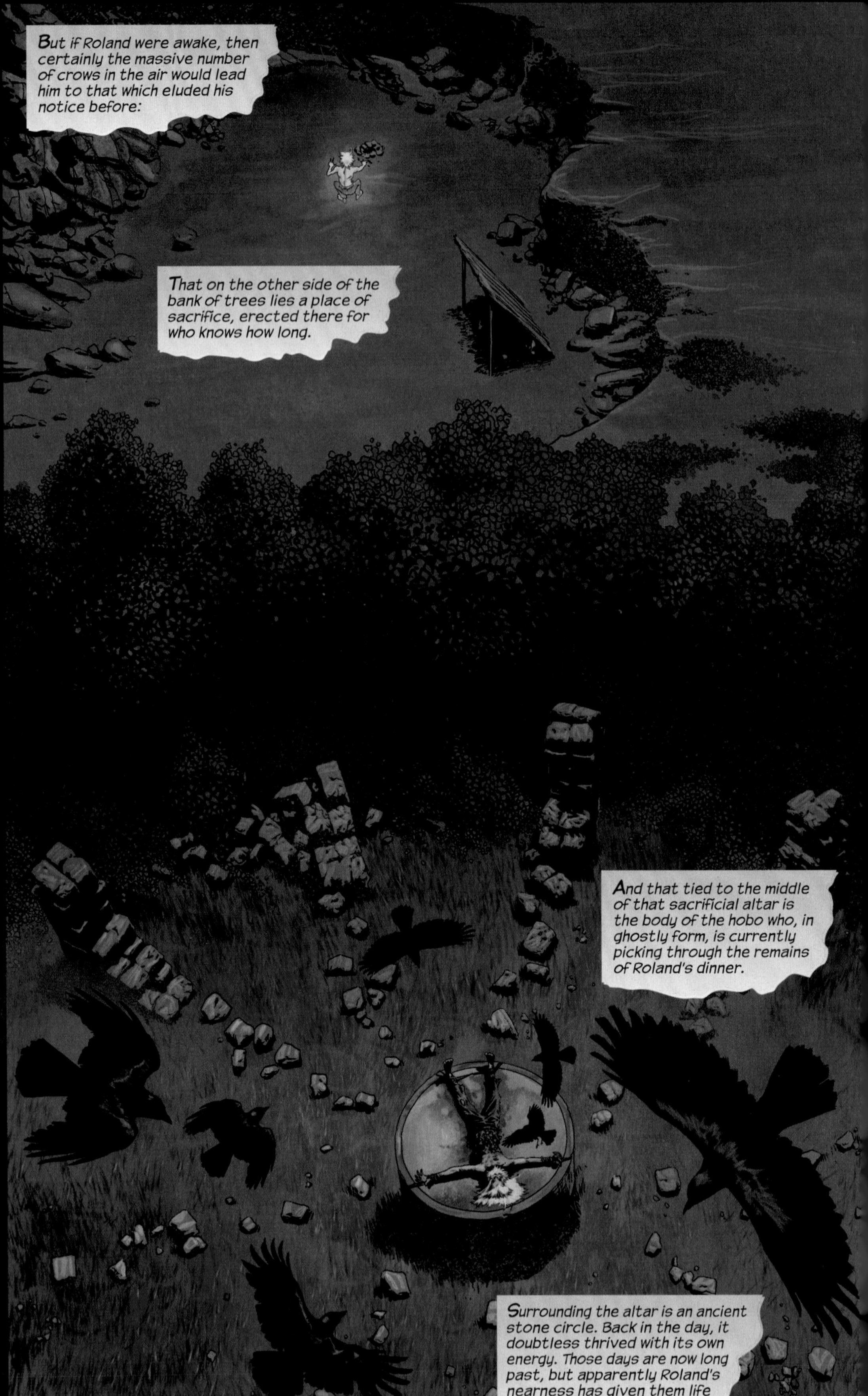
But if Roland were awake, then certainly the massive number of crows in the air would lead him to that which eluded his notice before:
That on the other side of the bank of trees lies a place of sacrifice, erected there for who knows how long.
And that tied to the middle of that sacrificial altar is the body of the hobo who, in ghostly form, is currently picking through the remains of Roland's dinner.
Surrounding the altar is an ancient stone circle. Back in the day, it doubtless thrived with its own energy. Those days are now long past, but apparently Roland's nearness has given them life long deprived of them.

One particularly aggressive crow descends upon the body and picks out the remains of an eyeball that it somehow missed on earlier trips.

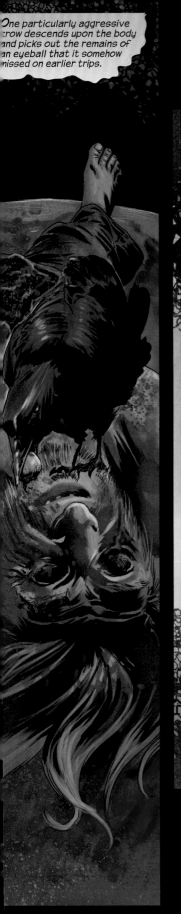

Somewhere deep in his sleep, Roland reacts to the eye's departure as if his own eyeball was being plucked out.

He twists and turns and moans even louder, the bad dreams resulting from the devil grass upon which he lies having its way with him.

In real life, he is a gunslinger of indeterminate years in pursuit of the black-clad man who continues to elude him.

But as tears roll down his face, he dreams he is a young man, and of the time when he was not alone.

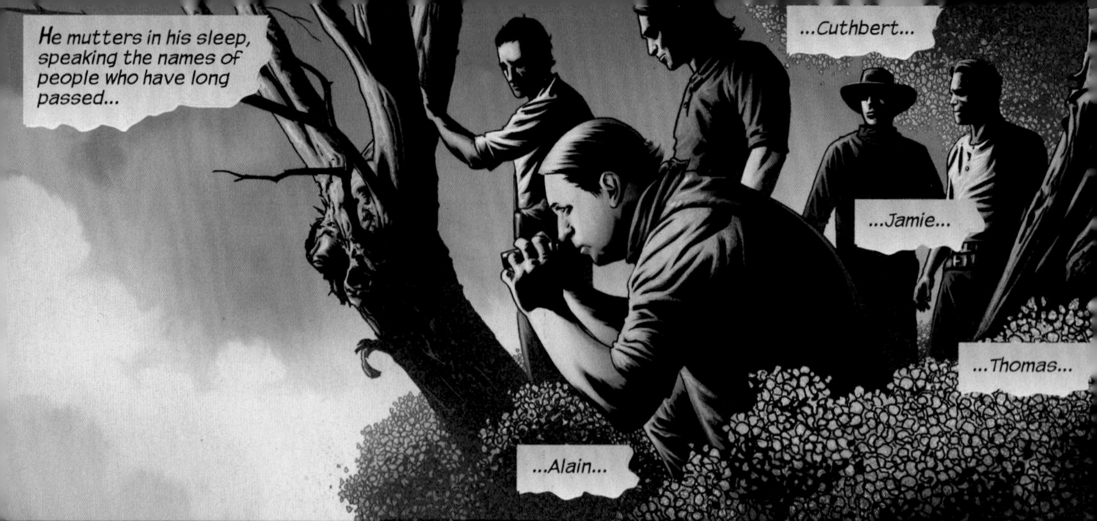
He mutters in his sleep, speaking the names of people who have long passed...
...Cuthbert...
...Jamie...
...Thomas...
...Alain...

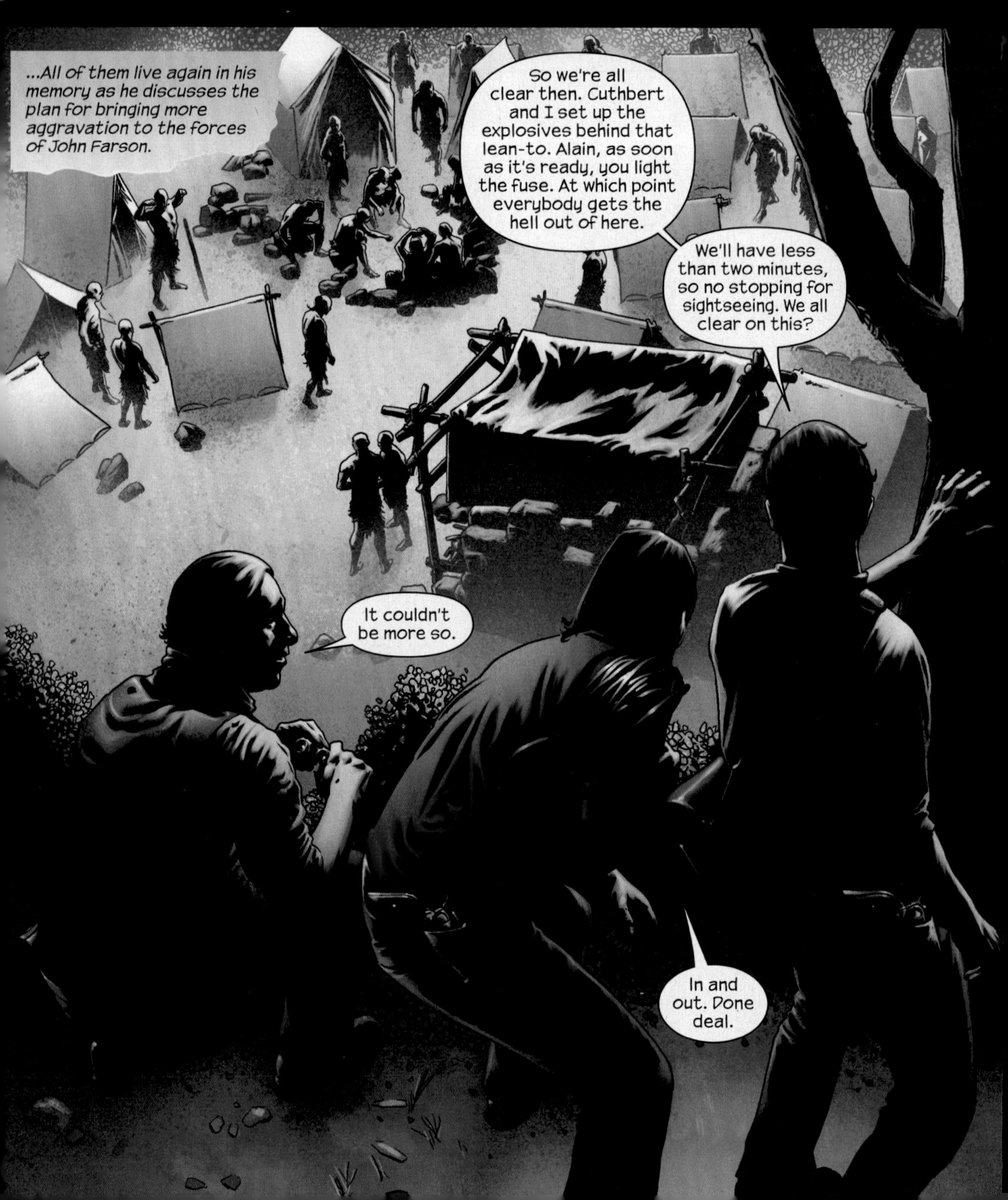
...All of them live again in his memory as he discusses the plan for bringing more aggravation to the forces of John Farson.
So we're all clear then. Cuthbert and I set up the explosives behind that lean-to. Alain, as soon as it's ready, you light the fuse. At which point everybody gets the hell out of here.
We'll have less than two minutes, so no stopping for sightseeing. We all clear on this?
It couldn't be more so.
In and out. Done deal.

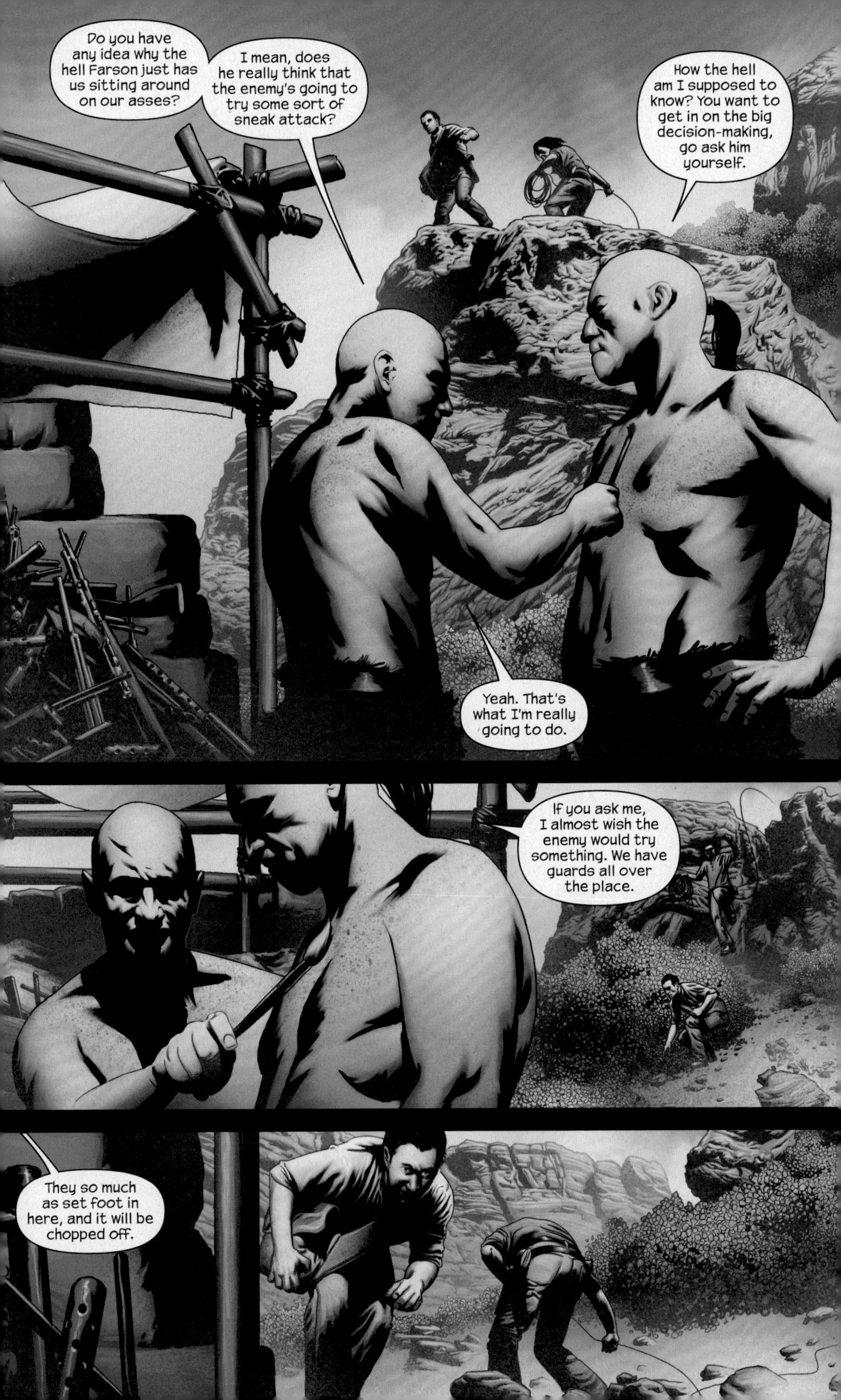
Do you have any idea why the hell Farson just has us sitting around on our asses?
I mean, does he really think that the enemy's going to try some sort of sneak attack?
How the hell am I supposed to know? You want to get in on the big decision-making, go ask him yourself.
Yeah. That's what I'm really going to do.
If you ask me, I almost wish the enemy would try something. We have guards all over the place.
They so much as set foot in here, and it will be chopped off.

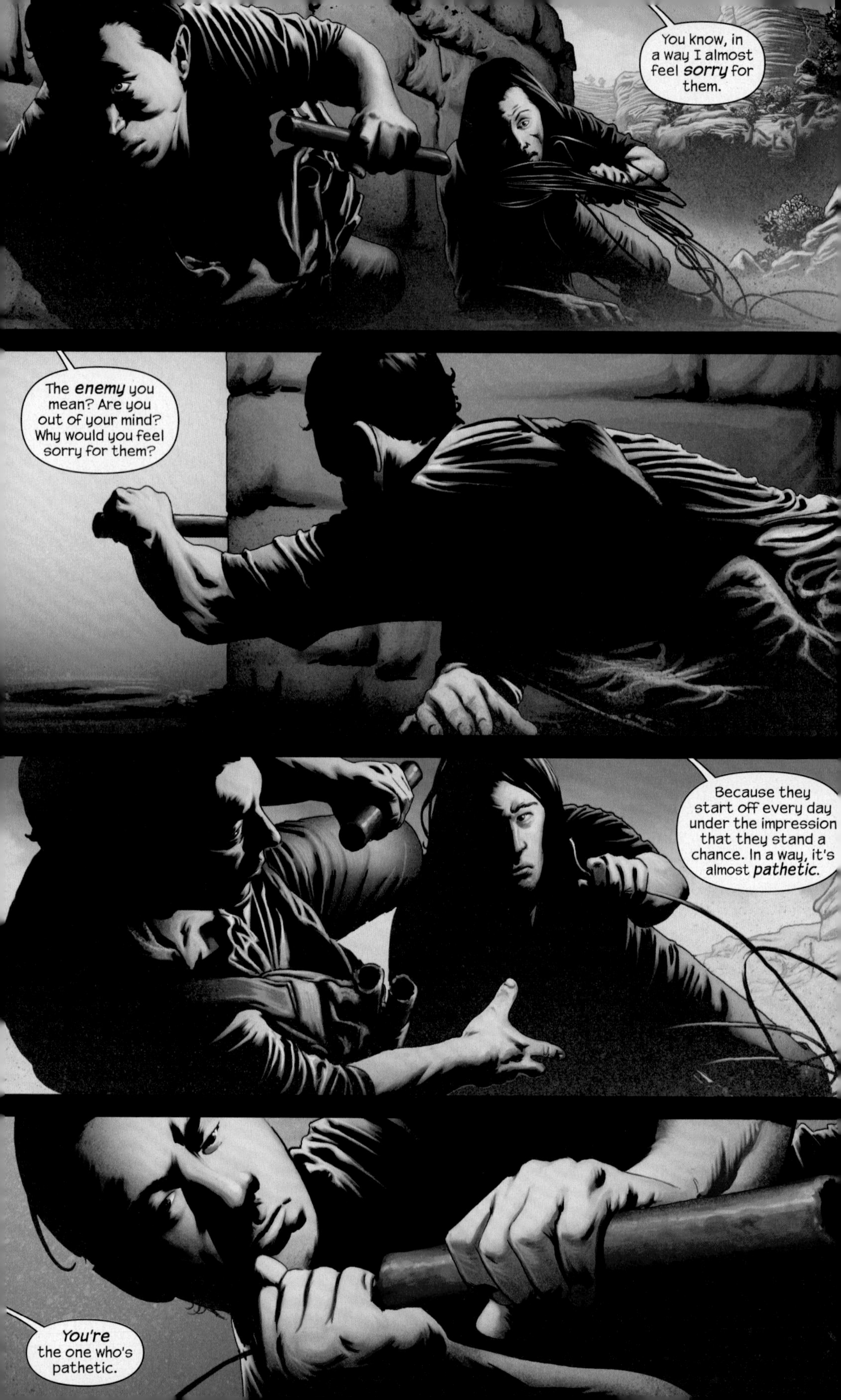
You know, in a way I almost feel *sorry* for them.
The *enemy* you mean? Are you out of your mind? Why would you feel sorry for them?
Because they start off every day under the impression that they stand a chance. In a way, it's almost *pathetic*.
You're the one who's pathetic.

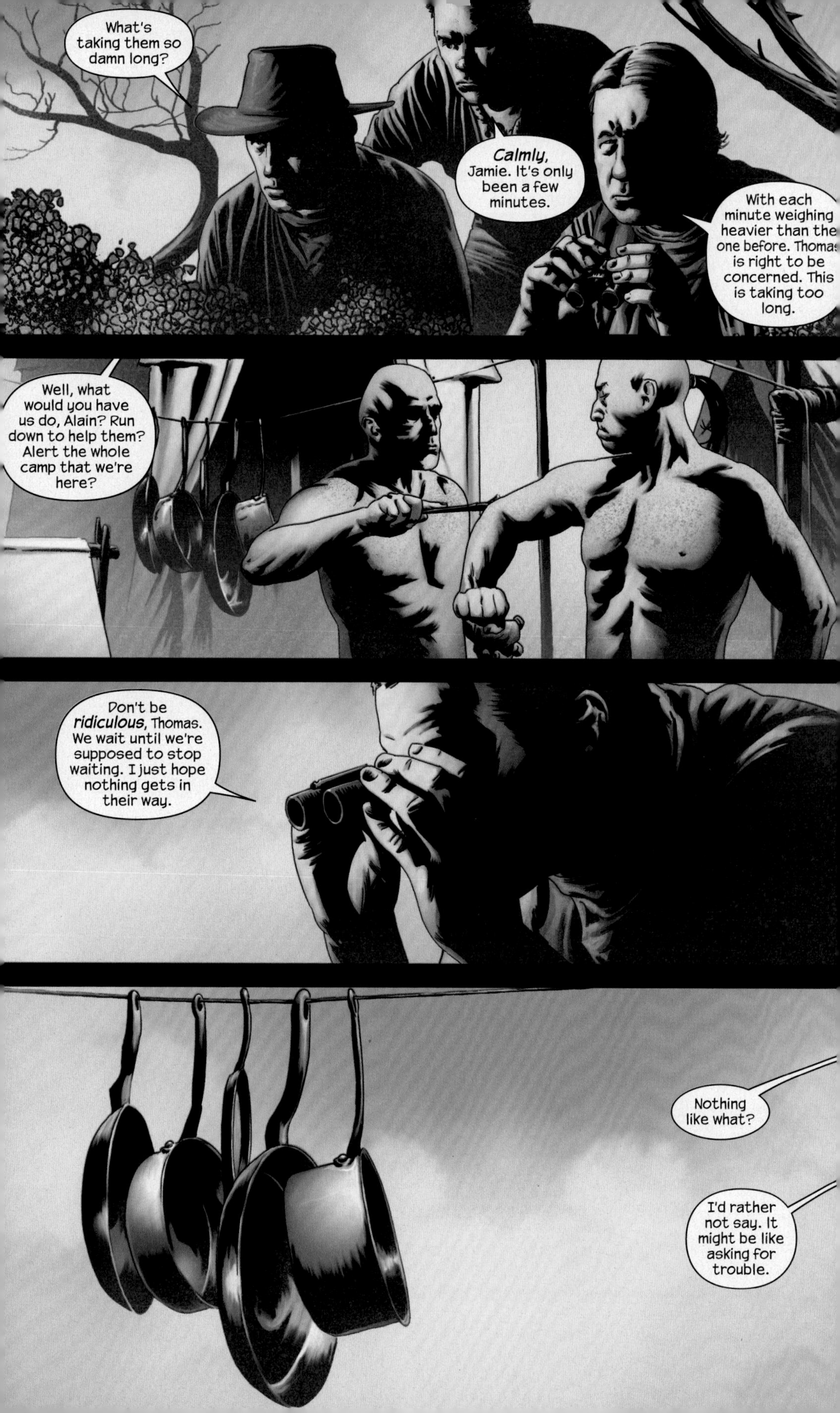
What's taking them so damn long?
Calmly, Jamie. It's only been a few minutes.
With each minute weighing heavier than the one before. Thomas is right to be concerned. This is taking too long.
Well, what would you have us do, Alain? Run down to help them? Alert the whole camp that we're here?
Don't be *ridiculous*, Thomas. We wait until we're supposed to stop waiting. I just hope nothing gets in their way.
Nothing like what?
I'd rather not say. It might be like asking for trouble.

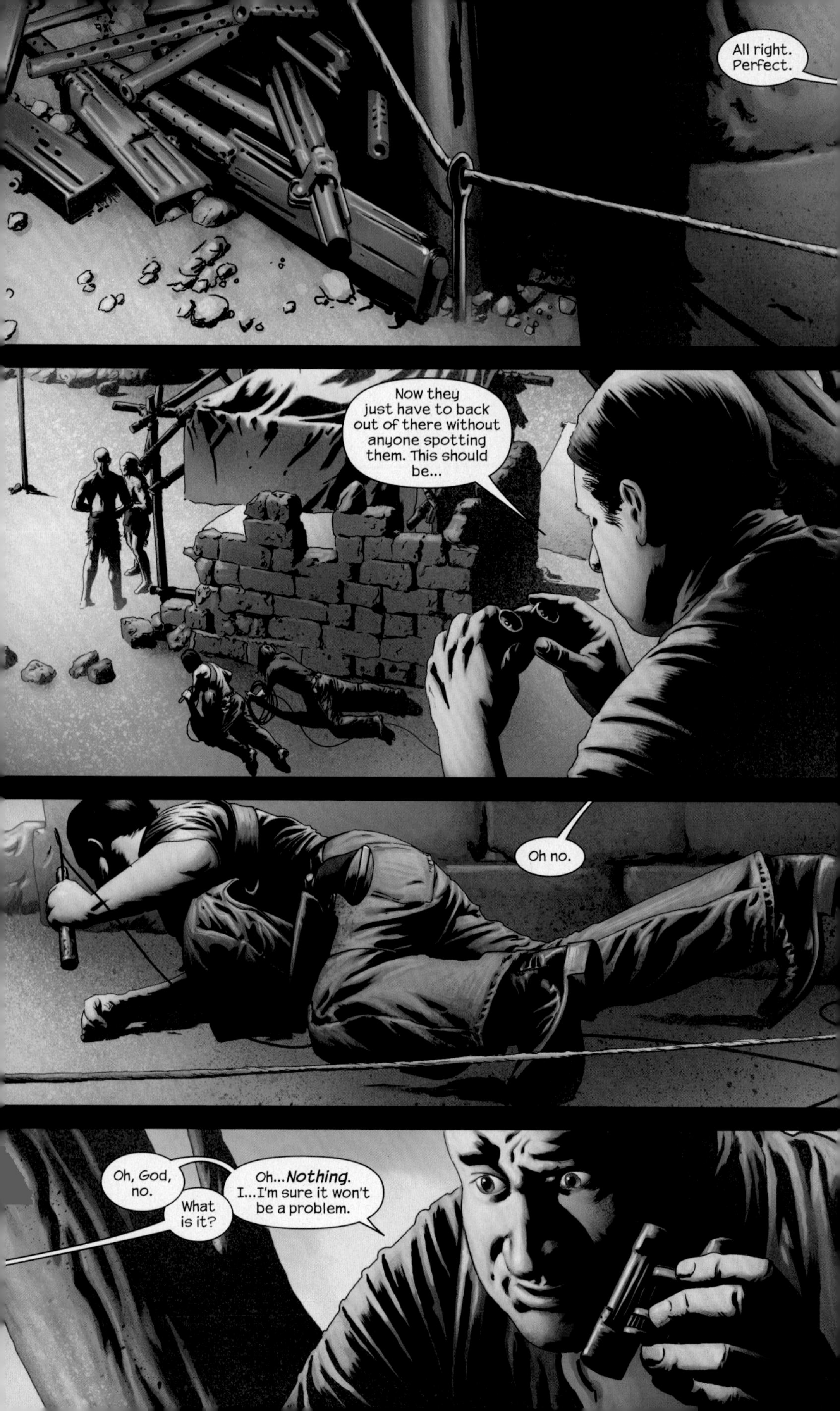
All right. Perfect.
Now they just have to back out of there without anyone spotting them. This should be...
Oh no.
Oh, God, no.
What is it?
Oh...*Nothing*. I...I'm sure it won't be a problem.

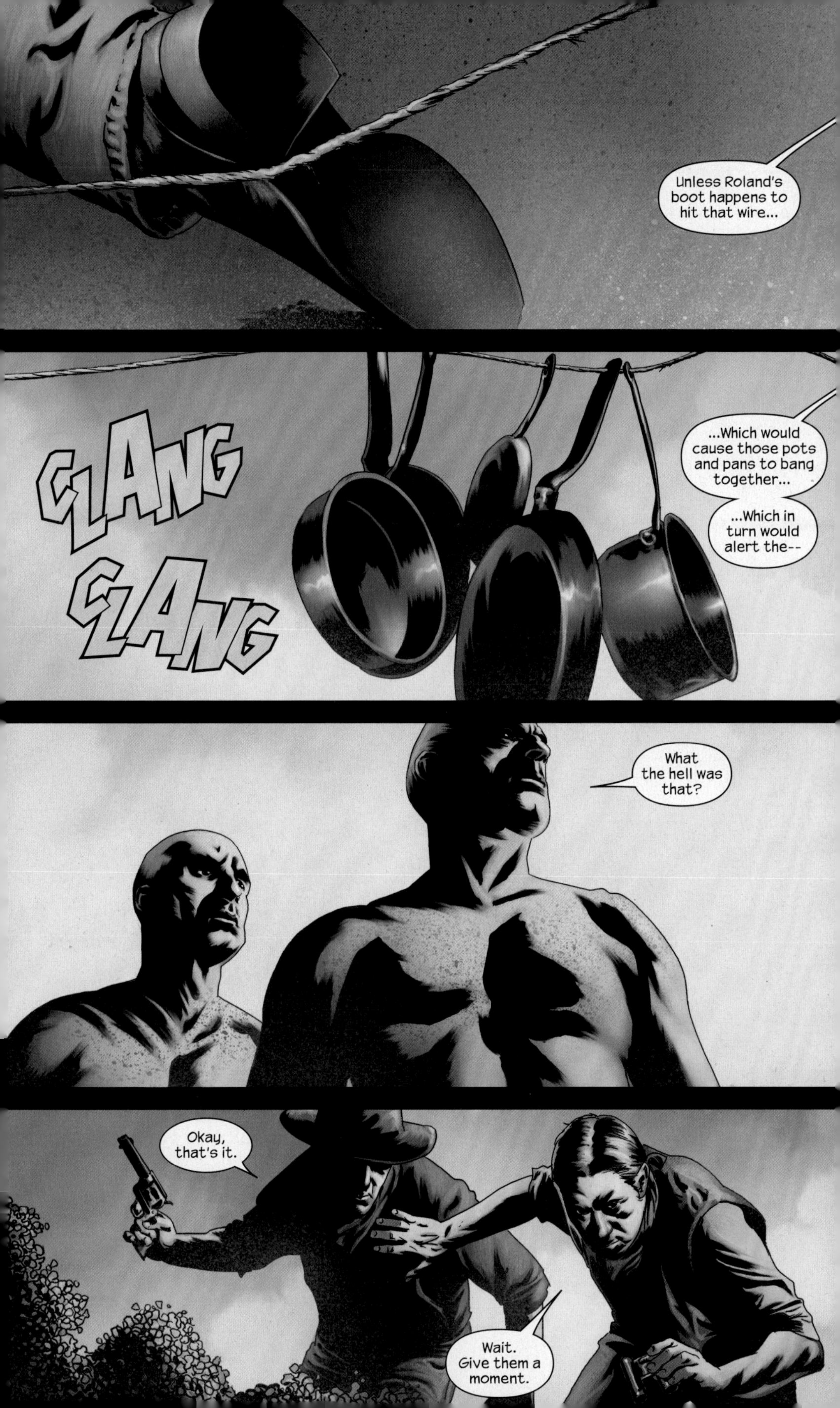
Unless Roland's boot happens to hit that wire...
CLANG
CLANG
...Which would cause those pots and pans to bang together...
...Which in turn would alert the--
What the hell was that?
Okay, that's it.
Wait. Give them a moment.

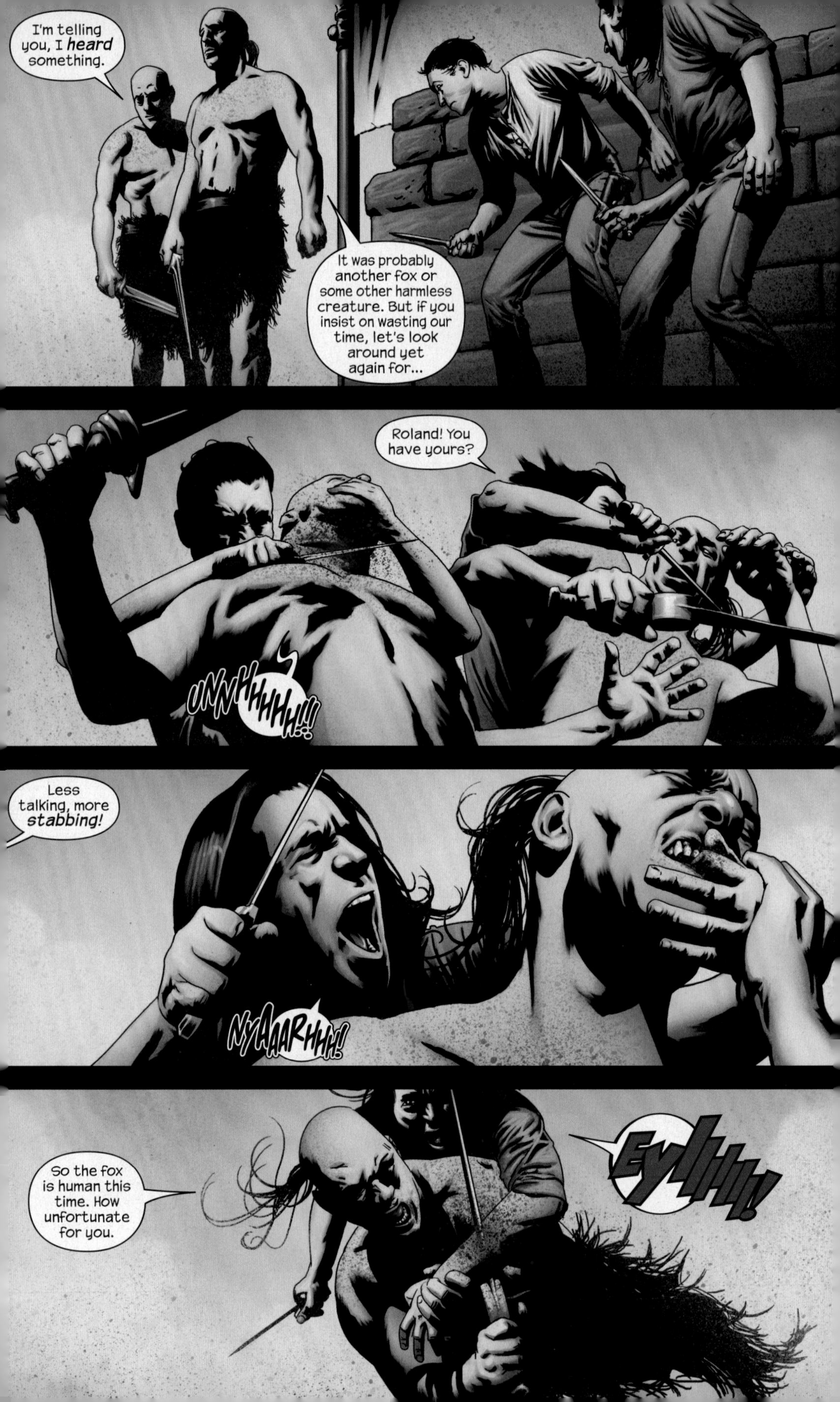
I'm telling you, I *heard* something.
It was probably another fox or some other harmless creature. But if you insist on wasting our time, let's look around yet again for...
Roland! You have yours?
UNNHHHHH!!!
Less talking, more *stabbing!*
NYAAARHHH!
So the fox is human this time. How unfortunate for you.
EYIIIII!

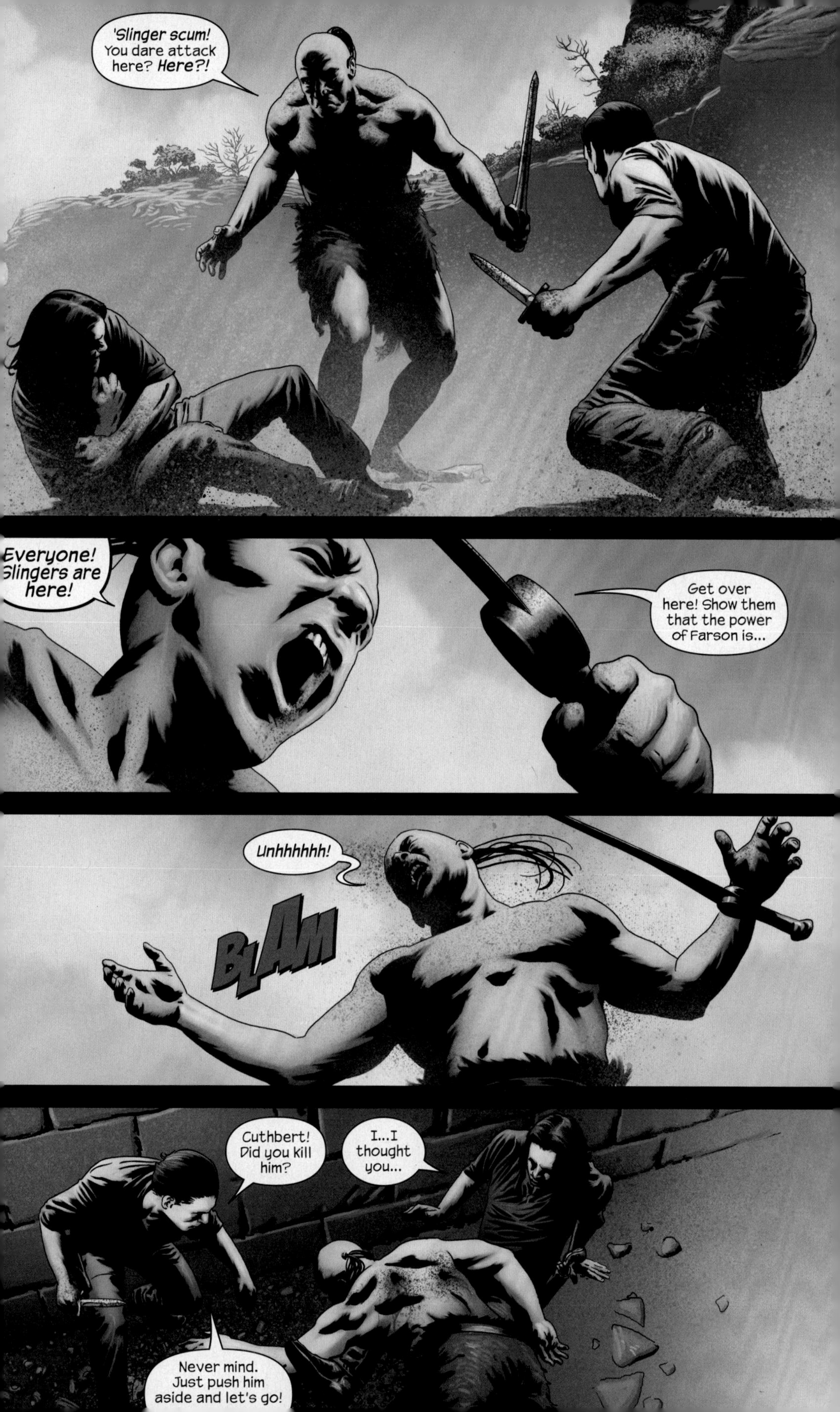
'Slinger scum! You dare attack here? Here?!
Everyone! Slingers are here!
Get over here! Show them that the power of Farson is...
Unhhhhhh!
BLAM
Cuthbert! Did you kill him?
I...I thought you...
Never mind. Just push him aside and let's go!

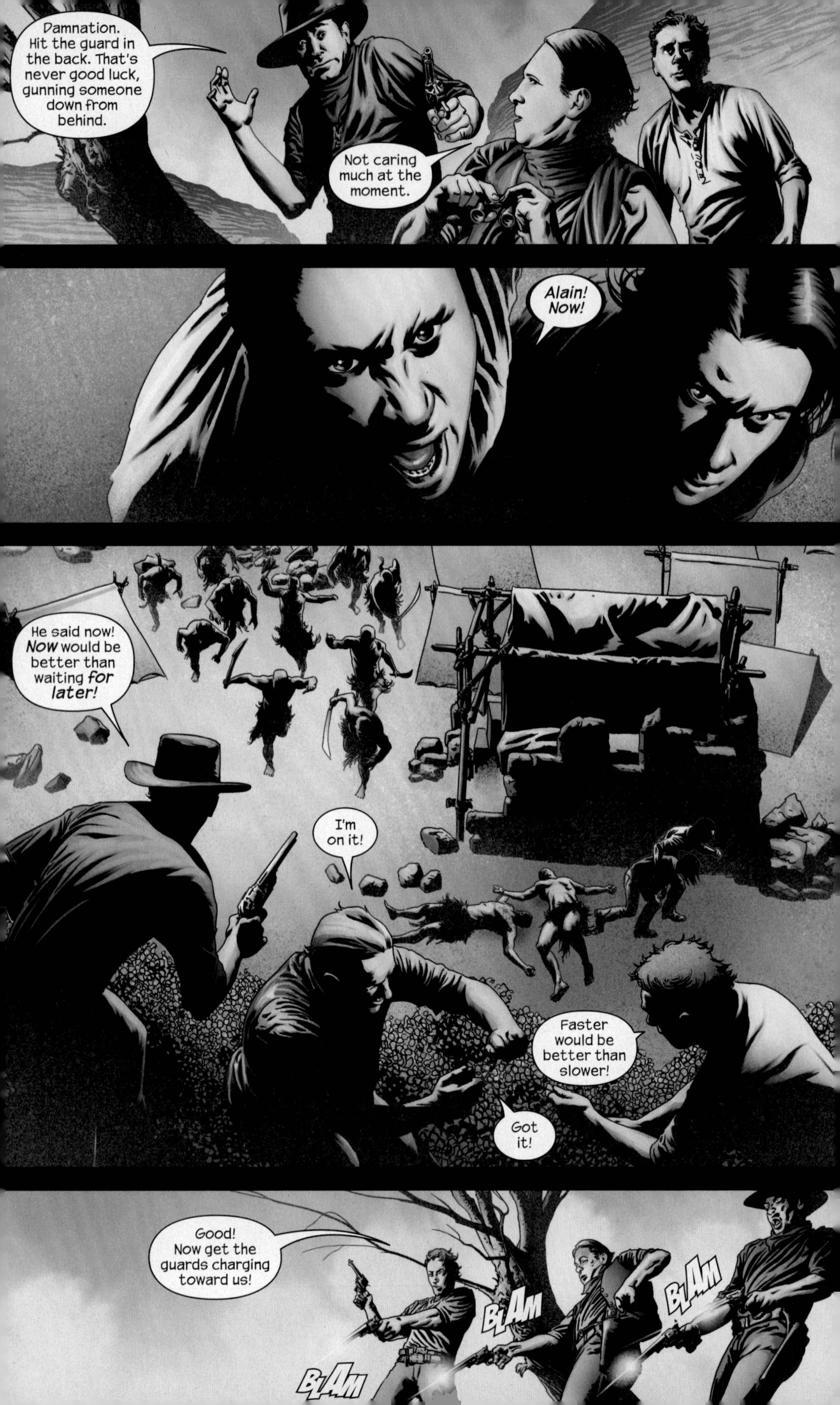
Damnation. Hit the guard in the back. That's never good luck, gunning someone down from behind.
Not caring much at the moment.
Alain! Now!
He said now! *Now* would be better than waiting *for later!*
I'm on it!
Faster would be better than slower!
Got it!
Good! Now get the guards charging toward us!
BLAM
BLAM
BLAM

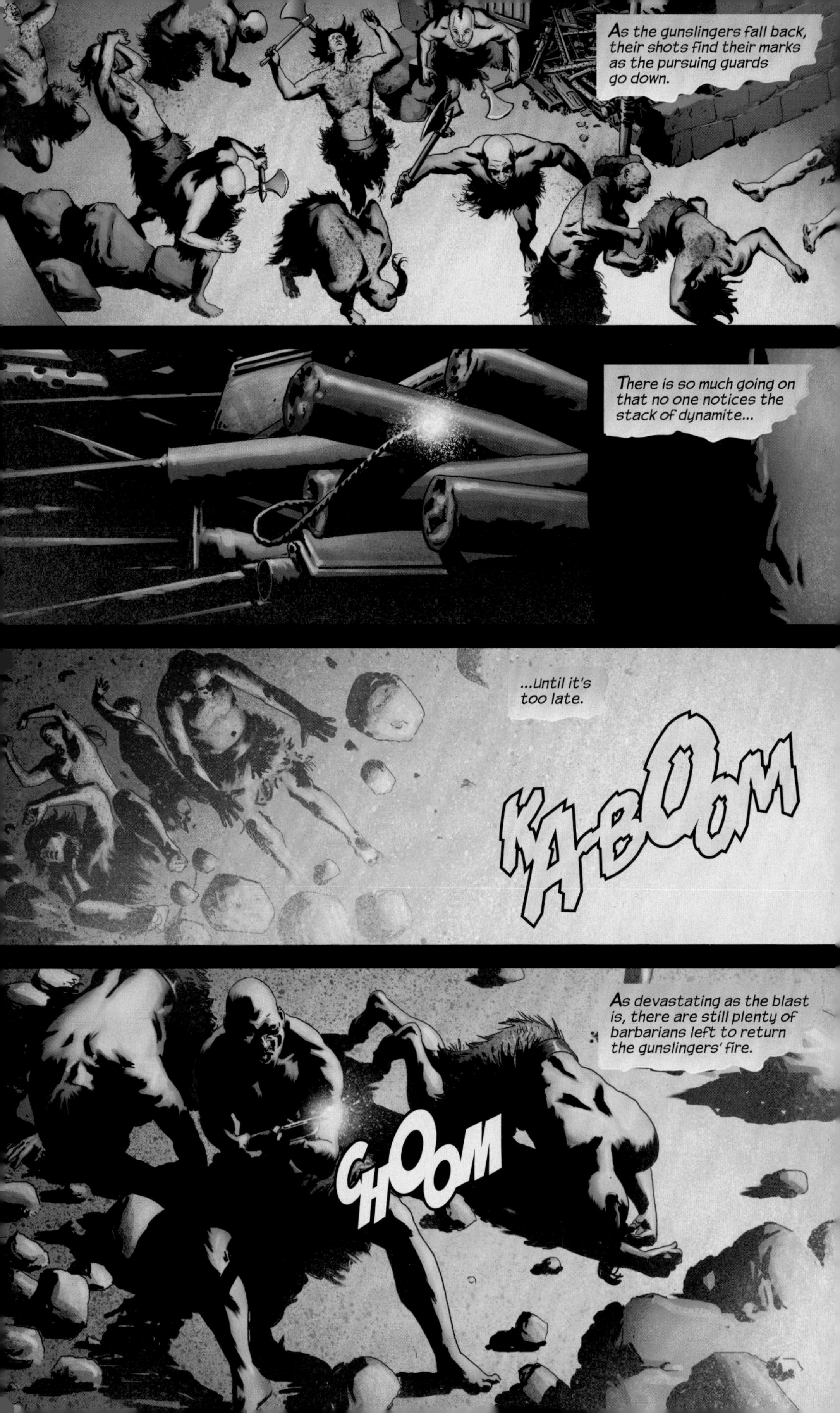

As the gunslingers fall back, their shots find their marks as the pursuing guards go down.
There is so much going on that no one notices the stack of dynamite...
...Until it's too late.
KA-BOOOM
As devastating as the blast is, there are still plenty of barbarians left to return the gunslingers' fire.
CHOOM

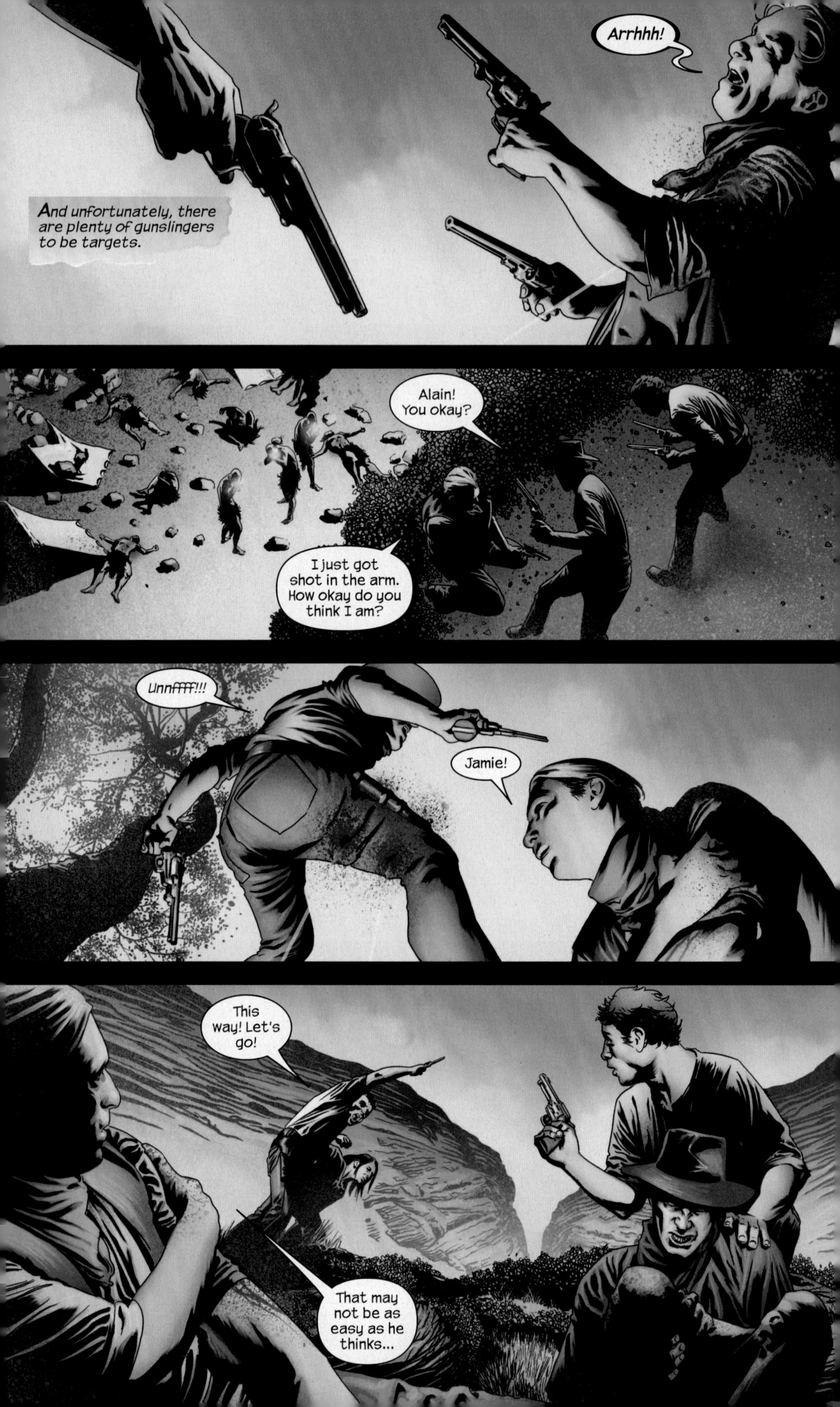
Arrhhh!
And unfortunately, there are plenty of gunslingers to be targets.
Alain! You okay?
I just got shot in the arm. How okay do you think I am?
Unnffff!!!
Jamie!
This way! Let's go!
That may not be as easy as he thinks...

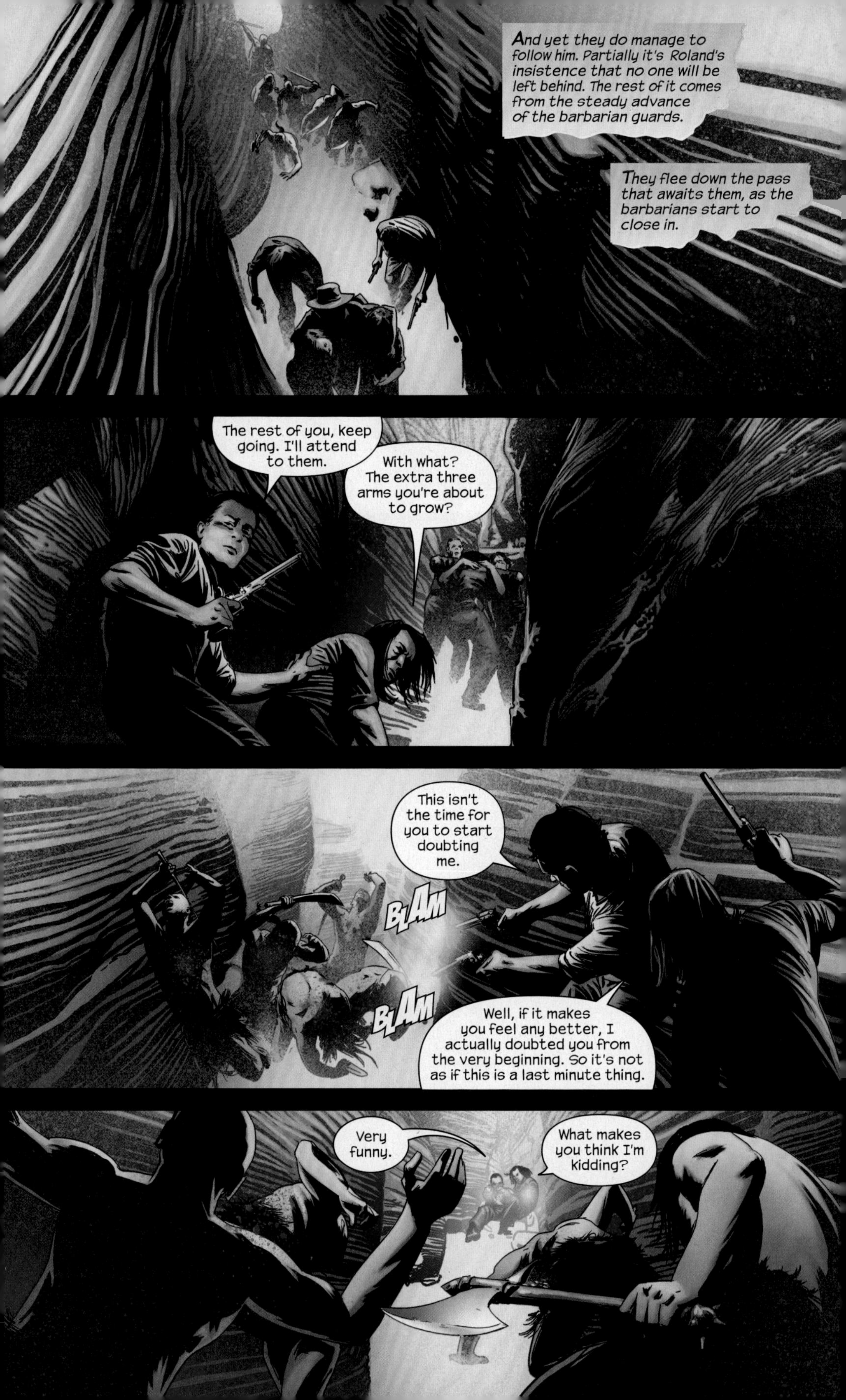
And yet they do manage to follow him. Partially it's Roland's insistence that no one will be left behind. The rest of it comes from the steady advance of the barbarian guards.
They flee down the pass that awaits them, as the barbarians start to close in.
The rest of you, keep going. I'll attend to them.
With what? The extra three arms you're about to grow?
This isn't the time for you to start doubting me.
BLAM
BLAM
Well, if it makes you feel any better, I actually doubted you from the very beginning. So it's not as if this is a last minute thing.
Very funny.
What makes you think I'm kidding?

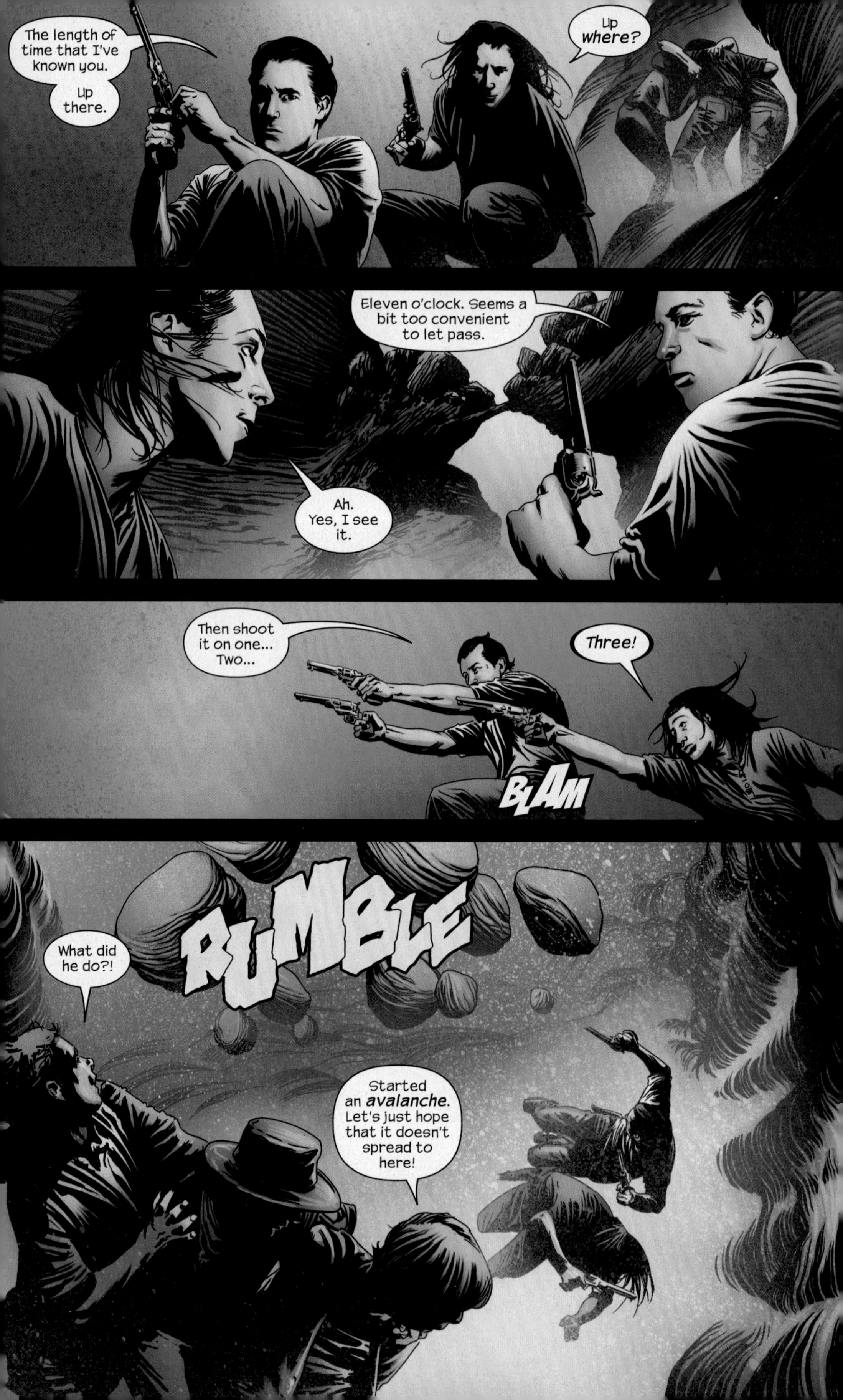
The length of time that I've known you.
Up there.
Up where?
Eleven o'clock. Seems a bit too convenient to let pass.
Ah. Yes, I see it.
Then shoot it on one... Two...
Three!
BLAM
RUMBLE
What did he do?!
Started an avalanche. Let's just hope that it doesn't spread to here!

STEPHEN KING

THE DARK TOWER
~ THE GUNSLINGER ~

EVIL GROUND

CHAPTER TWO

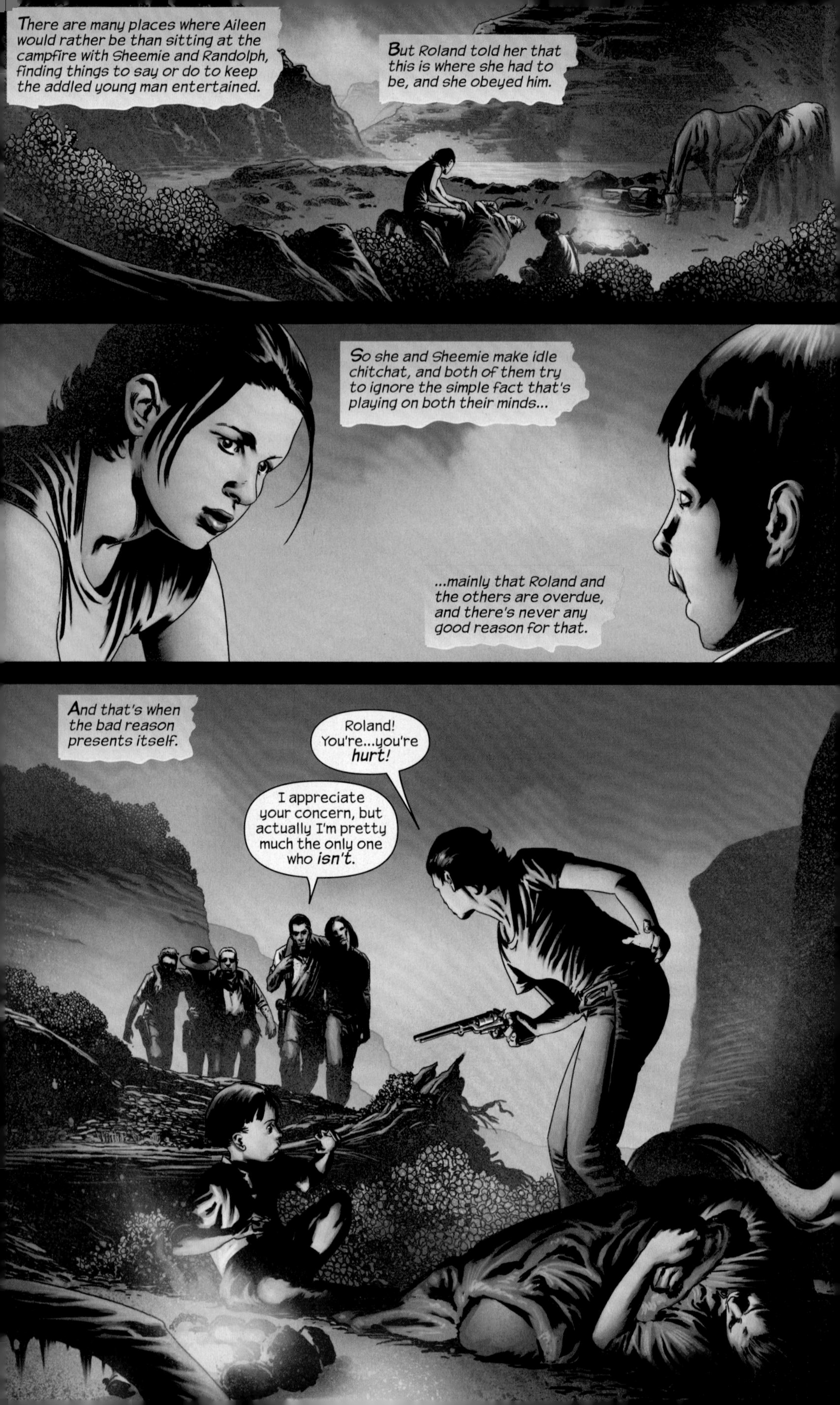
There are many places where Aileen would rather be than sitting at the campfire with Sheemie and Randolph, finding things to say or do to keep the addled young man entertained.
But Roland told her that this is where she had to be, and she obeyed him.
So she and Sheemie make idle chitchat, and both of them try to ignore the simple fact that's playing on both their minds...
...mainly that Roland and the others are overdue, and there's never any good reason for that.
And that's when the bad reason presents itself.
Roland! You're...you're hurt!
I appreciate your concern, but actually I'm pretty much the only one who isn't.

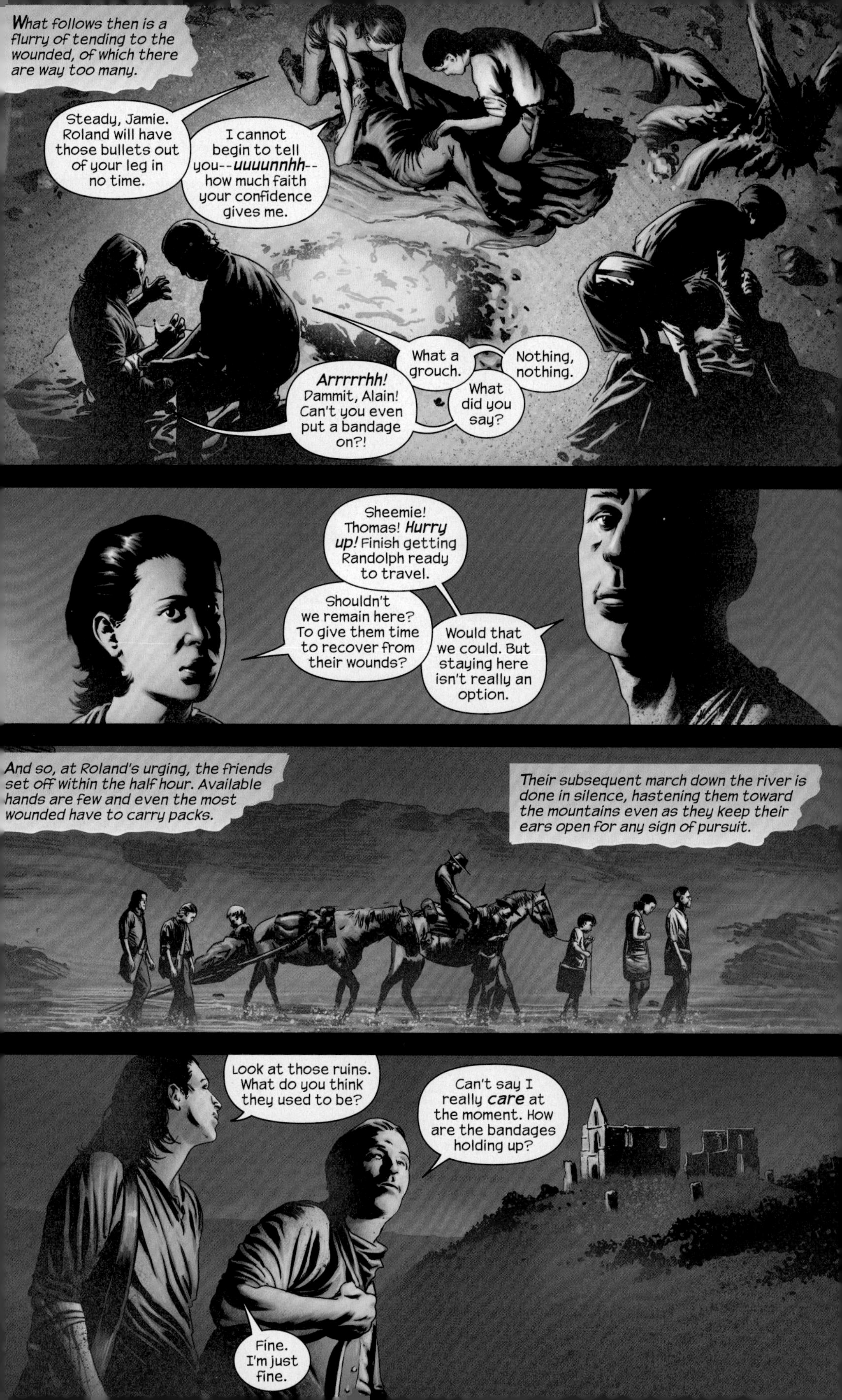
What follows then is a flurry of tending to the wounded, of which there are way too many.
Steady, Jamie. Roland will have those bullets out of your leg in no time.
I cannot begin to tell you--uuuunnhh--how much faith your confidence gives me.
Arrrrrhh! Dammit, Alain! Can't you even put a bandage on?!
What a grouch.
What did you say?
Nothing, nothing.
Sheemie! Thomas! Hurry up! Finish getting Randolph ready to travel.
Shouldn't we remain here? To give them time to recover from their wounds?
Would that we could. But staying here isn't really an option.
And so, at Roland's urging, the friends set off within the half hour. Available hands are few and even the most wounded have to carry packs.
Their subsequent march down the river is done in silence, hastening them toward the mountains even as they keep their ears open for any sign of pursuit.
Look at those ruins. What do you think they used to be?
Can't say I really care at the moment. How are the bandages holding up?
Fine. I'm just fine.

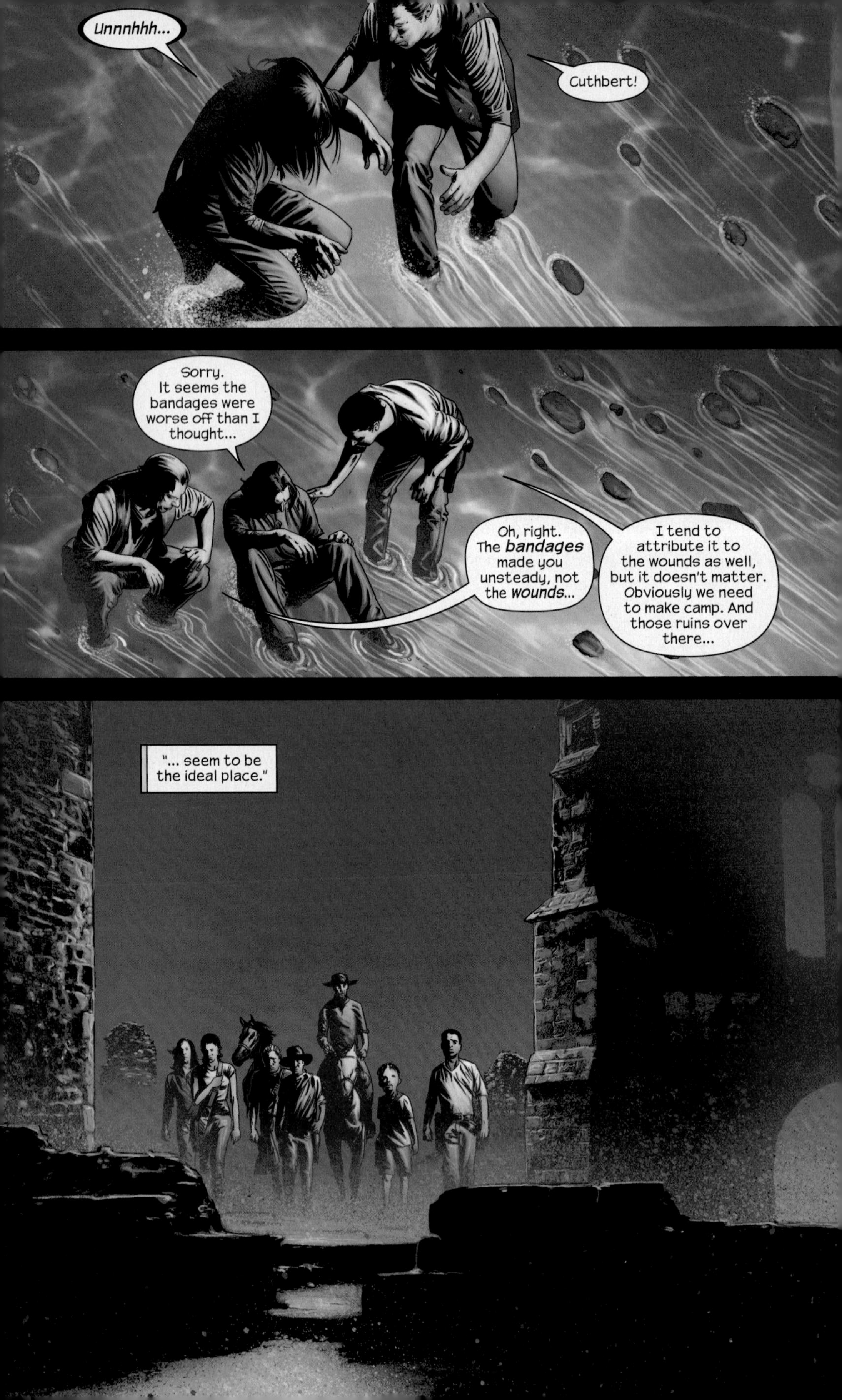
Unnnhhh...
Cuthbert!
Sorry. It seems the bandages were worse off than I thought...
Oh, right. The *bandages* made you unsteady, not the *wounds*...
I tend to attribute it to the wounds as well, but it doesn't matter. Obviously we need to make camp. And those ruins over there...
"... seem to be the ideal place."

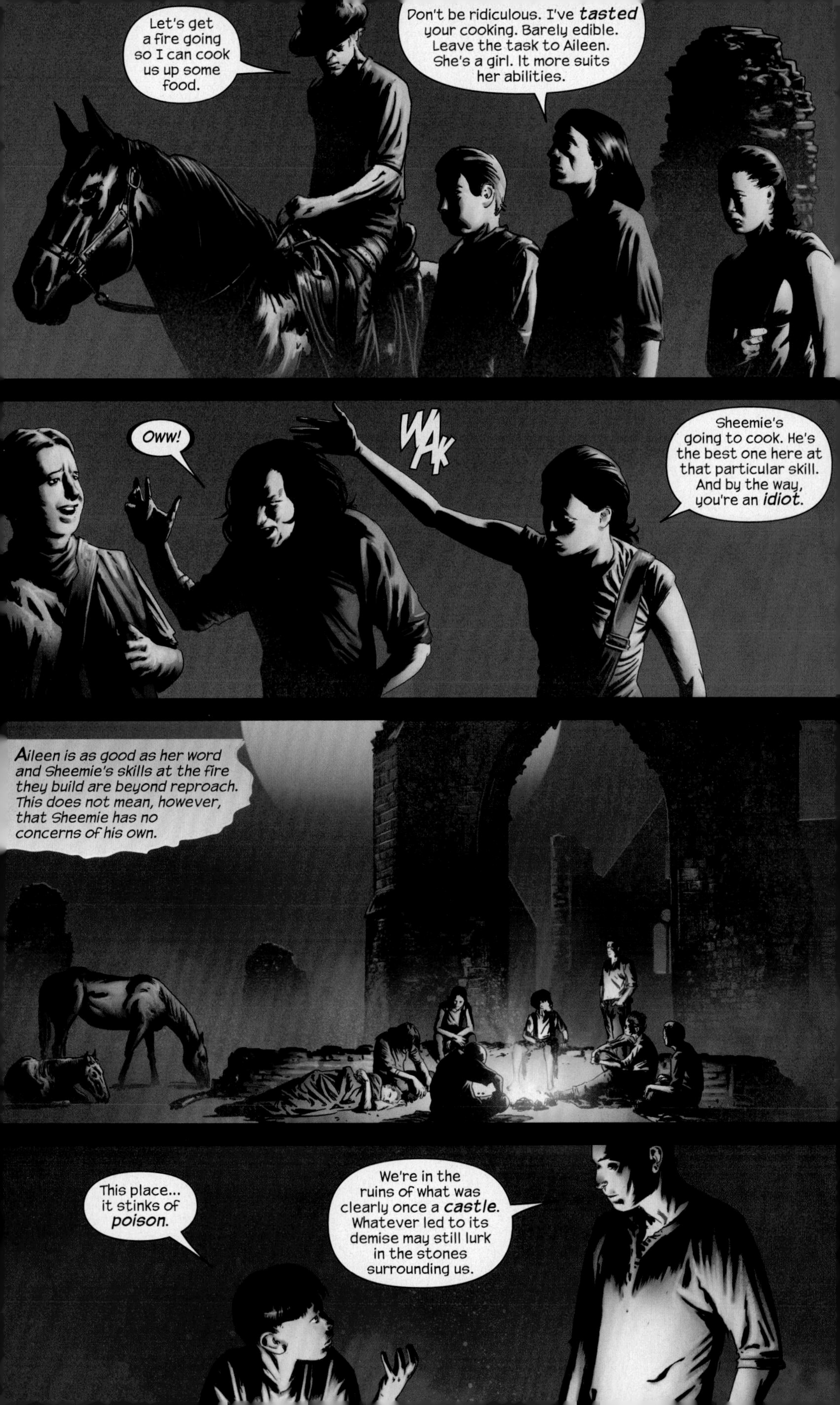

Let's get a fire going so I can cook us up some food.
Don't be ridiculous. I've tasted your cooking. Barely edible. Leave the task to Aileen. She's a girl. It more suits her abilities.
Oww!
WAK
Sheemie's going to cook. He's the best one here at that particular skill. And by the way, you're an idiot.
Aileen is as good as her word and Sheemie's skills at the fire they build are beyond reproach. This does not mean, however, that Sheemie has no concerns of his own.
This place... it stinks of poison.
We're in the ruins of what was clearly once a castle. Whatever led to its demise may still lurk in the stones surrounding us.

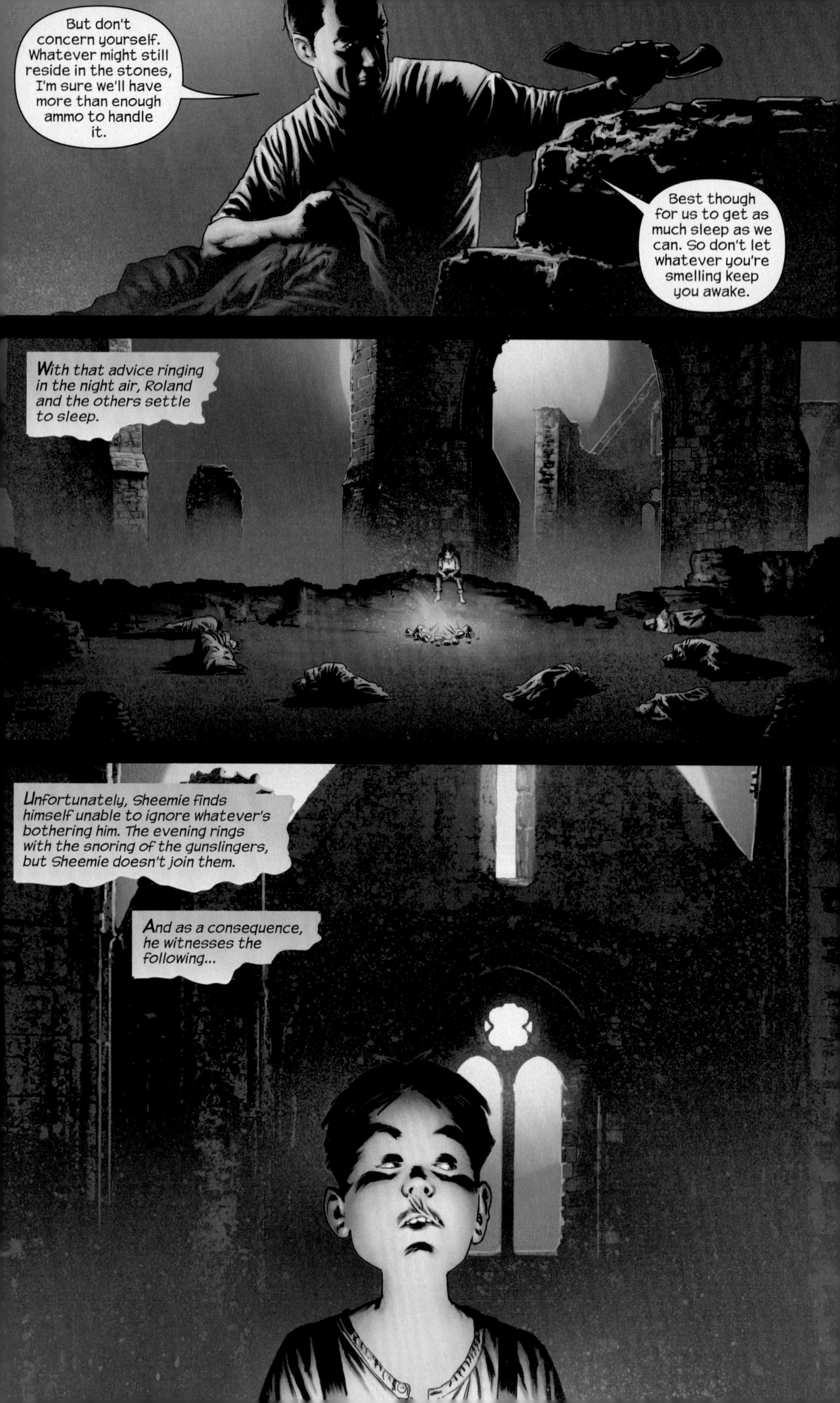
But don't concern yourself. Whatever might still reside in the stones, I'm sure we'll have more than enough ammo to handle it.
Best though for us to get as much sleep as we can. So don't let whatever you're smelling keep you awake.
With that advice ringing in the night air, Roland and the others settle to sleep.
Unfortunately, Sheemie finds himself unable to ignore whatever's bothering him. The evening rings with the snoring of the gunslingers, but Sheemie doesn't join them.
And as a consequence, he witnesses the following...

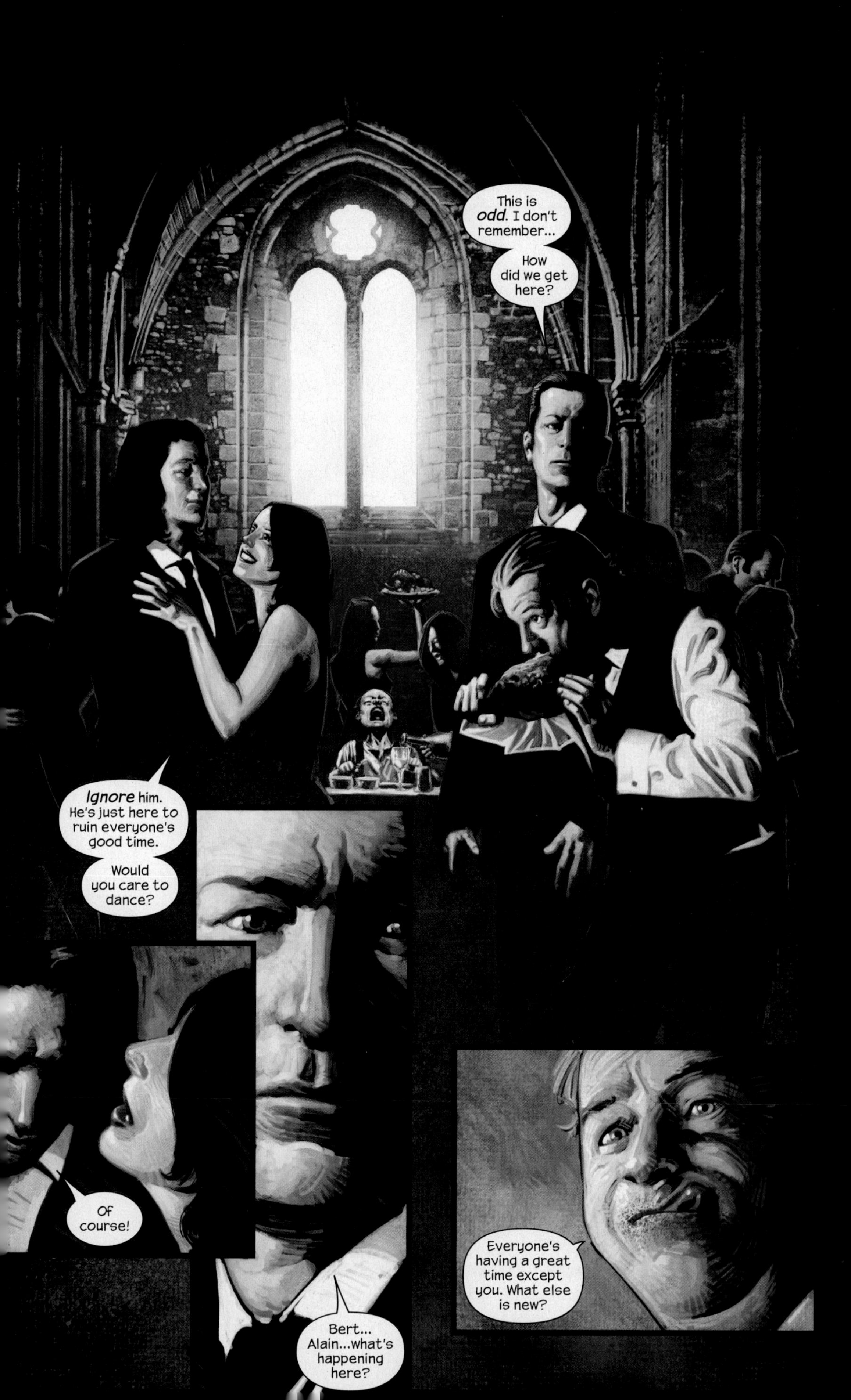

This is *odd*. I don't remember...
How did we get here?
Ignore him. He's just here to ruin everyone's good time.
Would you care to dance?
Of course!
Bert... Alain...what's happening here?
Everyone's having a great time except you. What else is new?

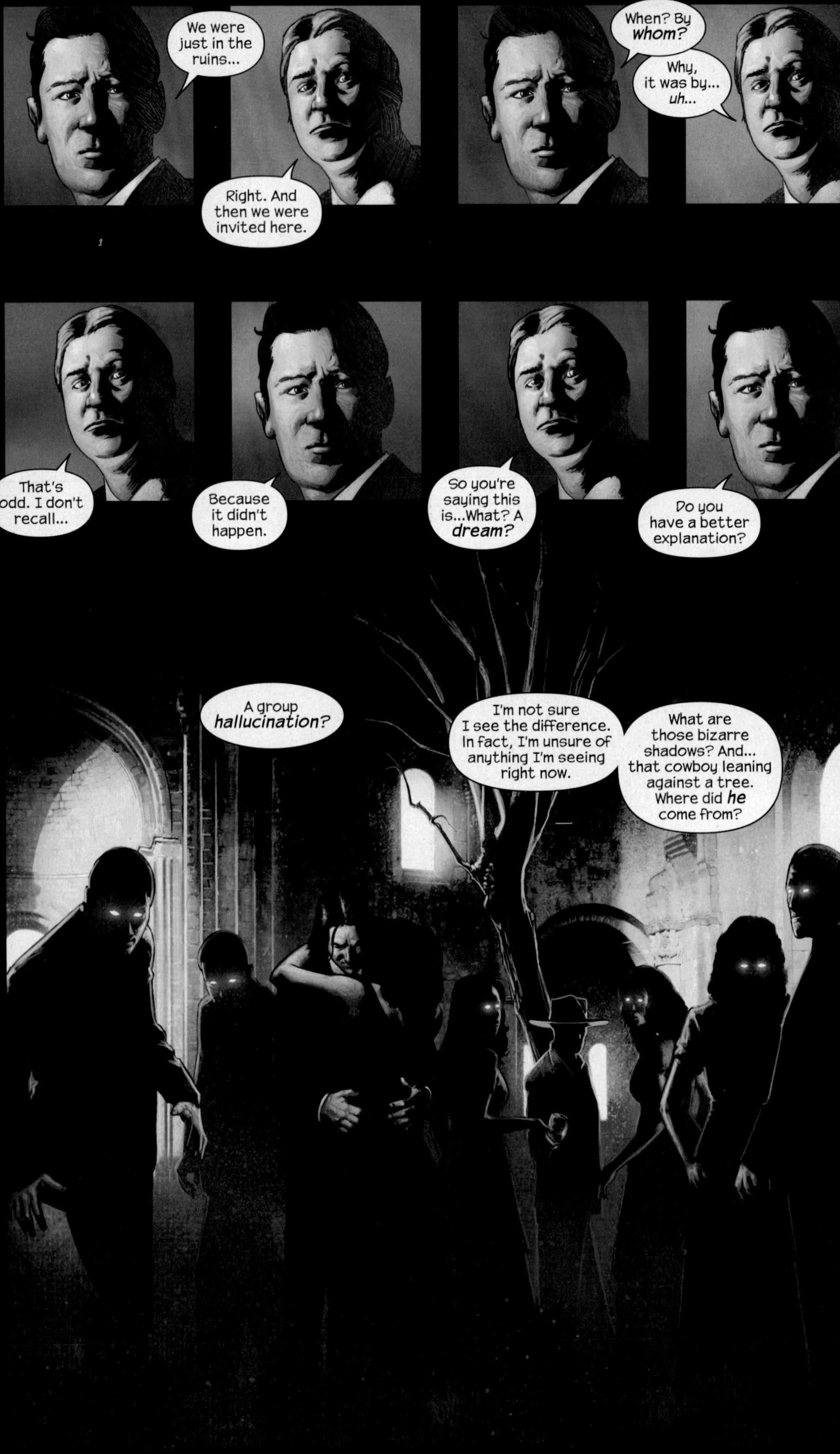

We were just in the ruins...
Right. And then we were invited here.
When? By *whom?*
Why, it was by... *uh...*
That's odd. I don't recall...
Because it didn't happen.
So you're saying this is...What? A *dream?*
Do you have a better explanation?
A group *hallucination?*
I'm not sure I see the difference. In fact, I'm unsure of anything I'm seeing right now.
What are those bizarre shadows? And... that cowboy leaning against a tree. Where did *he* come from?

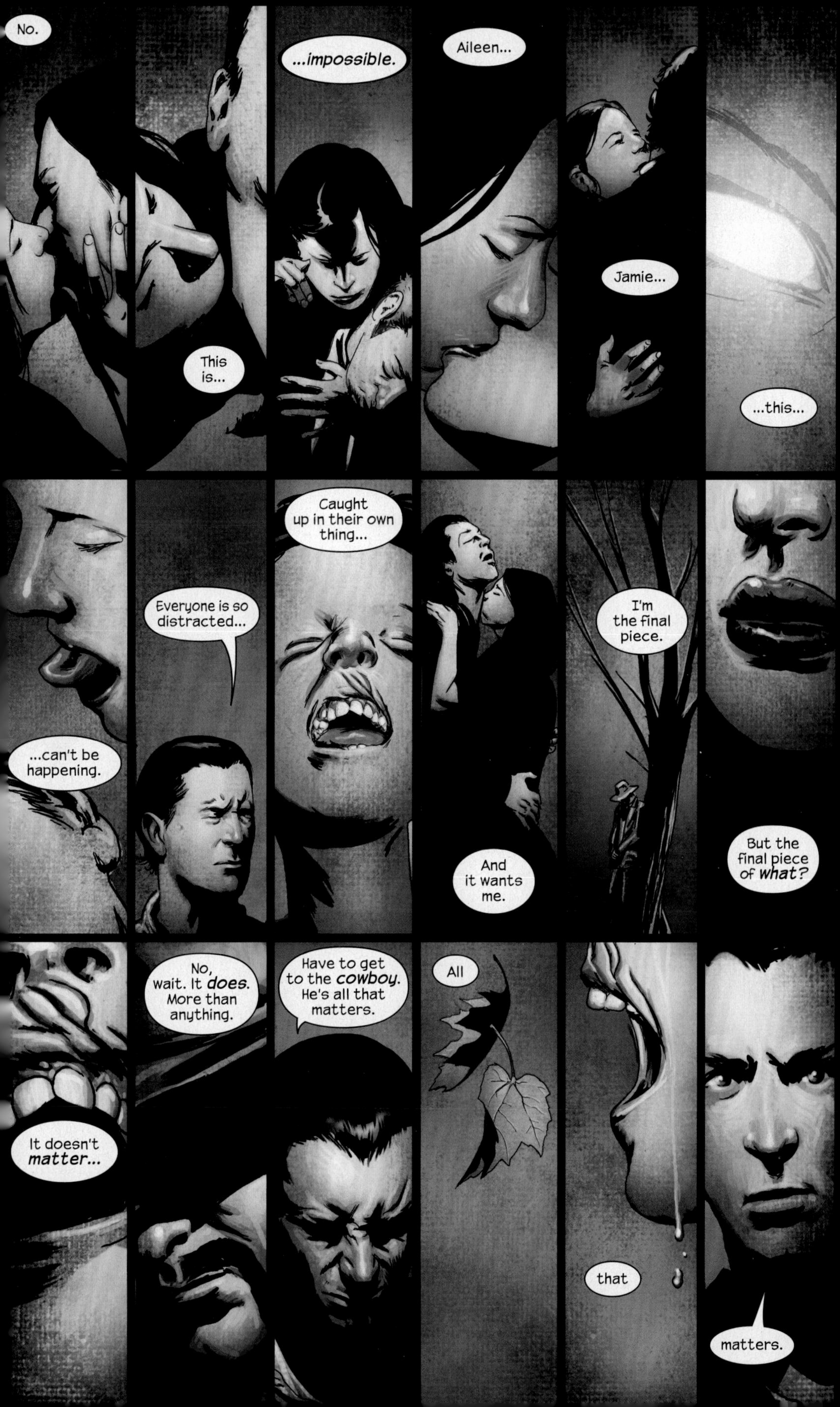
No.
This is...
...impossible.
Aileen...
Jamie...
...this...
...can't be happening.
Everyone is so distracted...
Caught up in their own thing...
And it wants me.
I'm the final piece.
But the final piece of *what?*
It doesn't *matter...*
No, wait. It *does.* More than anything.
Have to get to the *cowboy.* He's all that matters.
All
that
matters.

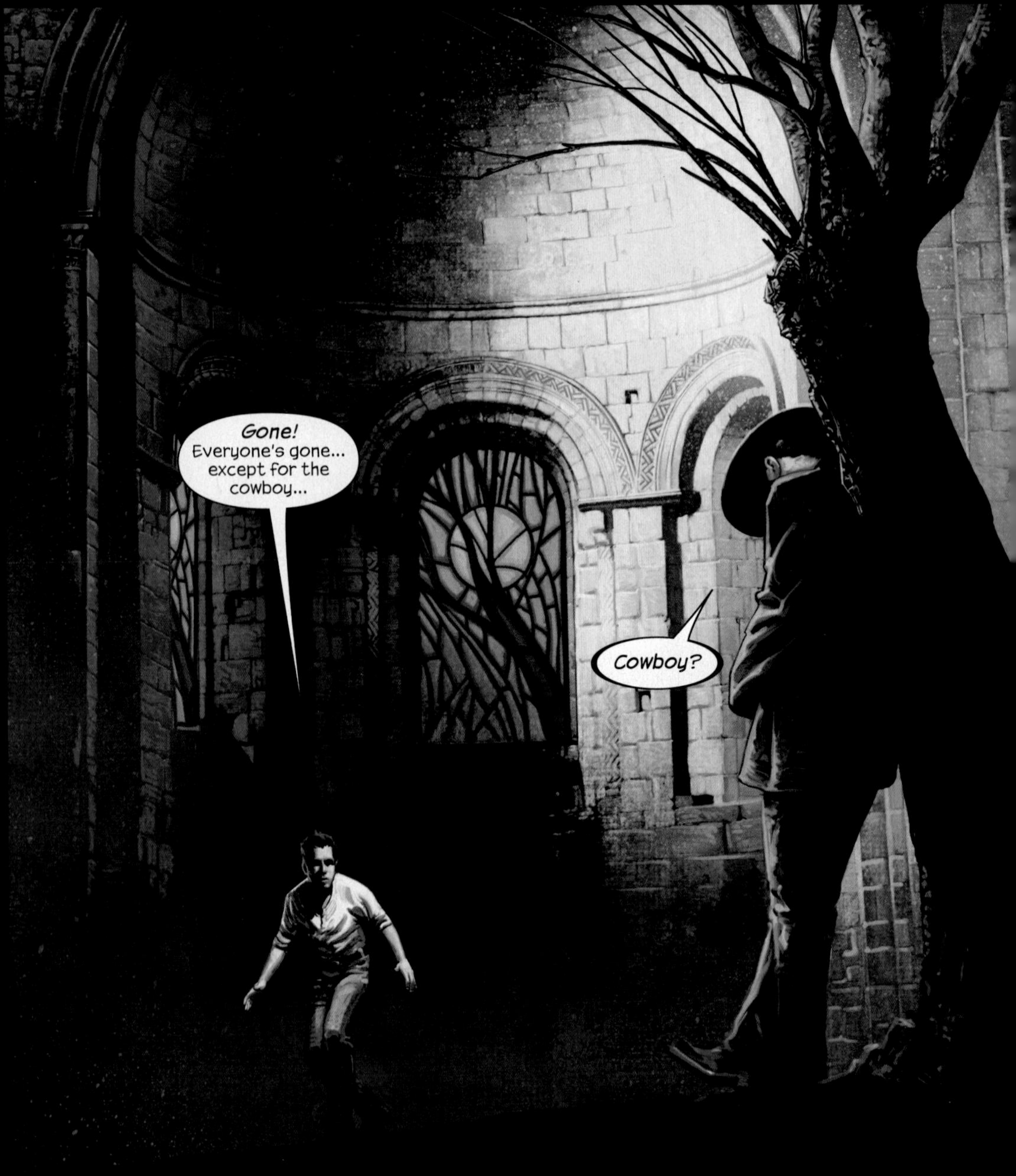
Gone! Everyone's gone... except for the cowboy...
Cowboy?

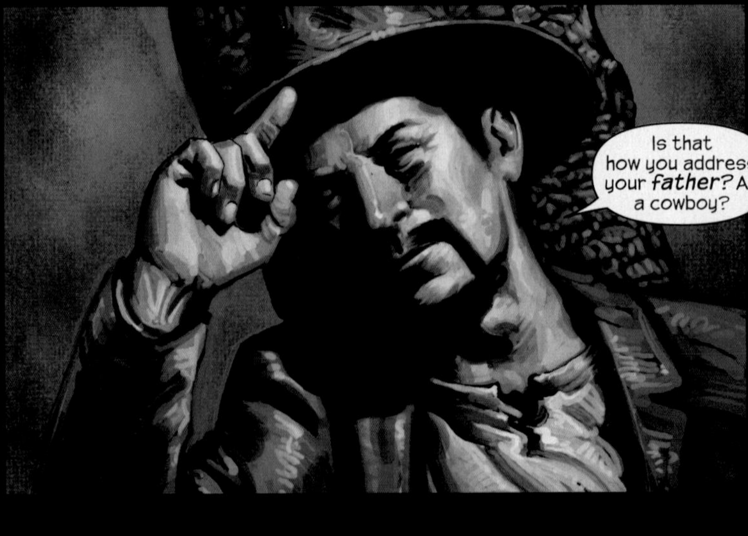
Is that how you address your father? As a cowboy?

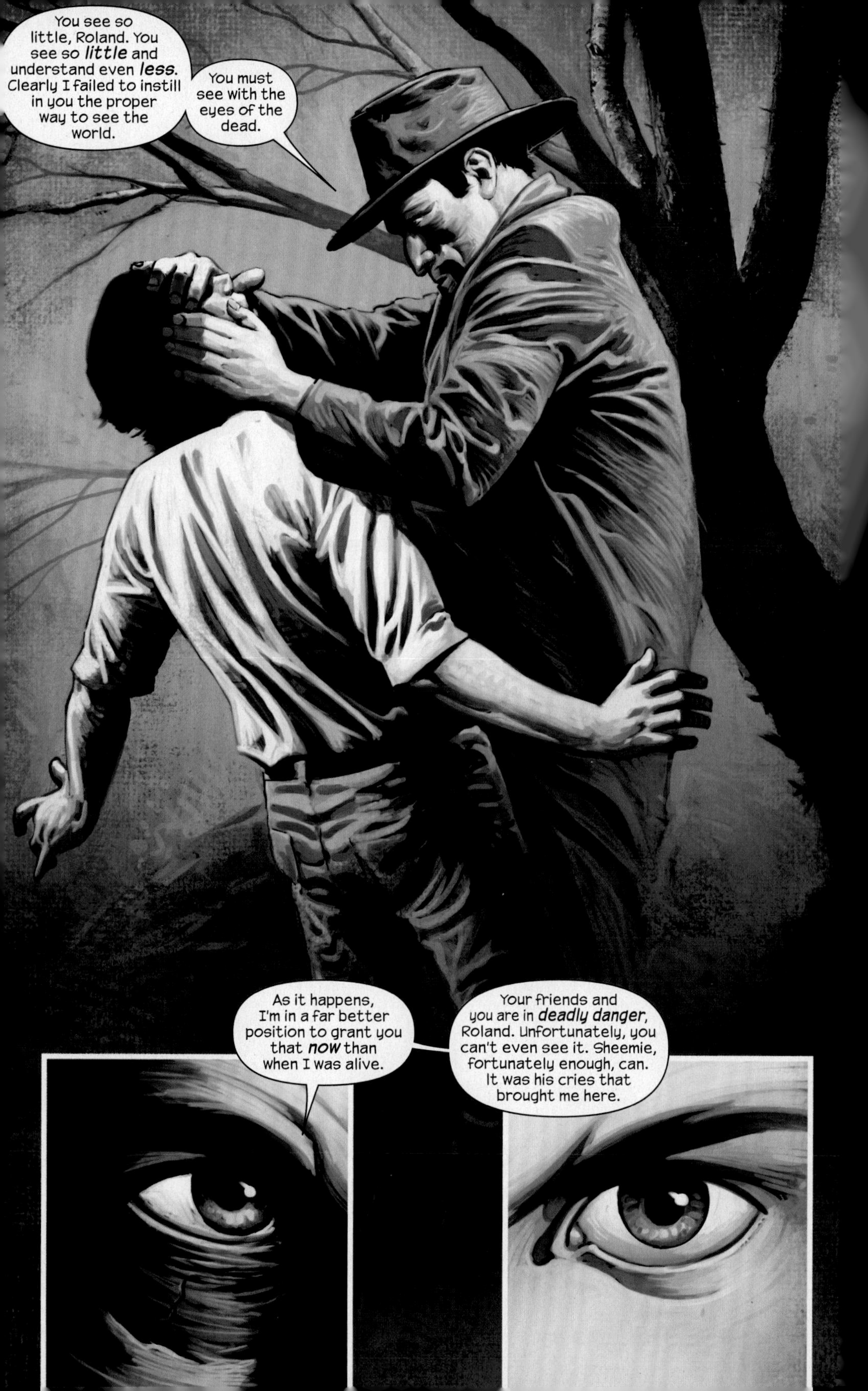
You see so little, Roland. You see so *little* and understand even *less*. Clearly I failed to instill in you the proper way to see the world.
You must see with the eyes of the dead.
As it happens, I'm in a far better position to grant you that *now* than when I was alive.
Your friends and you are in *deadly danger*, Roland. Unfortunately, you can't even see it. Sheemie, fortunately enough, can. It was his cries that brought me here.

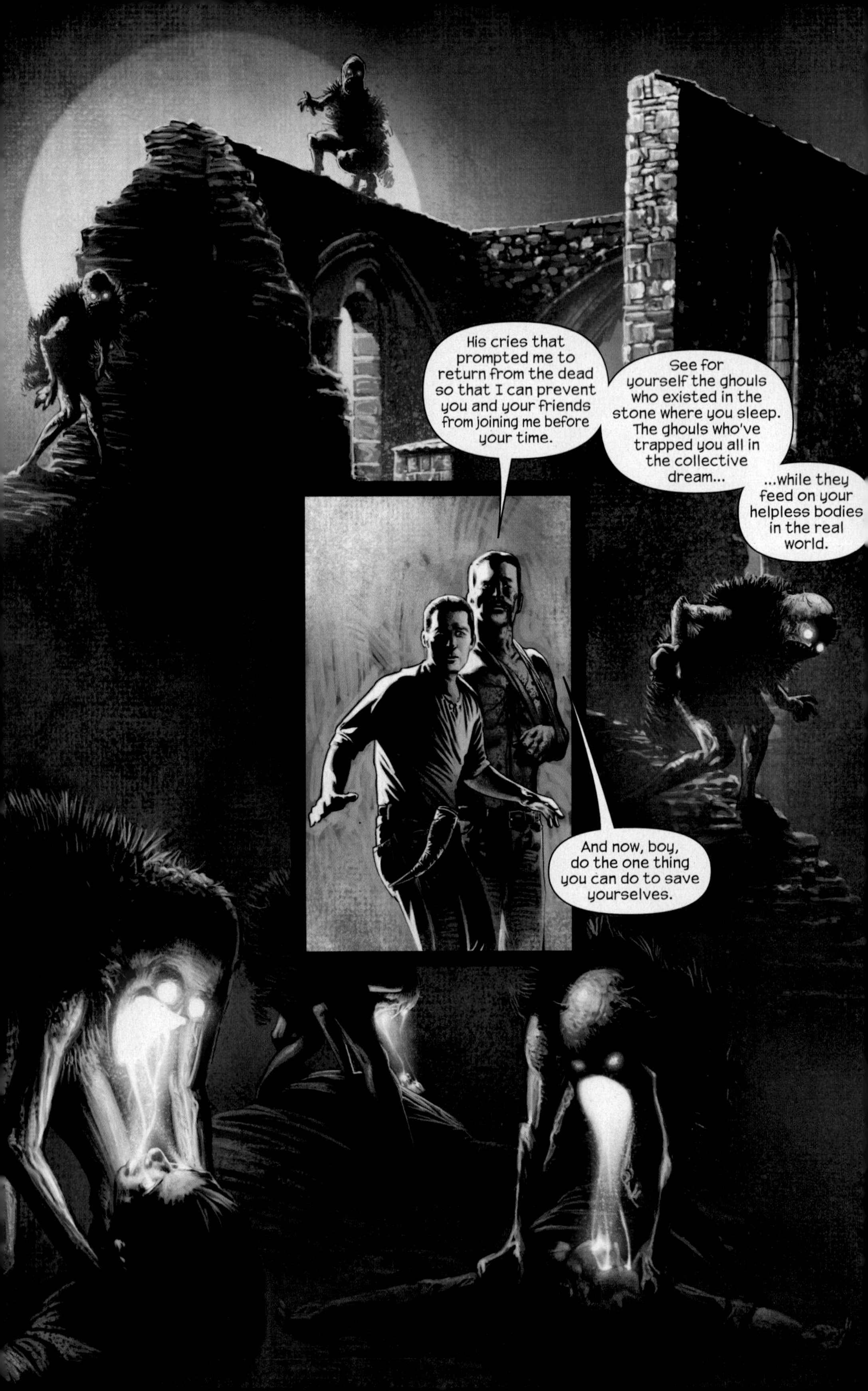
His cries that prompted me to return from the dead so that I can prevent you and your friends from joining me before your time.
See for yourself the ghouls who existed in the stone where you sleep. The ghouls who've trapped you all in the collective dream...
...while they feed on your helpless bodies in the real world.
And now, boy, do the one thing you can do to save yourselves.

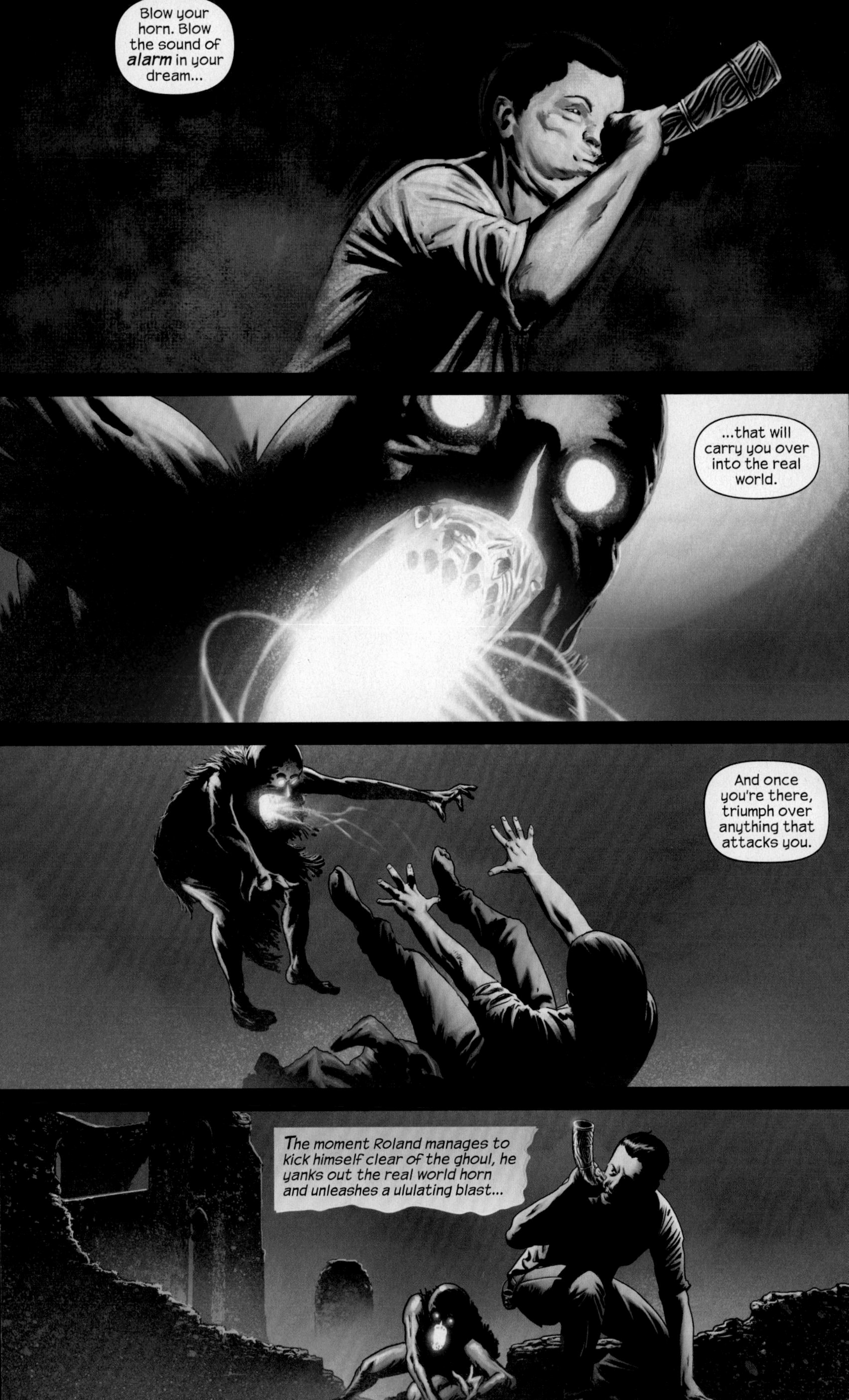
Blow your horn. Blow the sound of *alarm* in your dream...
...that will carry you over into the real world.
And once you're there, triumph over anything that attacks you.
The moment Roland manages to kick himself clear of the ghoul, he yanks out the real world horn and unleashes a ululating blast...

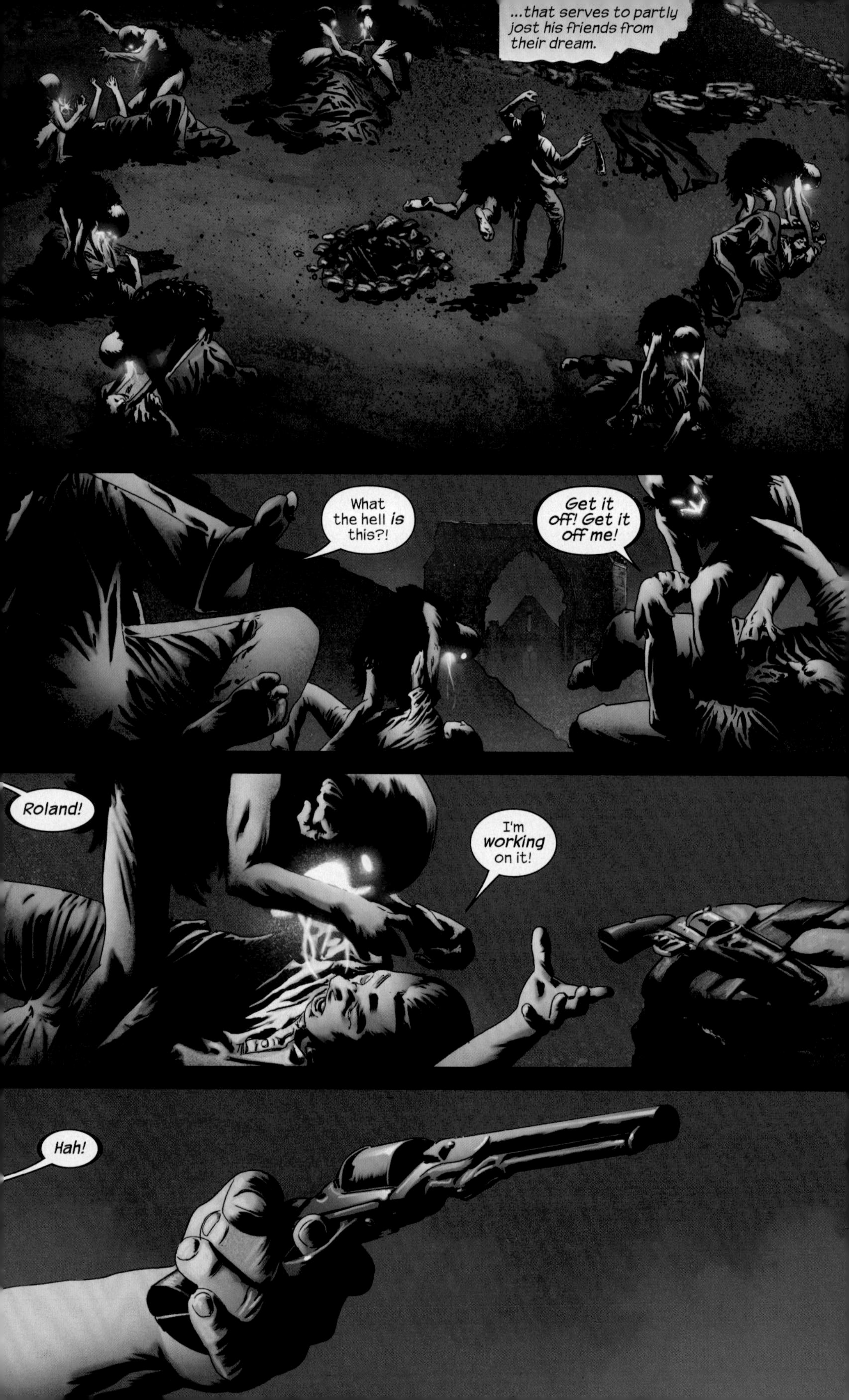
...that serves to partly jost his friends from their dream.
What the hell *is* this?!
Get it off! Get it off me!
Roland!
I'm *working* on it!
Hah!

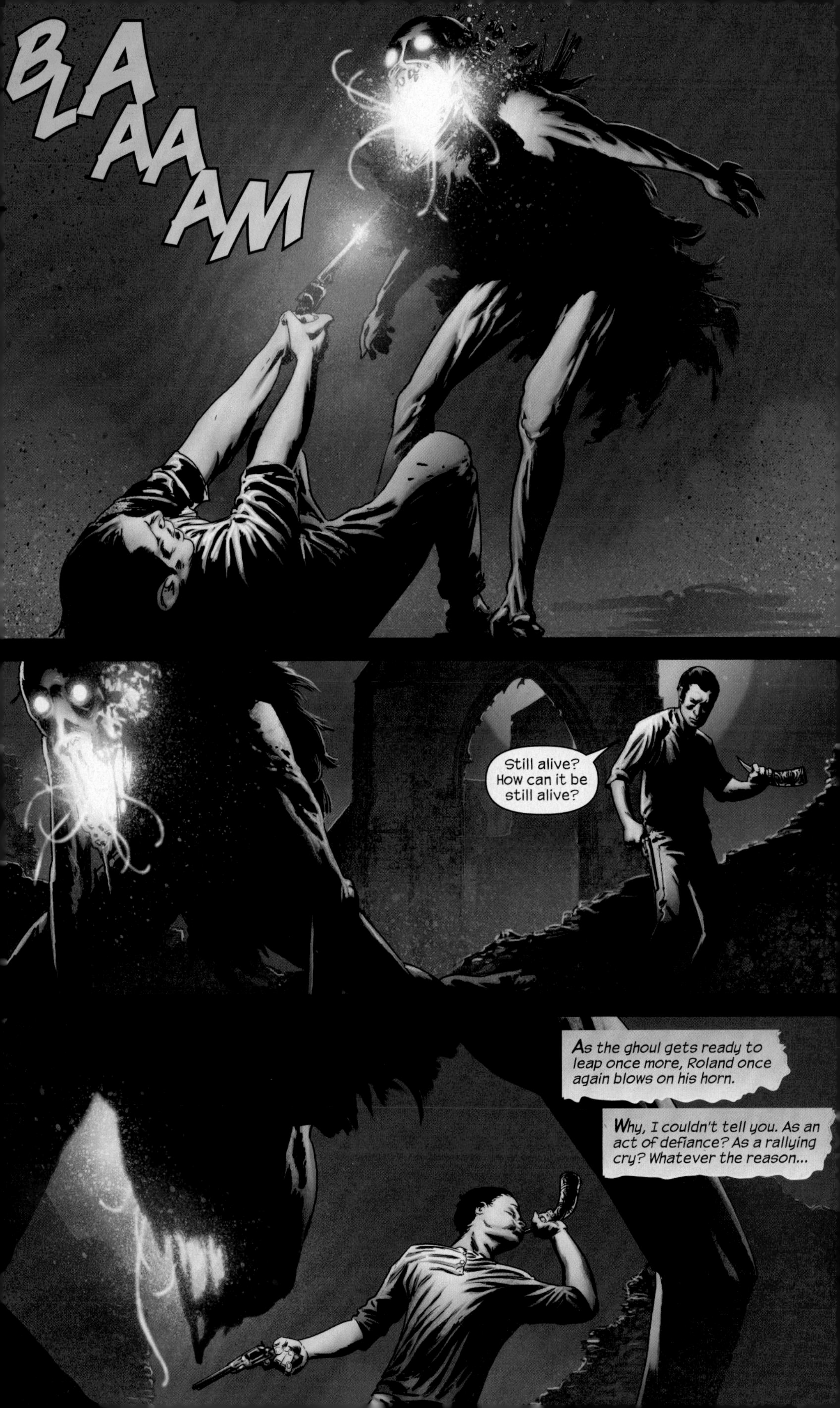
BLAAAAM
Still alive? How can it be still alive?
As the ghoul gets ready to leap once more, Roland once again blows on his horn.
Why, I couldn't tell you. As an act of defiance? As a rallying cry? Whatever the reason...

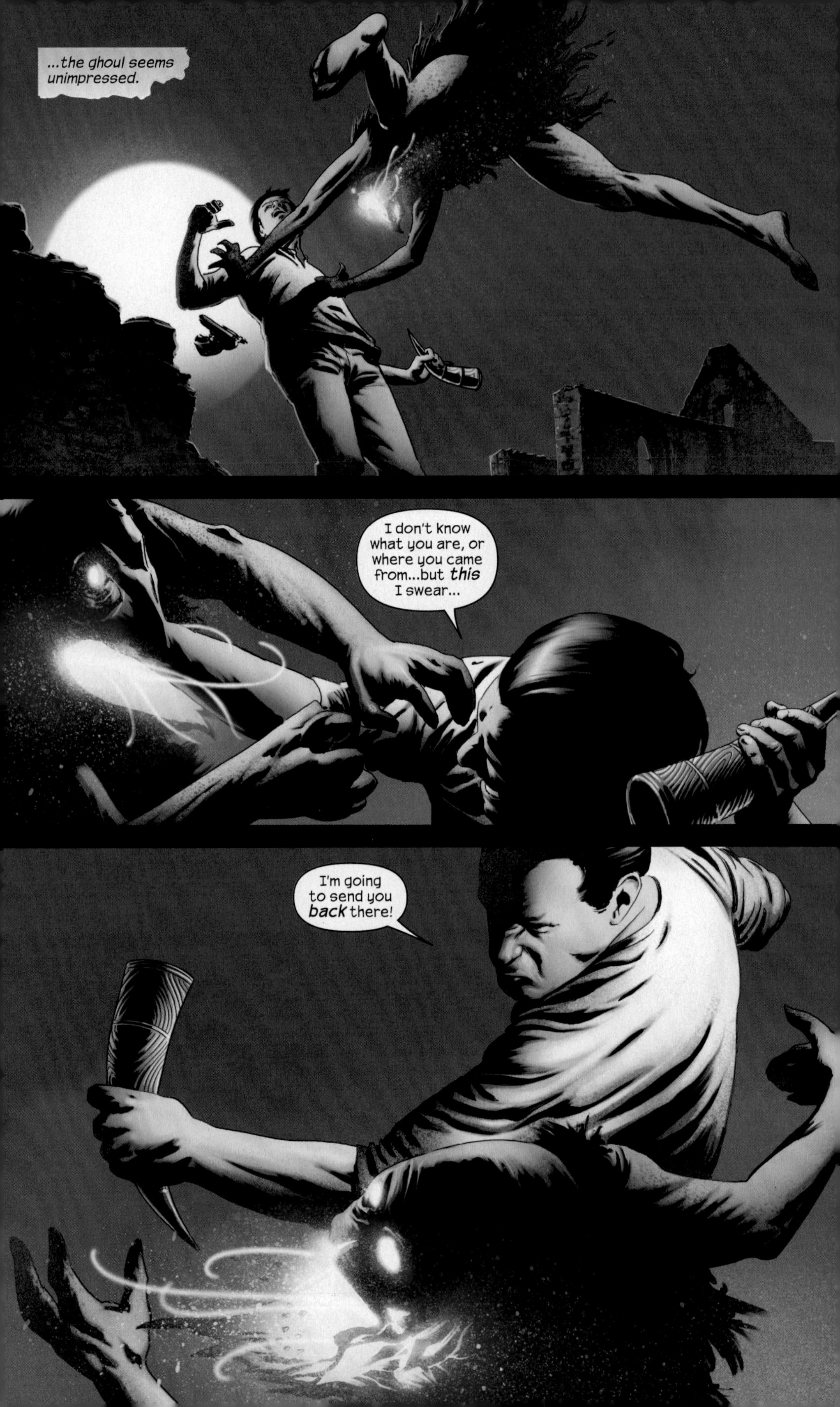

...the ghoul seems unimpressed.
I don't know what you are, or where you came from...but *this* I swear...
I'm going to send you *back* there!

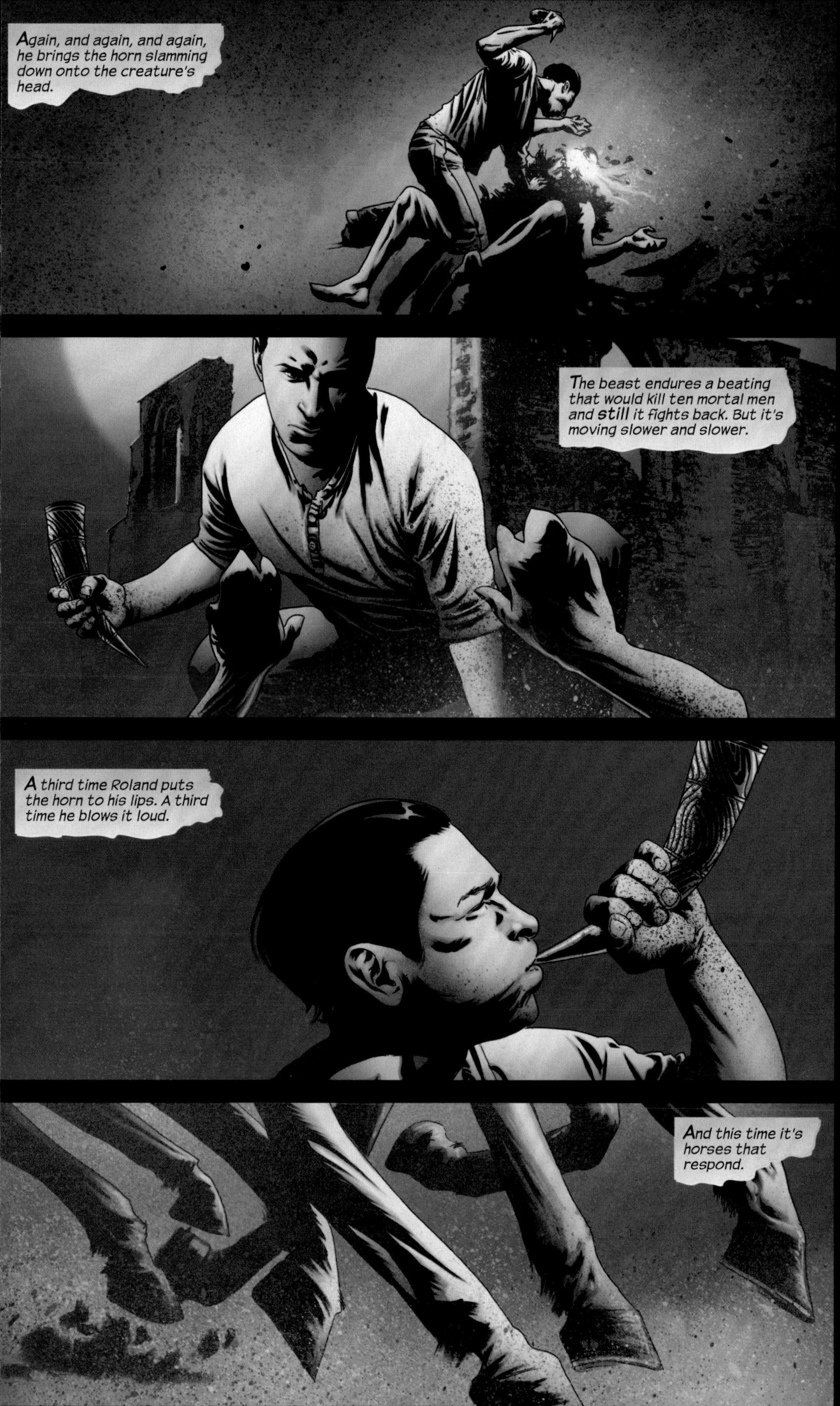
Again, and again, and again, he brings the horn slamming down onto the creature's head.
The beast endures a beating that would kill ten mortal men and still it fights back. But it's moving slower and slower.
A third time Roland puts the horn to his lips. A third time he blows it loud.
And this time it's horses that respond.

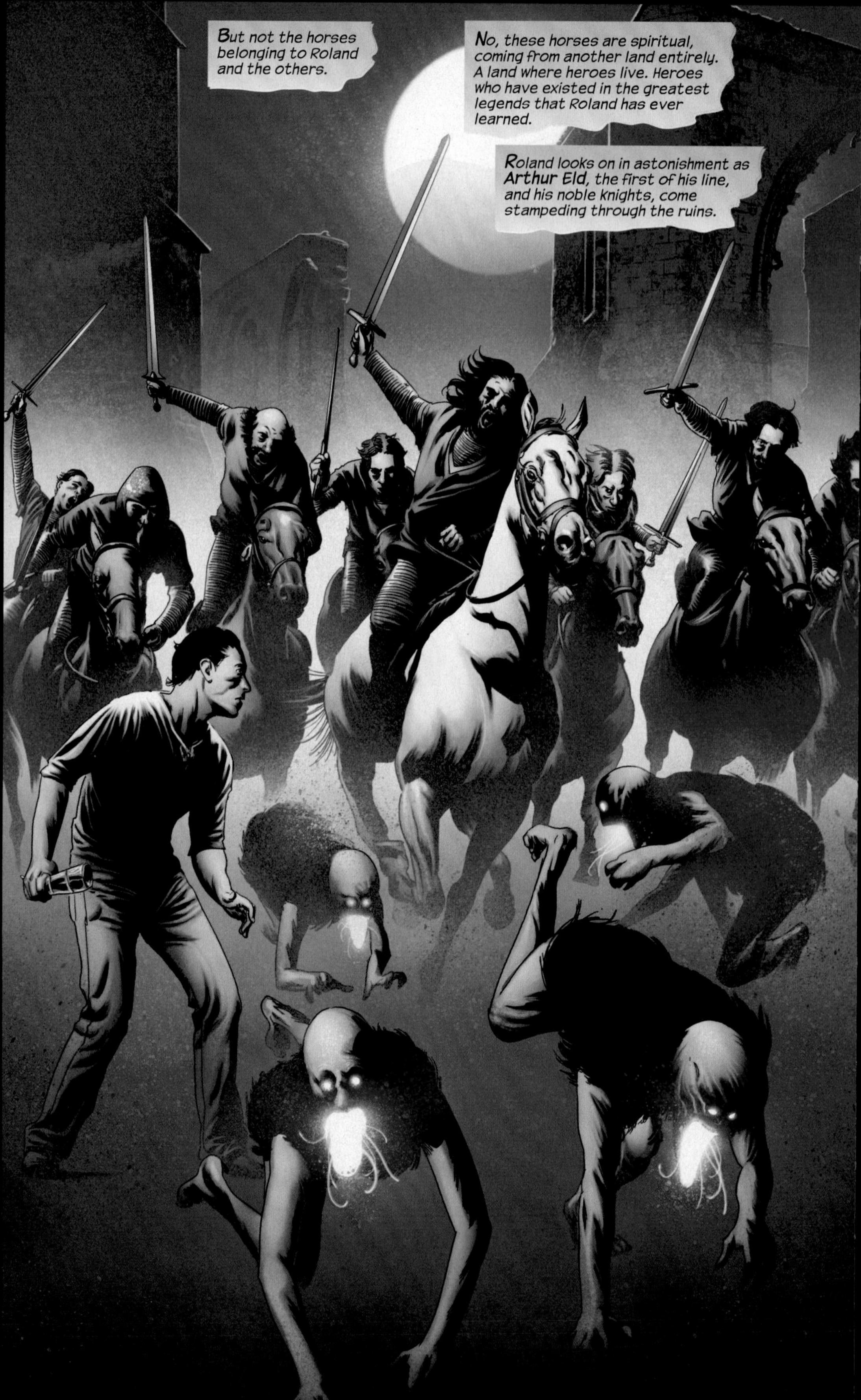
But not the horses belonging to Roland and the others.
No, these horses are spiritual, coming from another land entirely. A land where heroes live. Heroes who have existed in the greatest legends that Roland has ever learned.
Roland looks on in astonishment as Arthur Eld, the first of his line, and his noble knights, come stampeding through the ruins.

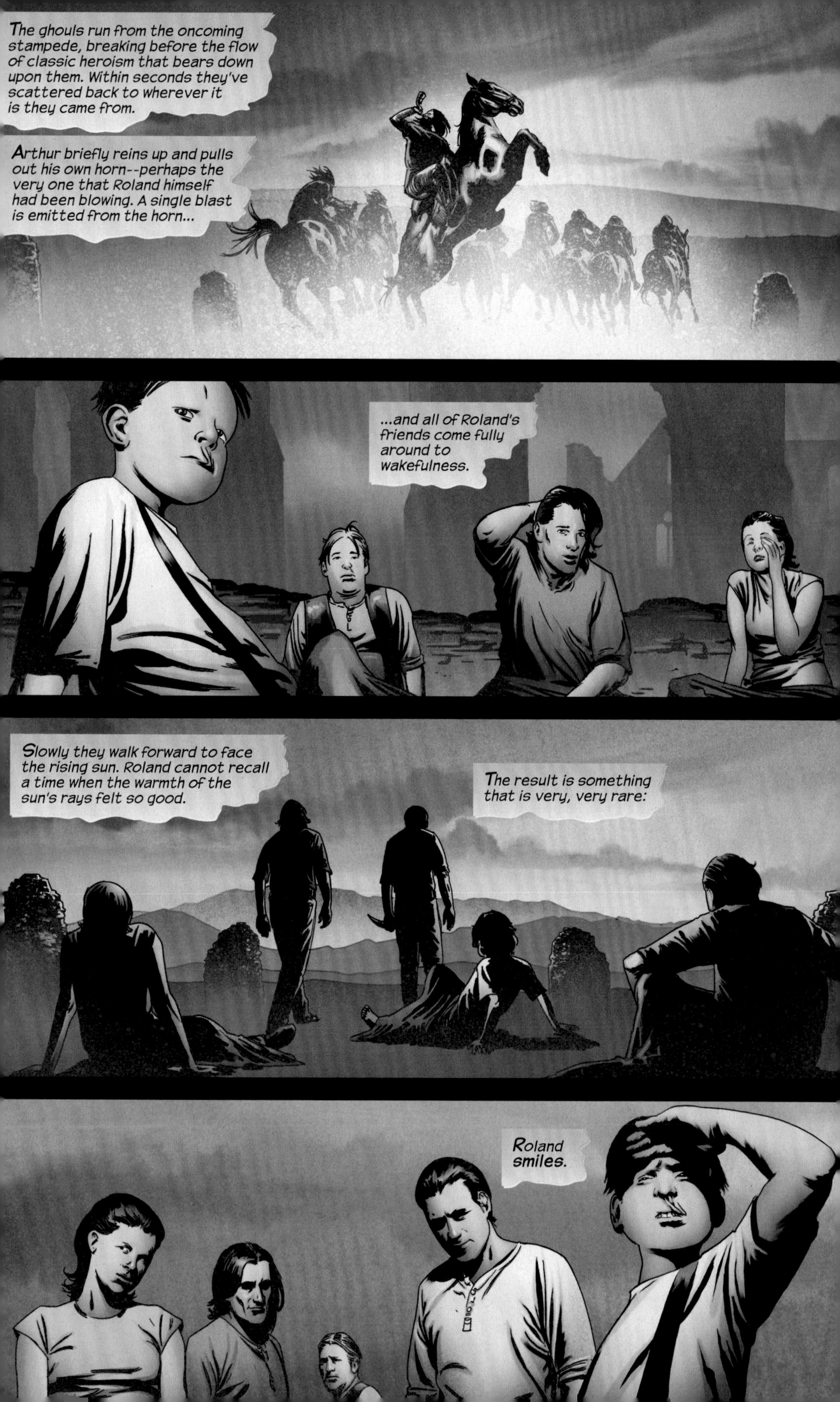

The ghouls run from the oncoming stampede, breaking before the flow of classic heroism that bears down upon them. Within seconds they've scattered back to wherever it is they came from.
Arthur briefly reins up and pulls out his own horn--perhaps the very one that Roland himself had been blowing. A single blast is emitted from the horn...
...and all of Roland's friends come fully around to wakefulness.
Slowly they walk forward to face the rising sun. Roland cannot recall a time when the warmth of the sun's rays felt so good.
The result is something that is very, very rare:
Roland smiles.

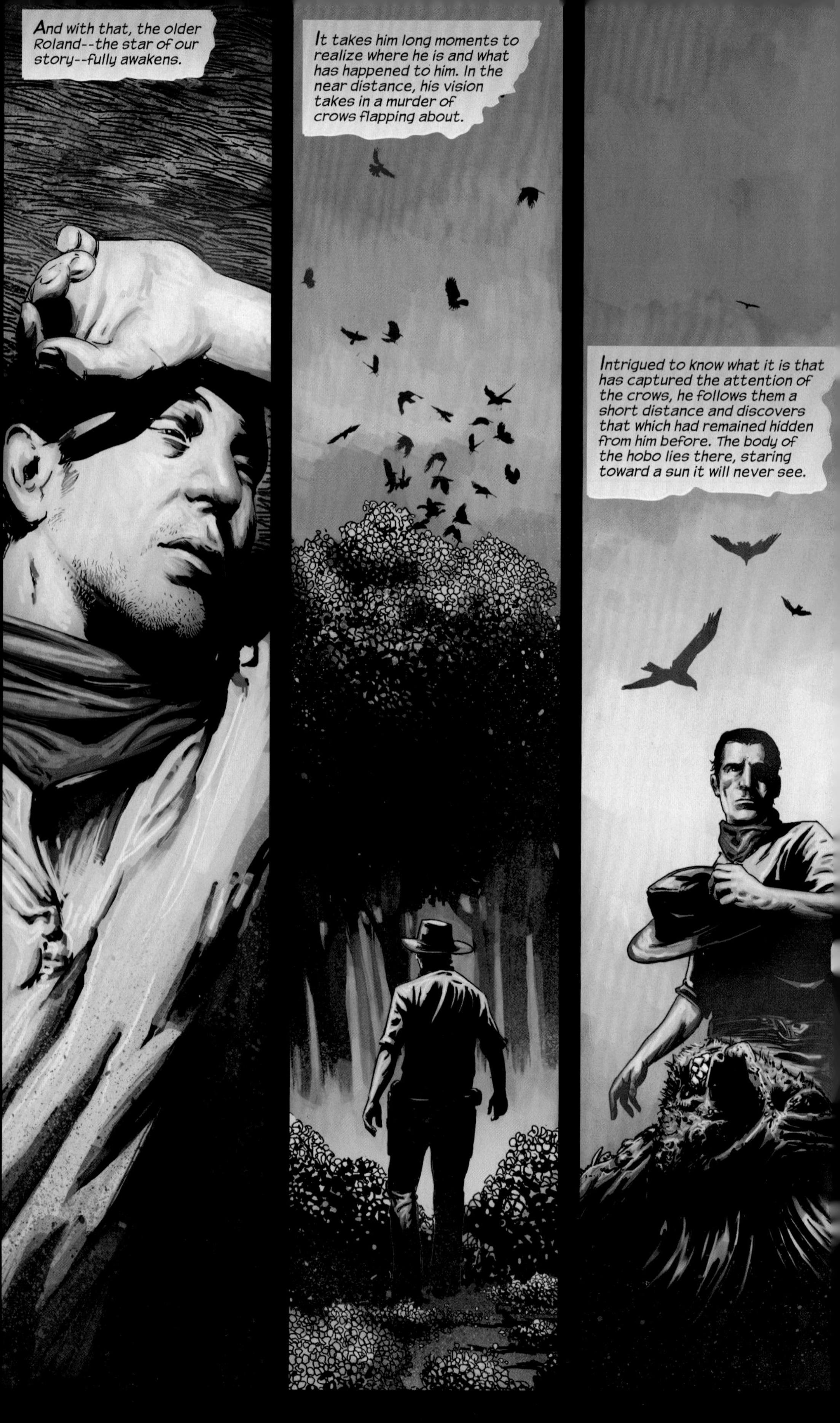
And with that, the older Roland--the star of our story--fully awakens.
It takes him long moments to realize where he is and what has happened to him. In the near distance, his vision takes in a murder of crows flapping about.
Intrigued to know what it is that has captured the attention of the crows, he follows them a short distance and discovers that which had remained hidden from him before. The body of the hobo lies there, staring toward a sun it will never see.

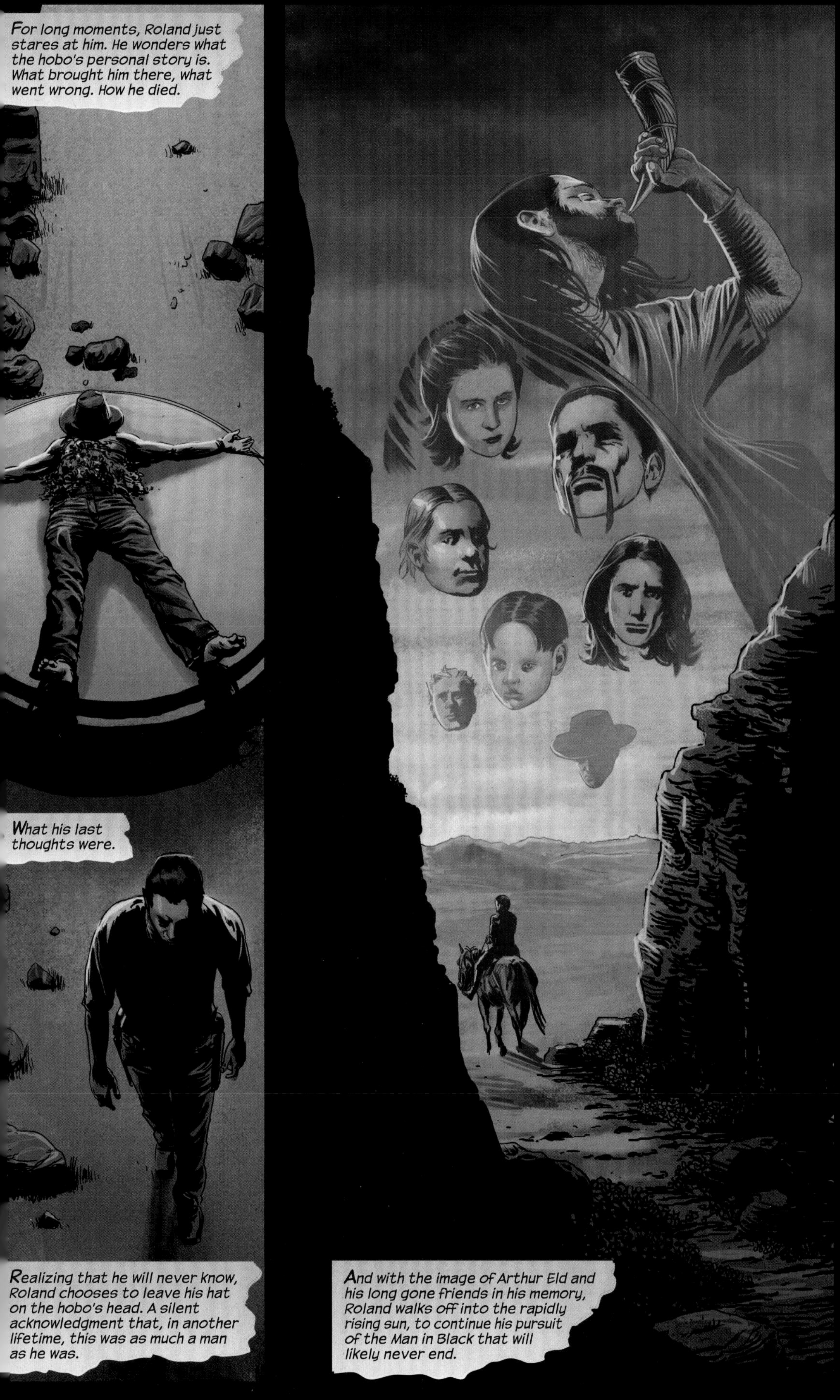
For long moments, Roland just stares at him. He wonders what the hobo's personal story is. What brought him there, what went wrong. How he died.
What his last thoughts were.
Realizing that he will never know, Roland chooses to leave his hat on the hobo's head. A silent acknowledgment that, in another lifetime, this was as much a man as he was.
And with the image of Arthur Eld and his long gone friends in his memory, Roland walks off into the rapidly rising sun, to continue his pursuit of the Man in Black that will likely never end.

'Roland nodded. . . "So fell Lord Perth," he said, "and the countryside did shake with that thunder.'

THE WASTE LANDS, 274

STEPHEN KING

THE DARK TOWER
~ THE GUNSLINGER ~

SO FELL
LORD PERTH

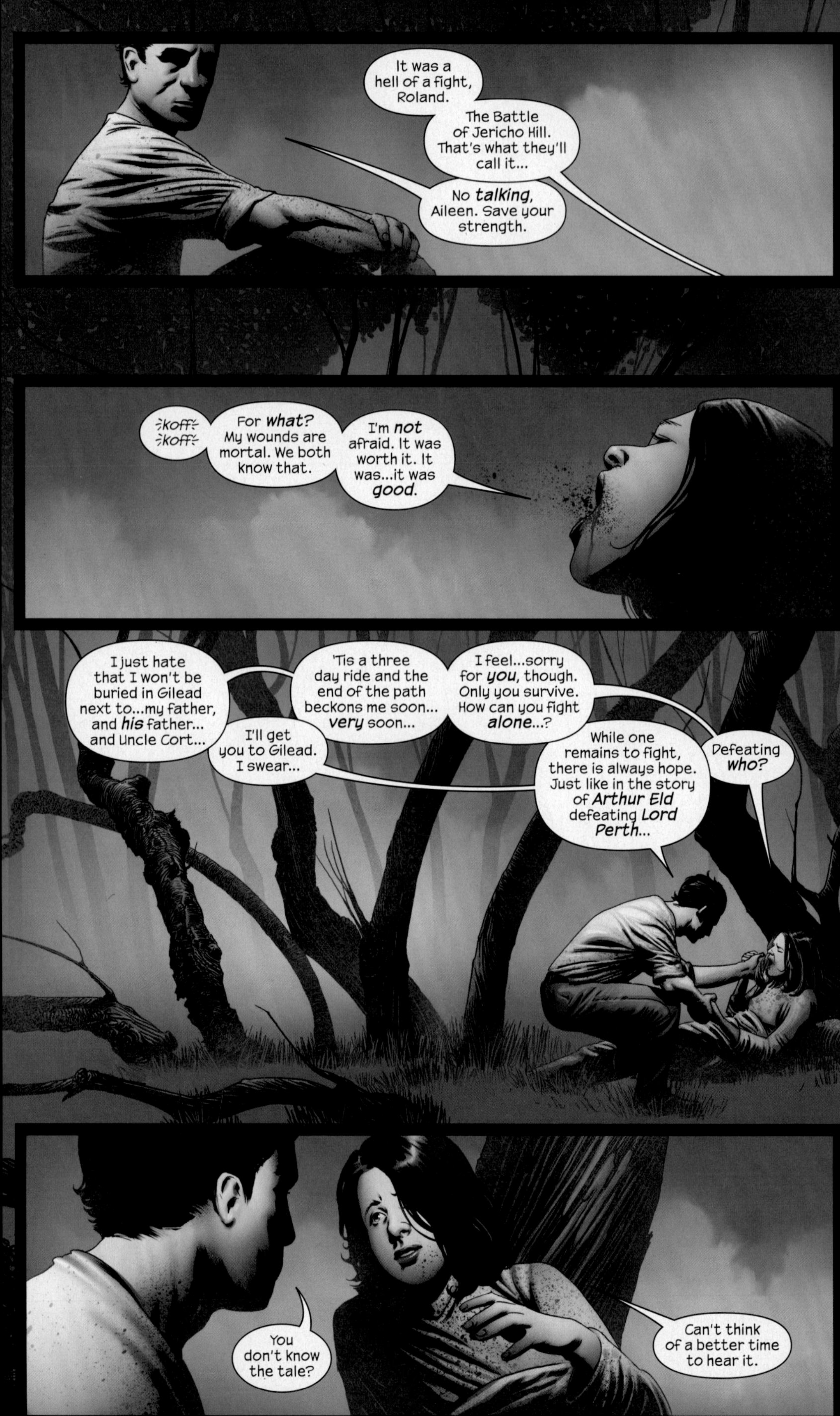
It was a hell of a fight, Roland.
The Battle of Jericho Hill. That's what they'll call it...
No talking, Aileen. Save your strength.
KOFF KOFF
For what? My wounds are mortal. We both know that.
I'm not afraid. It was worth it. It was...it was good.
I just hate that I won't be buried in Gilead next to...my father, and his father... and Uncle Cort...
'Tis a three day ride and the end of the path beckons me soon... very soon...
I'll get you to Gilead. I swear...
I feel...sorry for you, though. Only you survive. How can you fight alone...?
While one remains to fight, there is always hope. Just like in the story of Arthur Eld defeating Lord Perth...
Defeating who?
You don't know the tale?
Can't think of a better time to hear it.

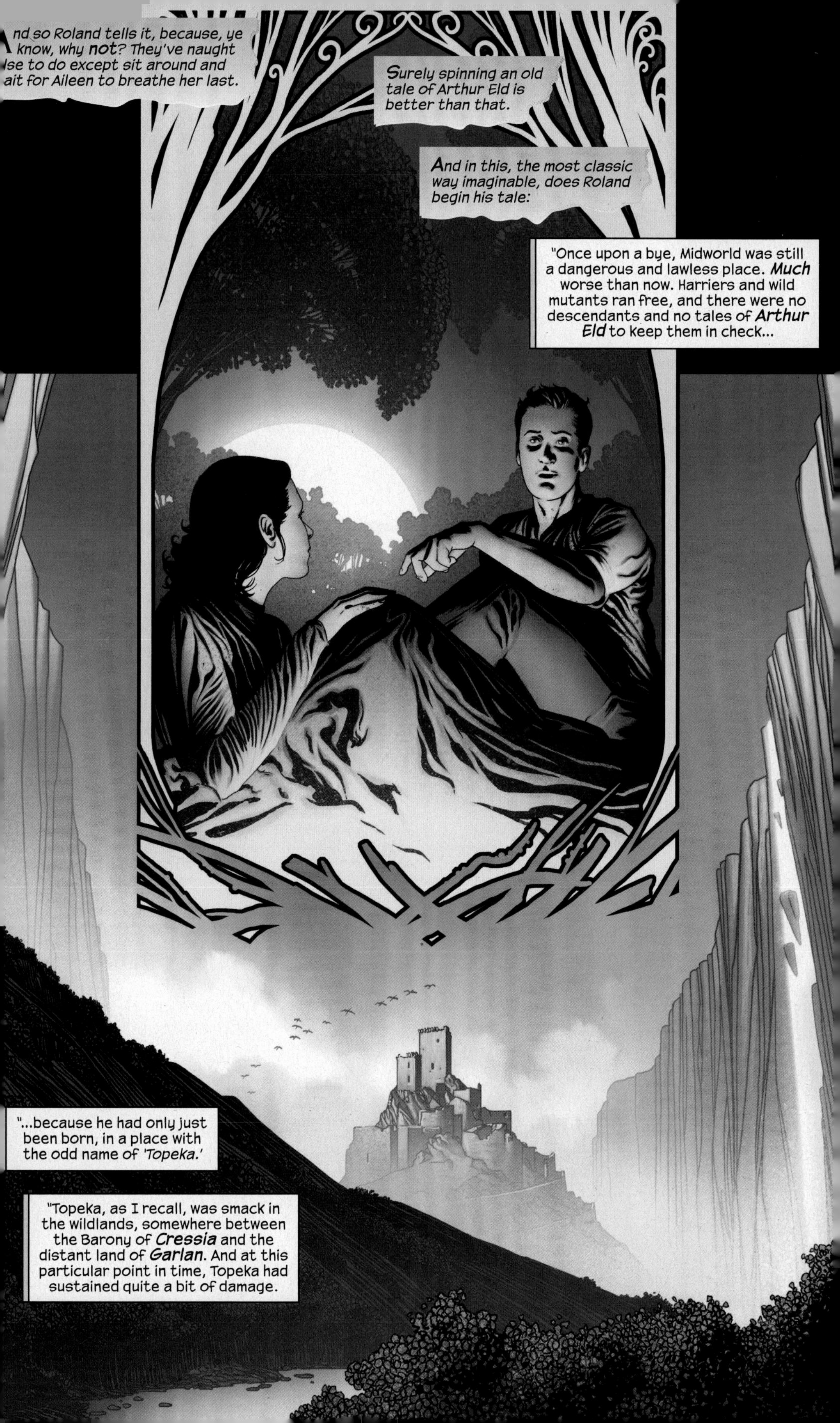
nd so Roland tells it, because, ye know, why not? They've naught lse to do except sit around and ait for Aileen to breathe her last.
Surely spinning an old tale of Arthur Eld is better than that.
And in this, the most classic way imaginable, does Roland begin his tale:
"Once upon a bye, Midworld was still a dangerous and lawless place. Much worse than now. Harriers and wild mutants ran free, and there were no descendants and no tales of Arthur Eld to keep them in check...
"...because he had only just been born, in a place with the odd name of 'Topeka.'
"Topeka, as I recall, was smack in the wildlands, somewhere between the Barony of Cressia and the distant land of Garlan. And at this particular point in time, Topeka had sustained quite a bit of damage.

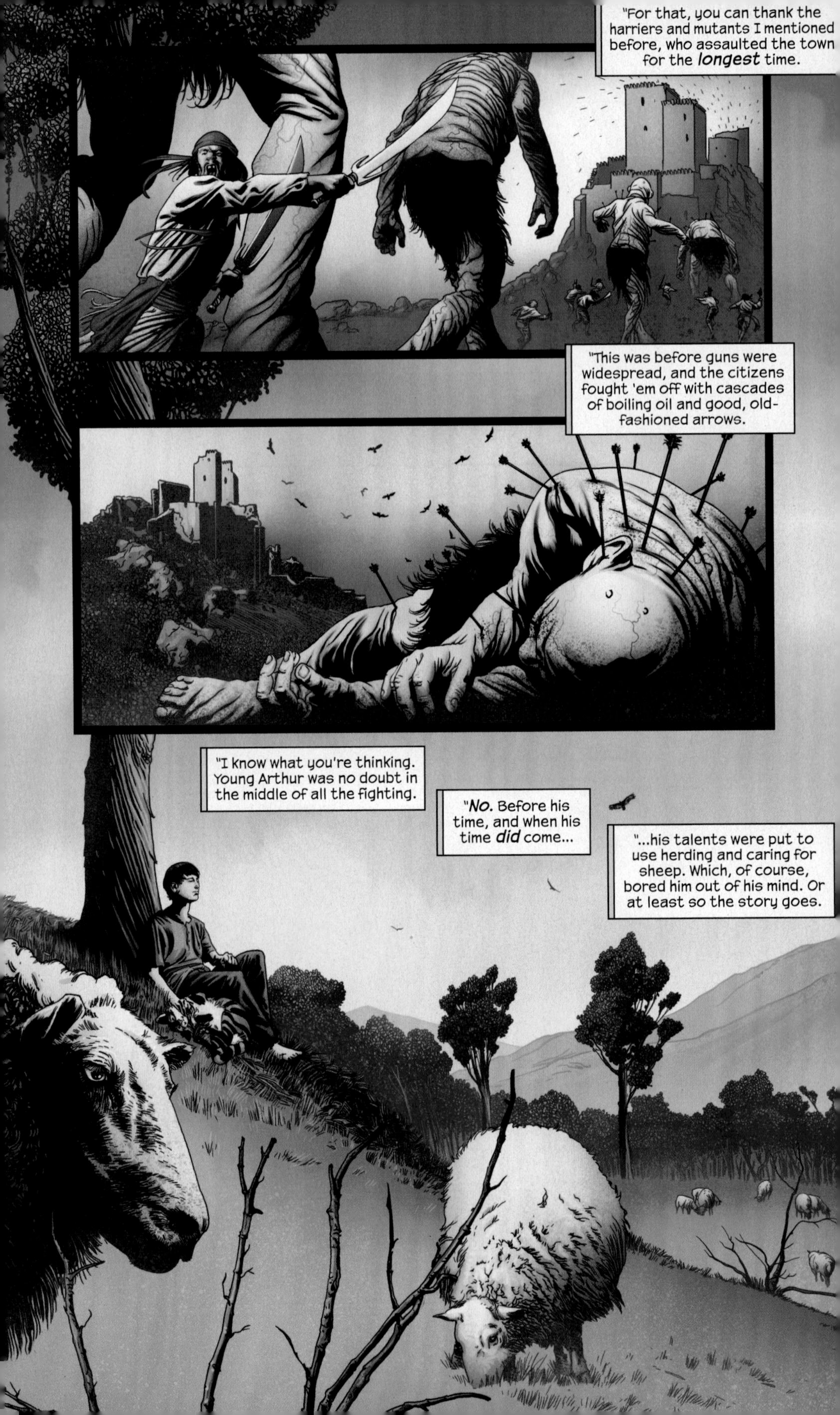
"For that, you can thank the harriers and mutants I mentioned before, who assaulted the town for the *longest* time.
"This was before guns were widespread, and the citizens fought 'em off with cascades of boiling oil and good, old-fashioned arrows.
"I know what you're thinking. Young Arthur was no doubt in the middle of all the fighting.
"*No.* Before his time, and when his time *did* come...
"...his talents were put to use herding and caring for sheep. Which, of course, bored him out of his mind. Or at least so the story goes.

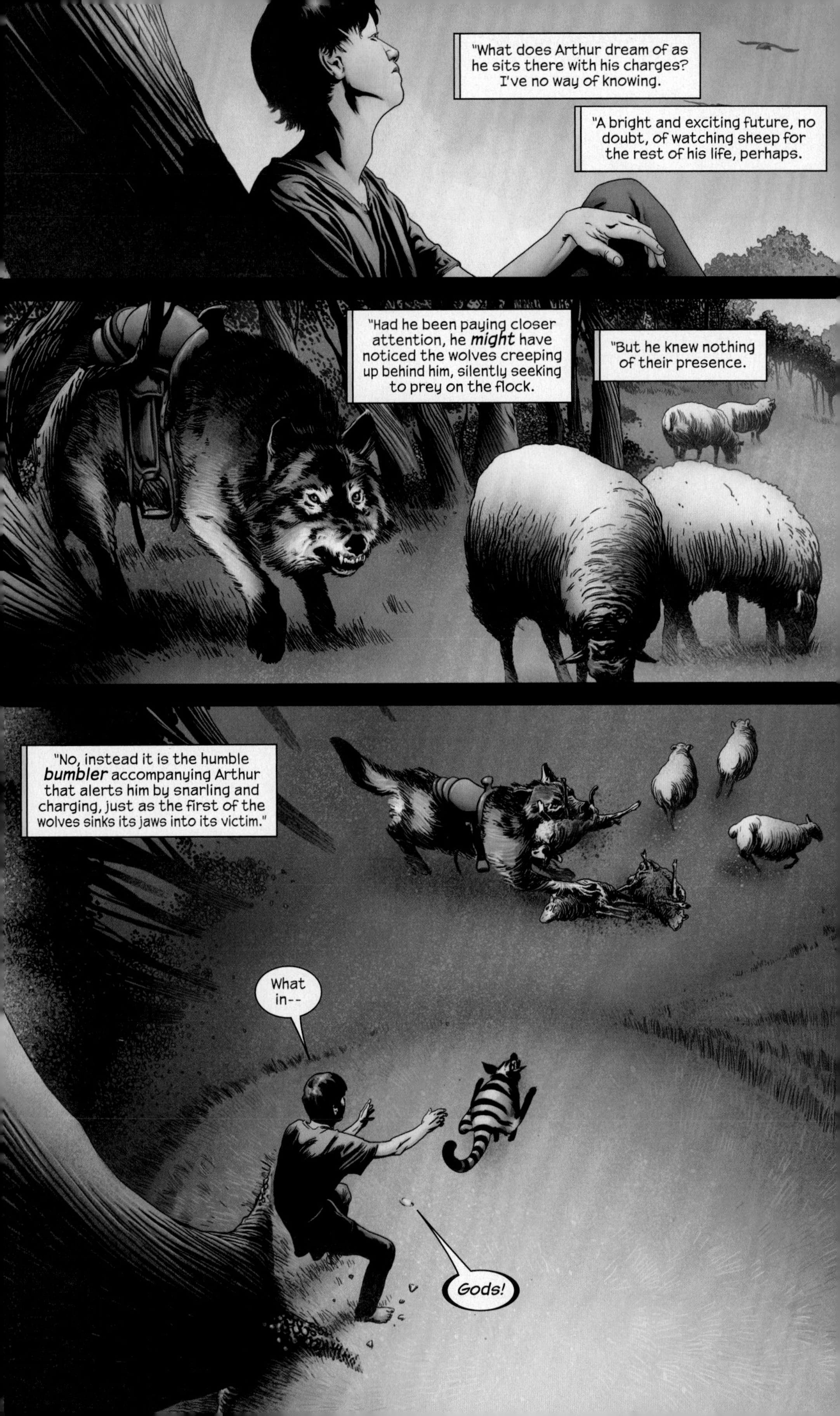

"What does Arthur dream of as he sits there with his charges? I've no way of knowing.
"A bright and exciting future, no doubt, of watching sheep for the rest of his life, perhaps.
"Had he been paying closer attention, he *might* have noticed the wolves creeping up behind him, silently seeking to prey on the flock.
"But he knew nothing of their presence.
"No, instead it is the humble *bumbler* accompanying Arthur that alerts him by snarling and charging, just as the first of the wolves sinks its jaws into its victim."
What in--
Gods!

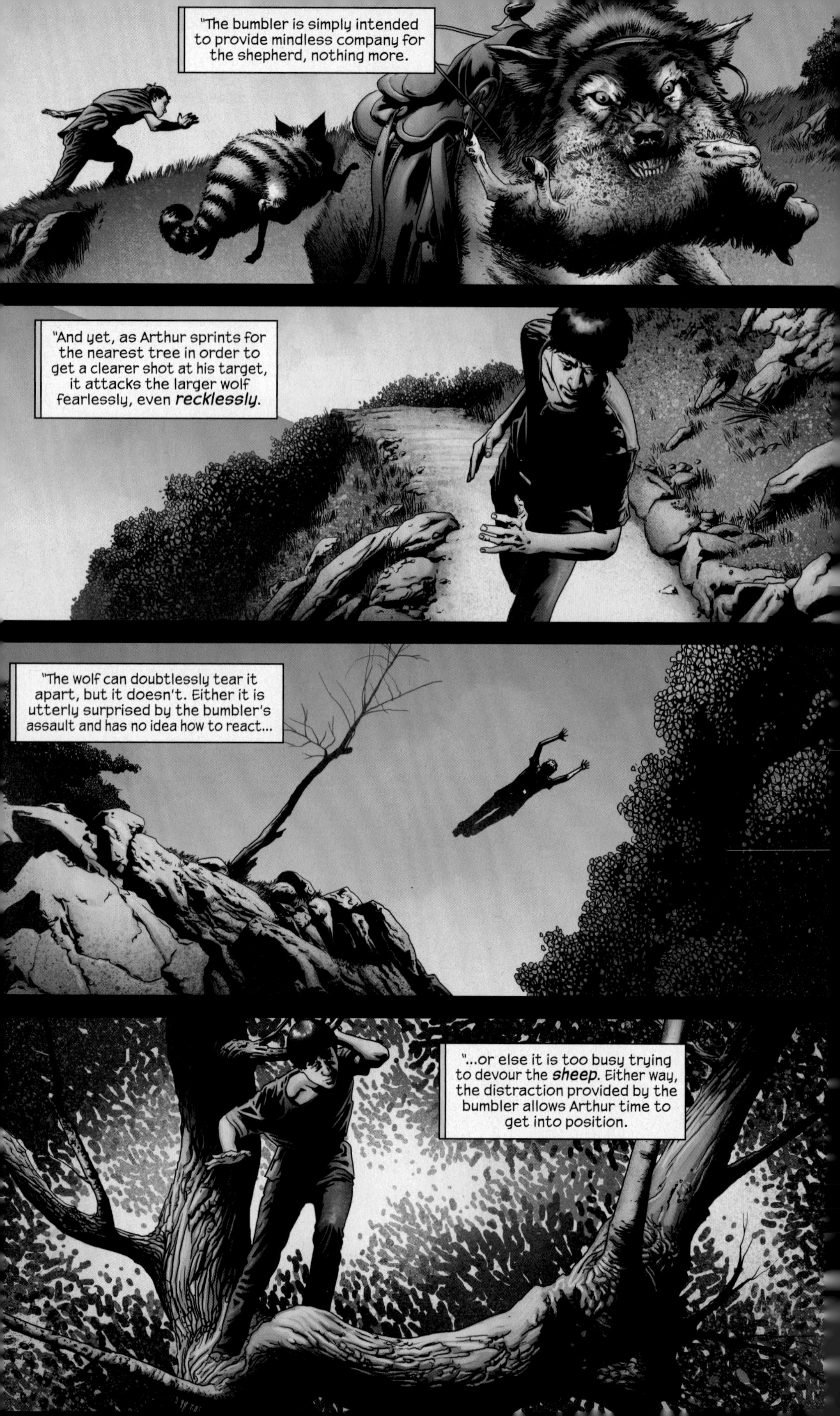
"The bumbler is simply intended to provide mindless company for the shepherd, nothing more.
"And yet, as Arthur sprints for the nearest tree in order to get a clearer shot at his target, it attacks the larger wolf fearlessly, even *recklessly*.
"The wolf can doubtlessly tear it apart, but it doesn't. Either it is utterly surprised by the bumbler's assault and has no idea how to react...
"...or else it is too busy trying to devour the *sheep*. Either way, the distraction provided by the bumbler allows Arthur time to get into position.

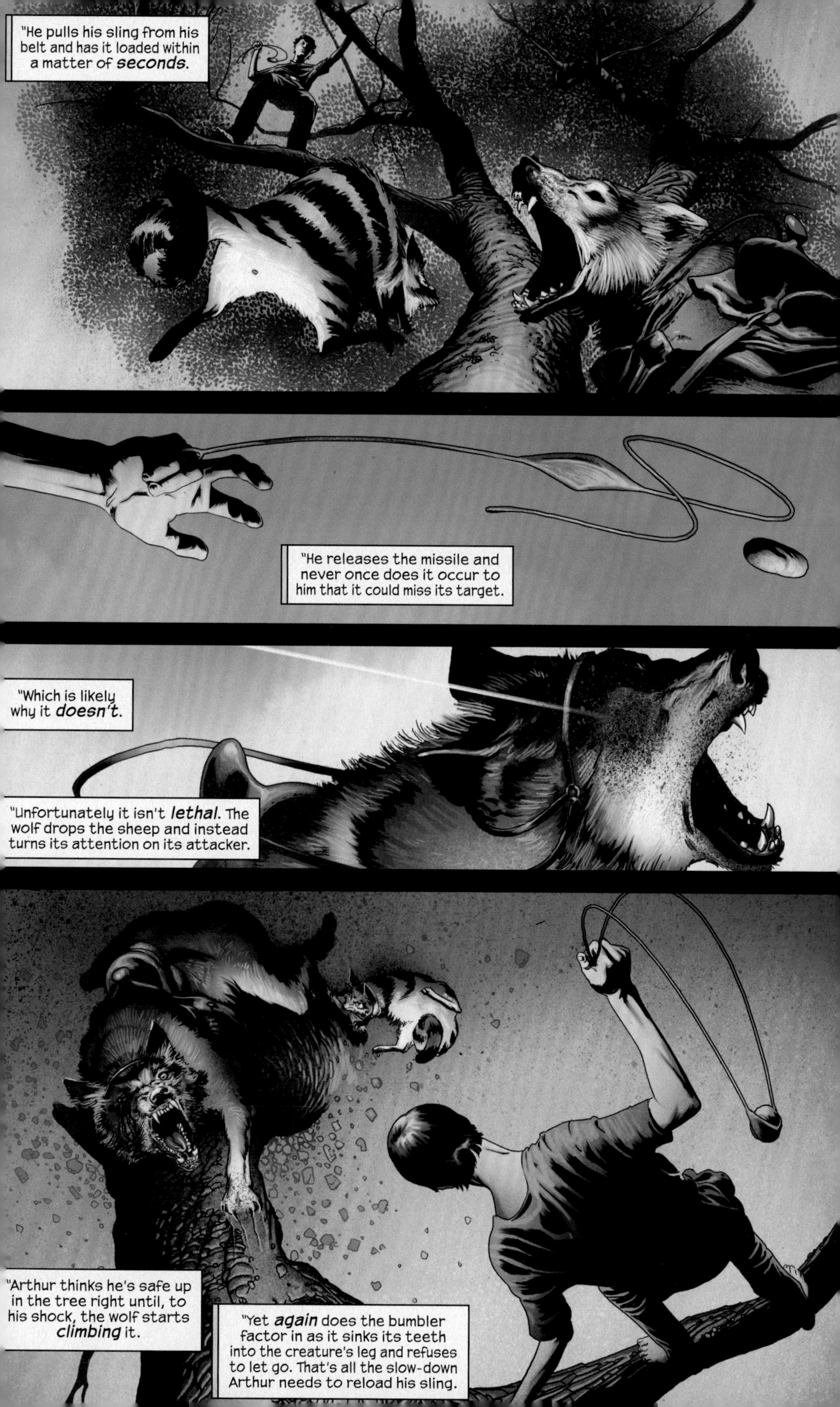
"He pulls his sling from his belt and has it loaded within a matter of *seconds*.
"He releases the missile and never once does it occur to him that it could miss its target.
"Which is likely why it *doesn't*.
"Unfortunately it isn't *lethal*. The wolf drops the sheep and instead turns its attention on its attacker.
"Arthur thinks he's safe up in the tree right until, to his shock, the wolf starts *climbing* it.
"Yet *again* does the bumbler factor in as it sinks its teeth into the creature's leg and refuses to let go. That's all the slow-down Arthur needs to reload his sling.

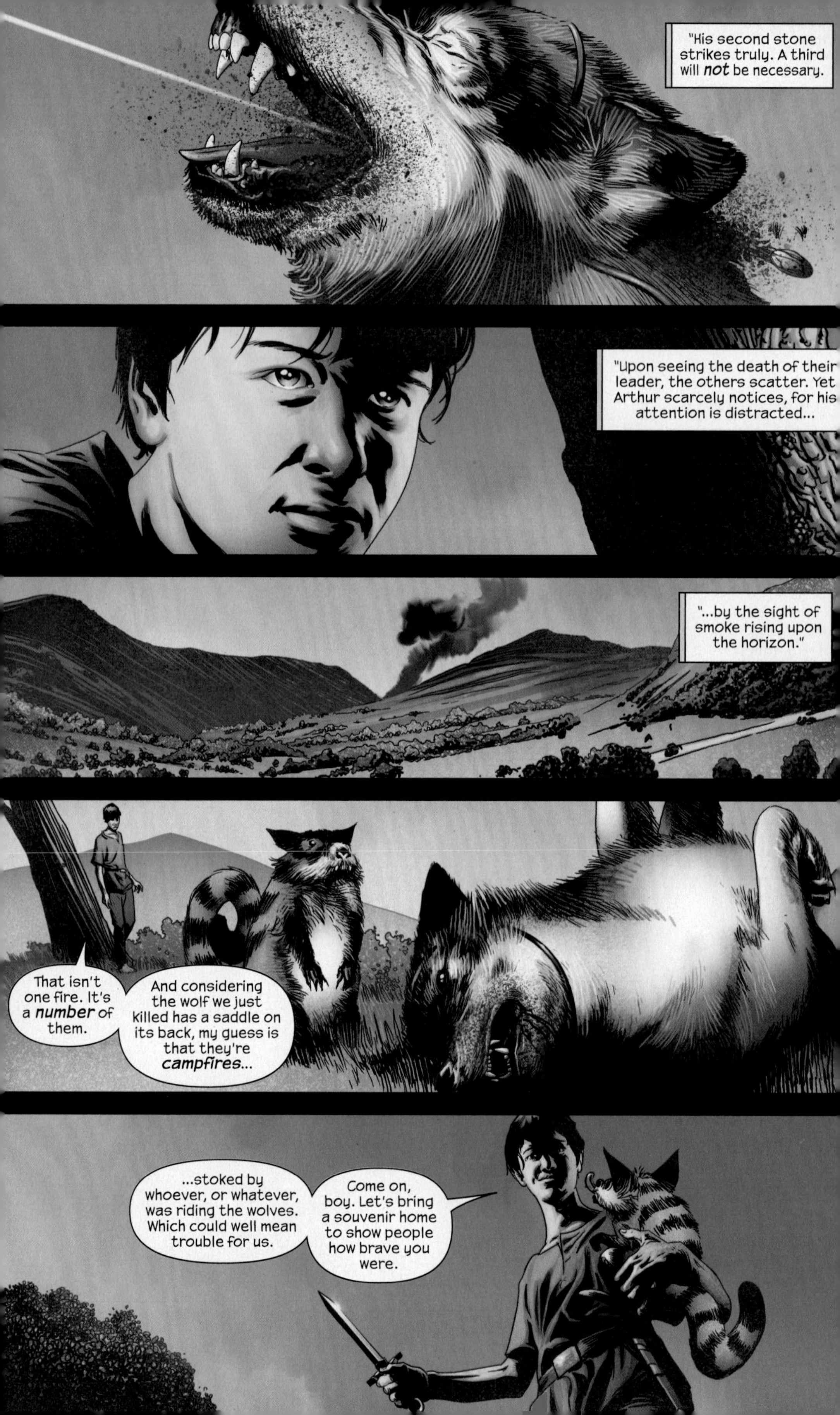
"His second stone strikes truly. A third will *not* be necessary.
"Upon seeing the death of their leader, the others scatter. Yet Arthur scarcely notices, for his attention is distracted...
"...by the sight of smoke rising upon the horizon."
That isn't one fire. It's a *number* of them.
And considering the wolf we just killed has a saddle on its back, my guess is that they're *campfires*...
...stoked by whoever, or whatever, was riding the wolves. Which could well mean trouble for us.
Come on, boy. Let's bring a souvenir home to show people how brave you were.

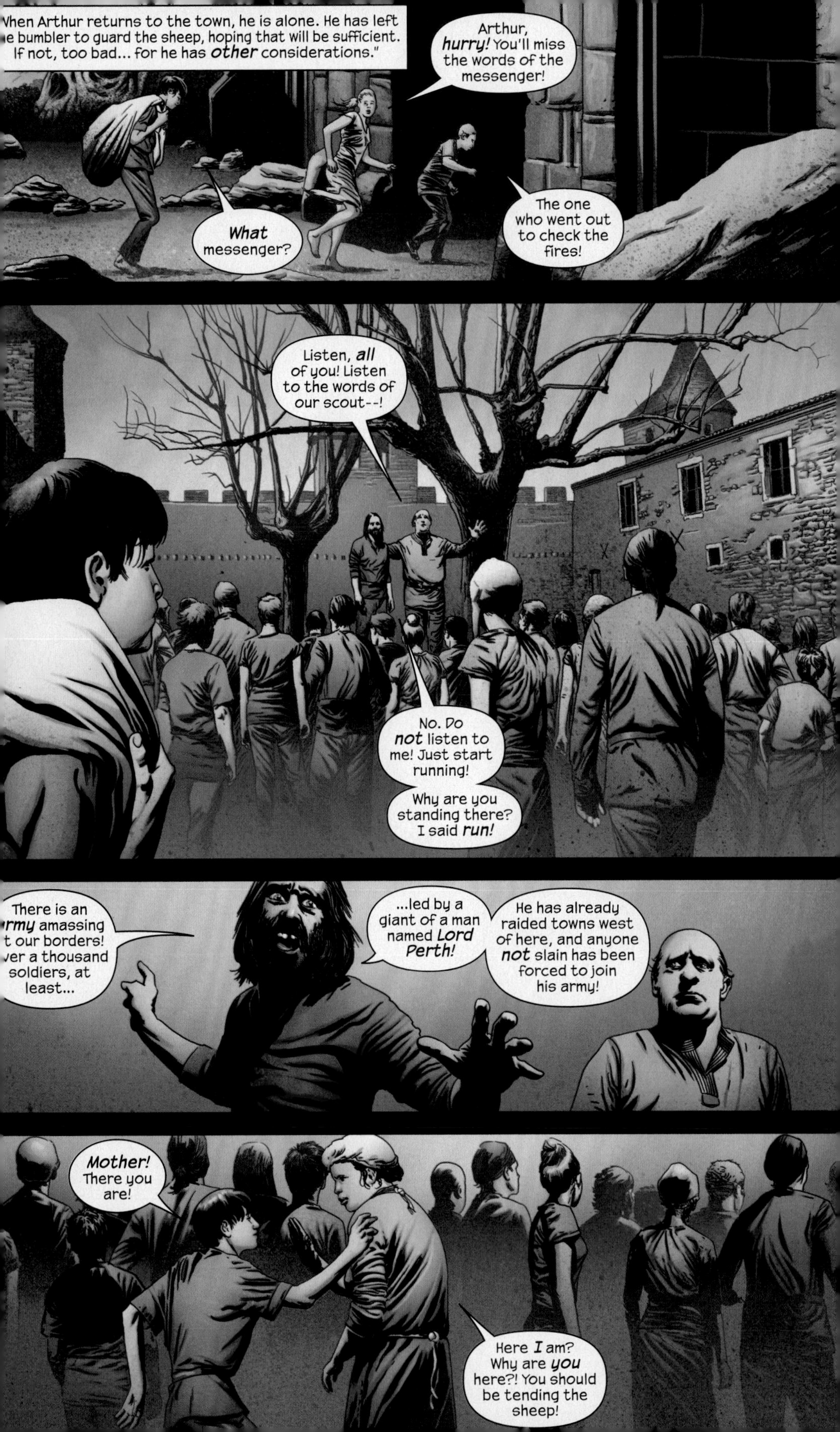

Vhen Arthur returns to the town, he is alone. He has left e bumbler to guard the sheep, hoping that will be sufficient. If not, too bad... for he has other considerations."
Arthur, hurry! You'll miss the words of the messenger!
What messenger?
The one who went out to check the fires!
Listen, all of you! Listen to the words of our scout--!
No. Do not listen to me! Just start running!
Why are you standing there? I said run!
There is an rmy amassing t our borders! ver a thousand soldiers, at least...
...led by a giant of a man named Lord Perth!
He has already raided towns west of here, and anyone not slain has been forced to join his army!
Mother! There you are!
Here I am? Why are you here?! You should be tending the sheep!

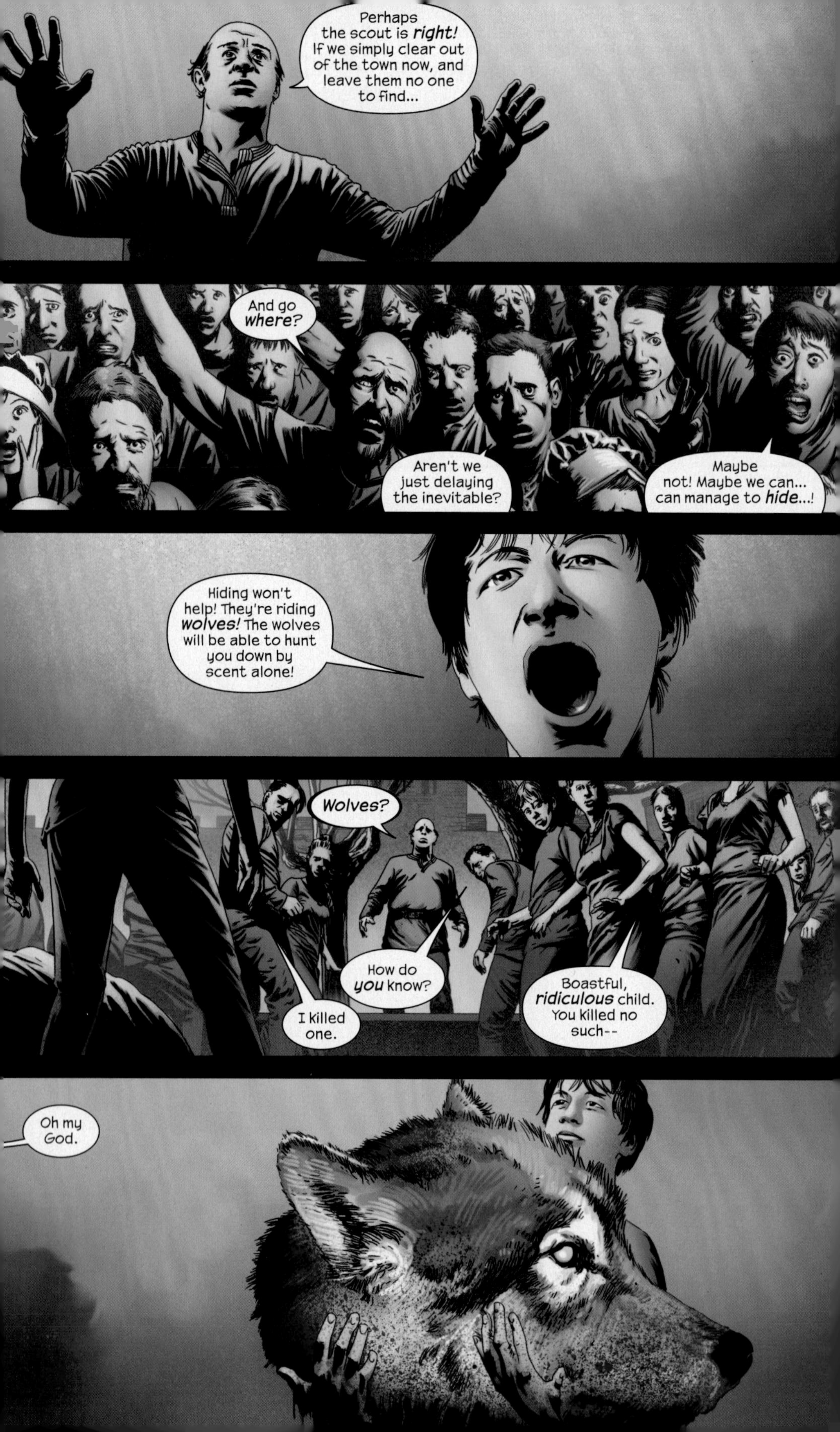
Perhaps the scout is *right!* If we simply clear out of the town now, and leave them no one to find...
And go *where?*
Aren't we just delaying the inevitable?
Maybe not! Maybe we can... can manage to *hide*...!
Hiding won't help! They're riding *wolves!* The wolves will be able to hunt you down by scent alone!
Wolves?
How do *you* know?
I killed one.
Boastful, *ridiculous* child. You killed no such--
Oh my God.

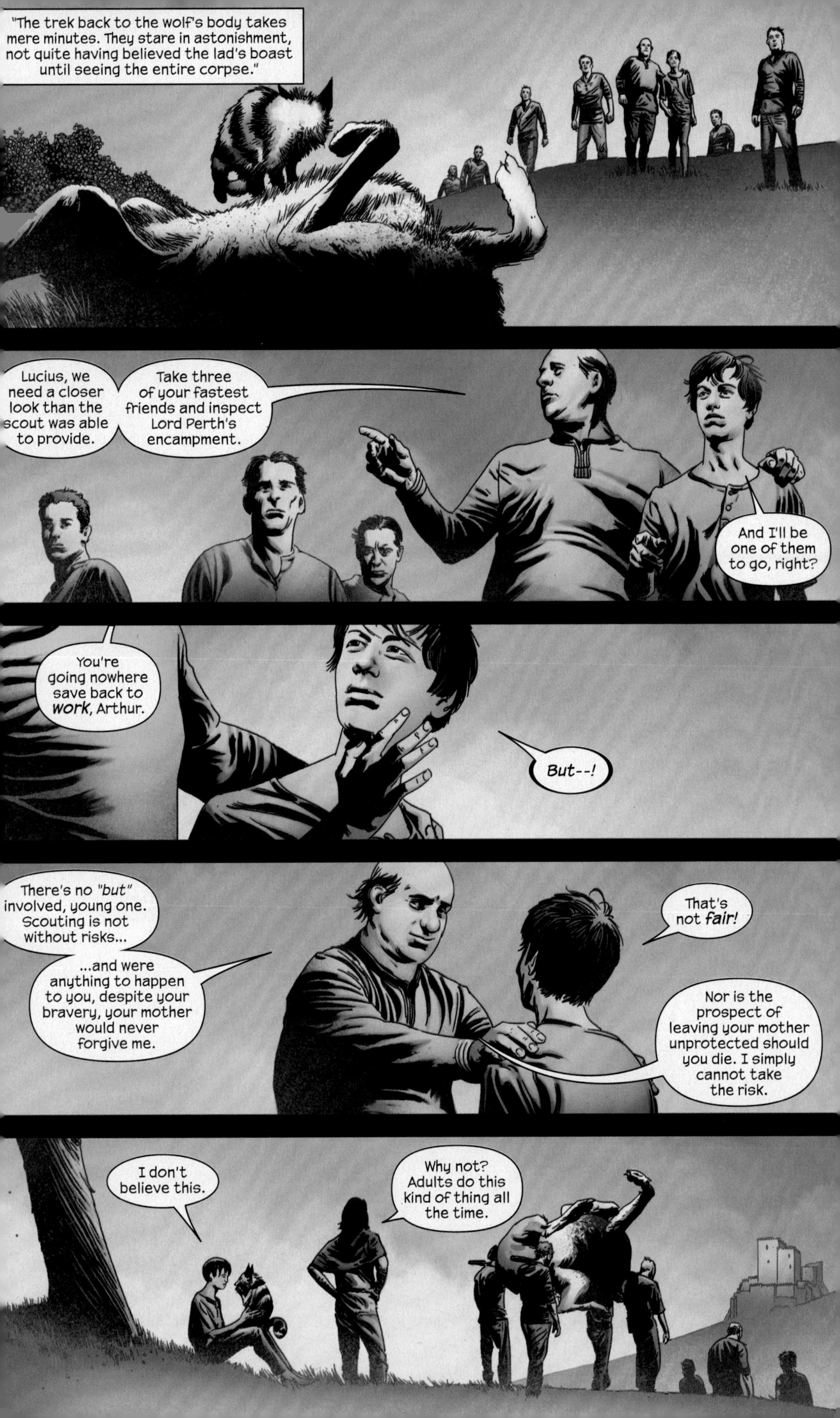
"The trek back to the wolf's body takes mere minutes. They stare in astonishment, not quite having believed the lad's boast until seeing the entire corpse."
Lucius, we need a closer look than the scout was able to provide.
Take three of your fastest friends and inspect Lord Perth's encampment.
And I'll be one of them to go, right?
You're going nowhere save back to *work*, Arthur.
But--!
There's no *"but"* involved, young one. Scouting is not without risks...
...and were anything to happen to you, despite your bravery, your mother would never forgive me.
That's not *fair!*
Nor is the prospect of leaving your mother unprotected should you die. I simply cannot take the risk.
I don't believe this.
Why not? Adults do this kind of thing all the time.

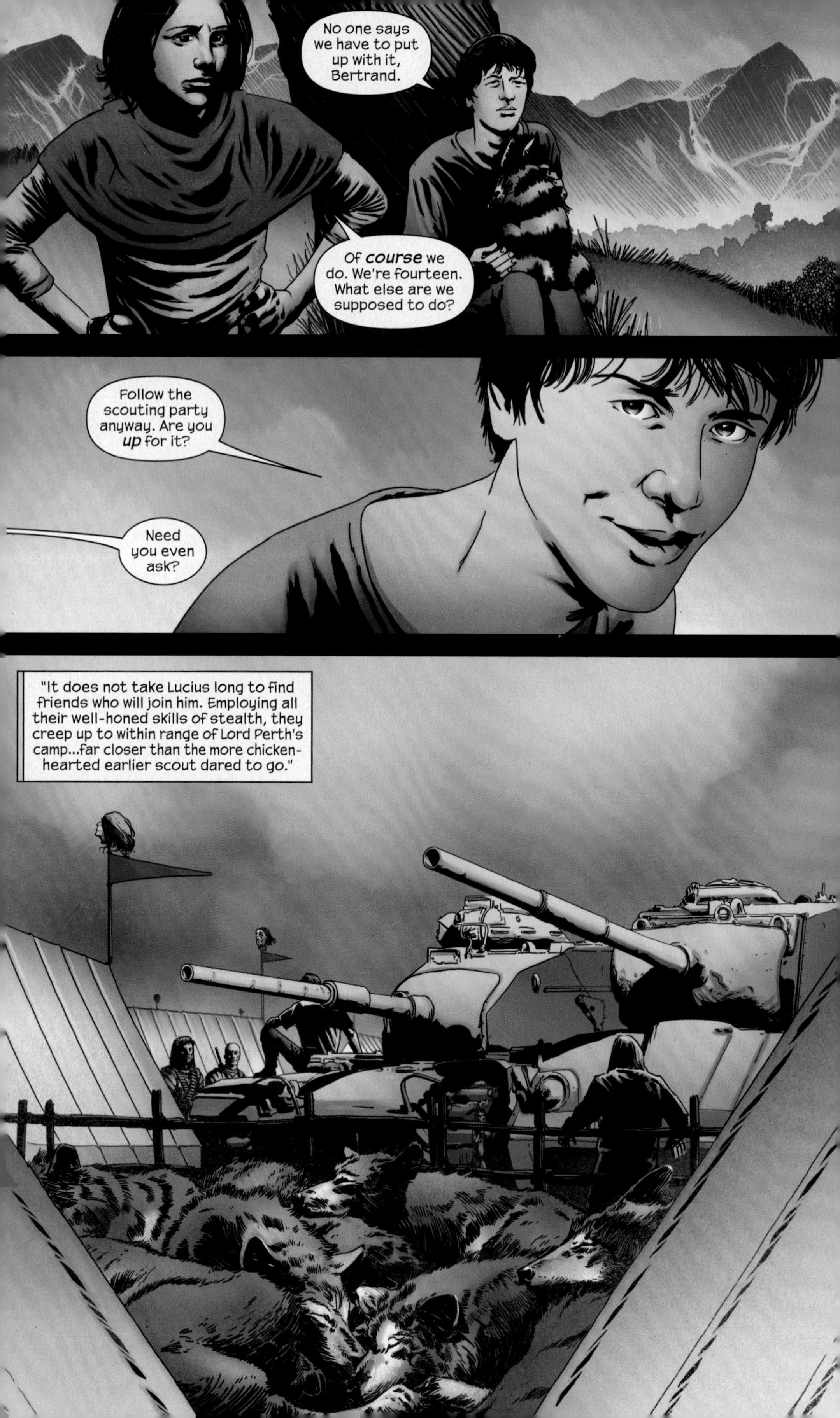
No one says we have to put up with it, Bertrand.
Of course we do. We're fourteen. What else are we supposed to do?
Follow the scouting party anyway. Are you up for it?
Need you even ask?
"It does not take Lucius long to find friends who will join him. Employing all their well-honed skills of stealth, they creep up to within range of Lord Perth's camp...far closer than the more chicken-hearted earlier scout dared to go."

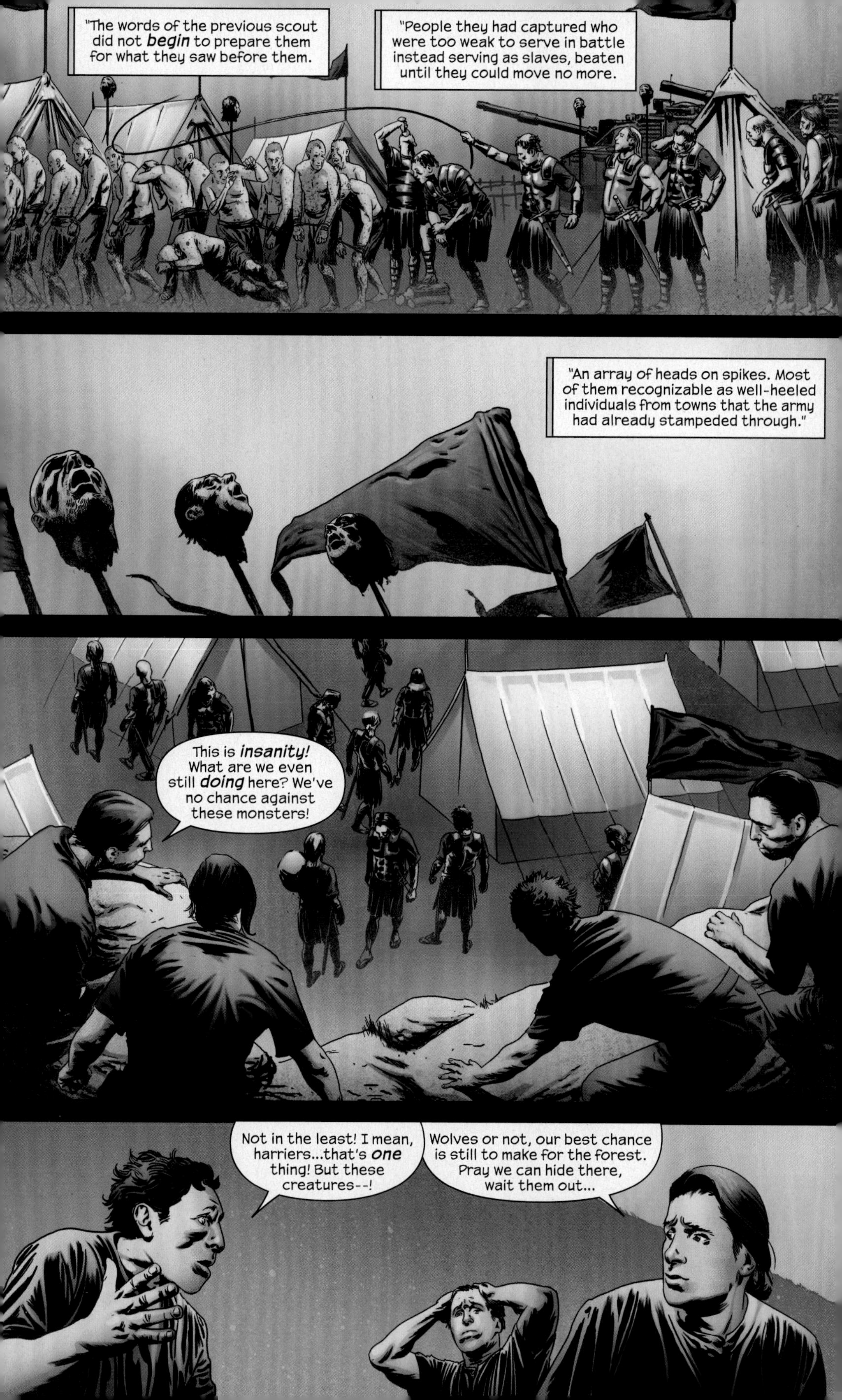
"The words of the previous scout did not *begin* to prepare them for what they saw before them.
"People they had captured who were too weak to serve in battle instead serving as slaves, beaten until they could move no more.
"An array of heads on spikes. Most of them recognizable as well-heeled individuals from towns that the army had already stampeded through."
This is *insanity!* What are we even still *doing* here? We've no chance against these monsters!
Not in the least! I mean, harriers...that's *one* thing! But these creatures--!
Wolves or not, our best chance is still to make for the forest. Pray we can hide there, wait them out...

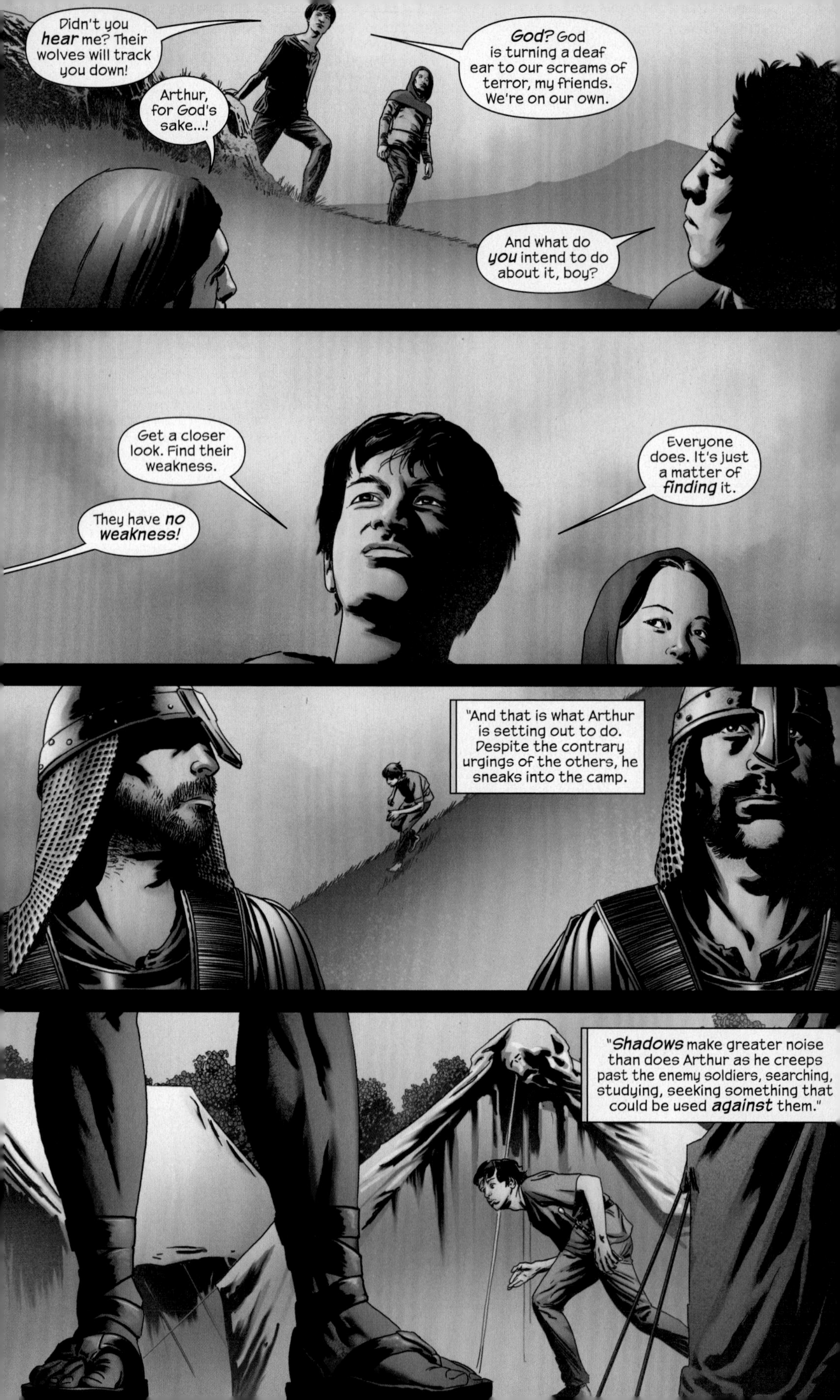

Didn't you **hear** me? Their wolves will track you down!
Arthur, for God's sake...!
God? God is turning a deaf ear to our screams of terror, my friends. We're on our own.
And what do **you** intend to do about it, boy?
Get a closer look. Find their weakness.
They have **no weakness!**
Everyone does. It's just a matter of **finding** it.
"And that is what Arthur is setting out to do. Despite the contrary urgings of the others, he sneaks into the camp.
"**Shadows** make greater noise than does Arthur as he creeps past the enemy soldiers, searching, studying, seeking something that could be used **against** them."

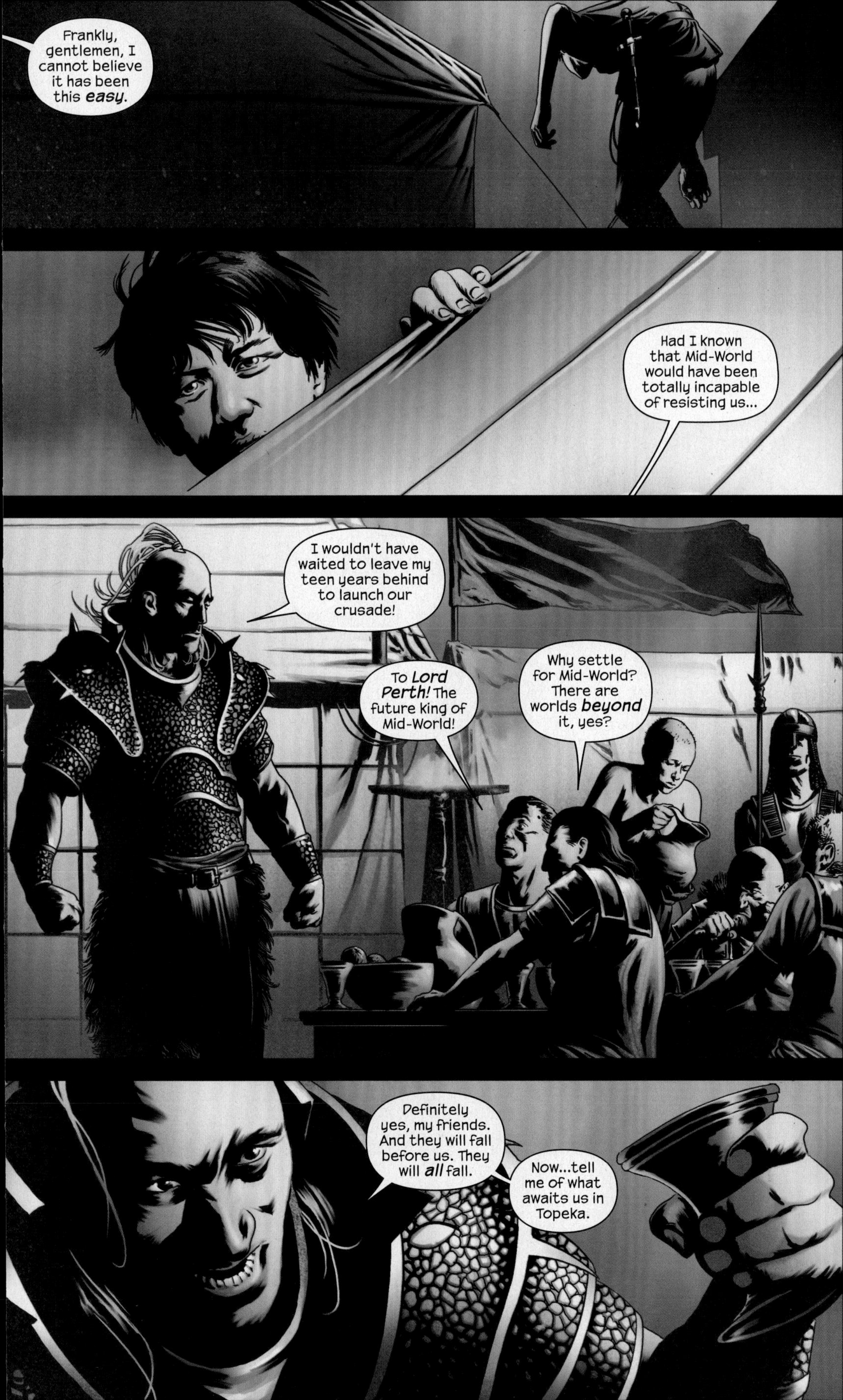

Frankly, gentlemen, I cannot believe it has been this *easy*.
Had I known that Mid-World would have been totally incapable of resisting us...
I wouldn't have waited to leave my teen years behind to launch our crusade!
To *Lord Perth!* The future king of Mid-World!
Why settle for Mid-World? There are worlds *beyond* it, yes?
Definitely yes, my friends. And they will fall before us. They will *all* fall.
Now...tell me of what awaits us in Topeka.

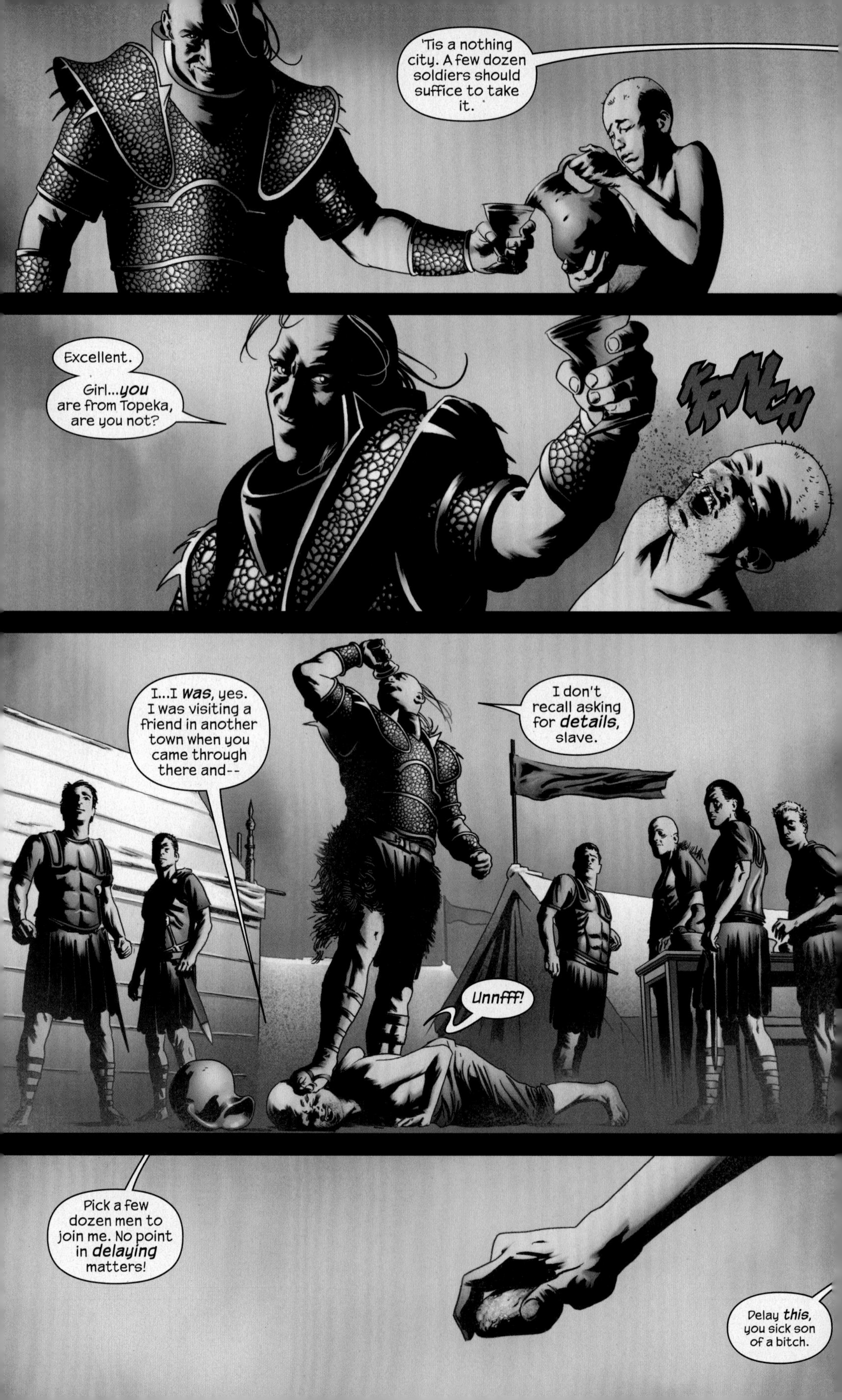
'Tis a nothing city. A few dozen soldiers should suffice to take it.
Excellent.
Girl...*you* are from Topeka, are you not?
KRNCH
I...I *was*, yes. I was visiting a friend in another town when you came through there and--
I don't recall asking for *details*, slave.
Unnfff!
Pick a few dozen men to join me. No point in *delaying* matters!
Delay *this*, you sick son of a bitch.

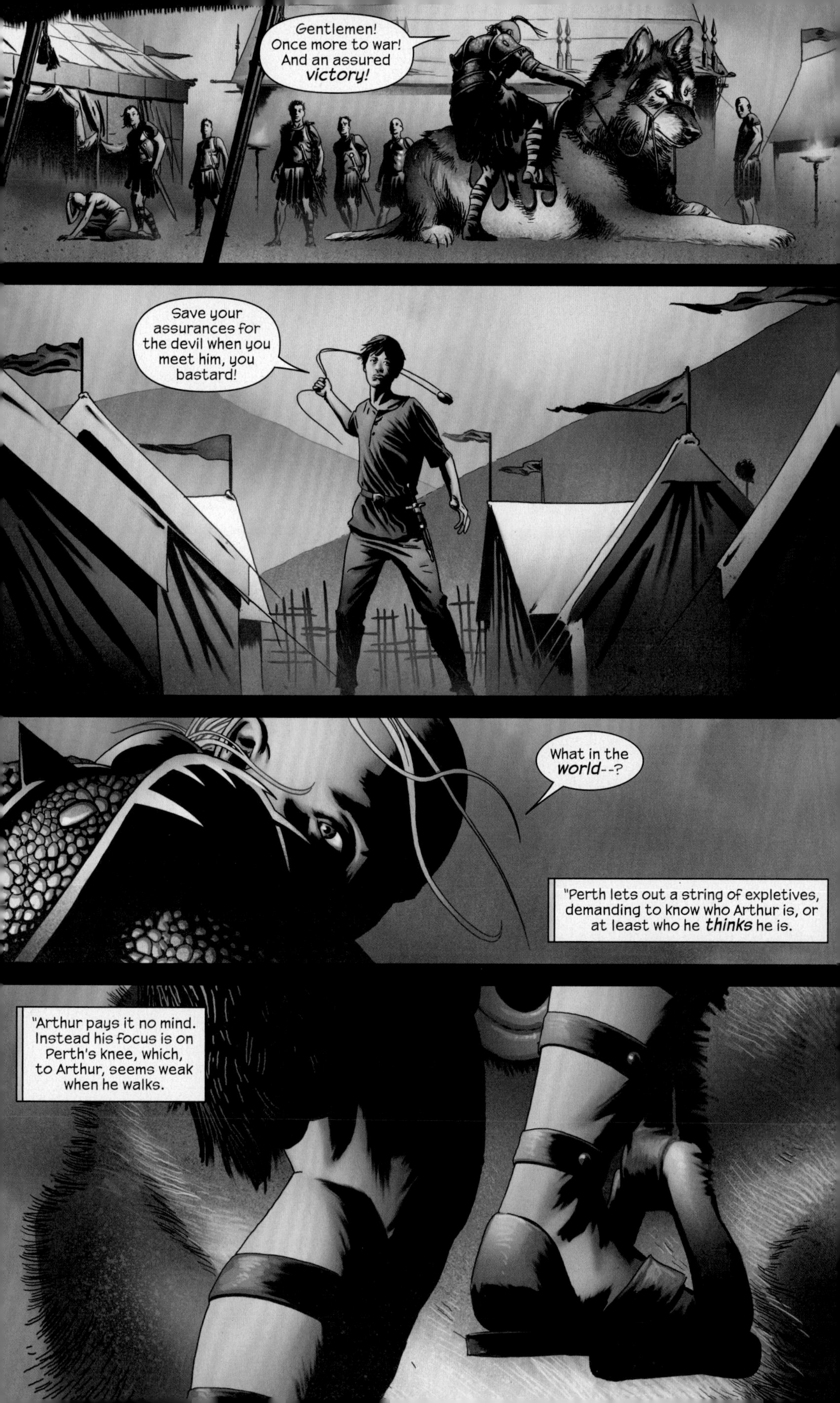
Gentlemen! Once more to war! And an assured victory!
Save your assurances for the devil when you meet him, you bastard!
What in the world--?
"Perth lets out a string of expletives, demanding to know who Arthur is, or at least who he thinks he is.
"Arthur pays it no mind. Instead his focus is on Perth's knee, which, to Arthur, seems weak when he walks.

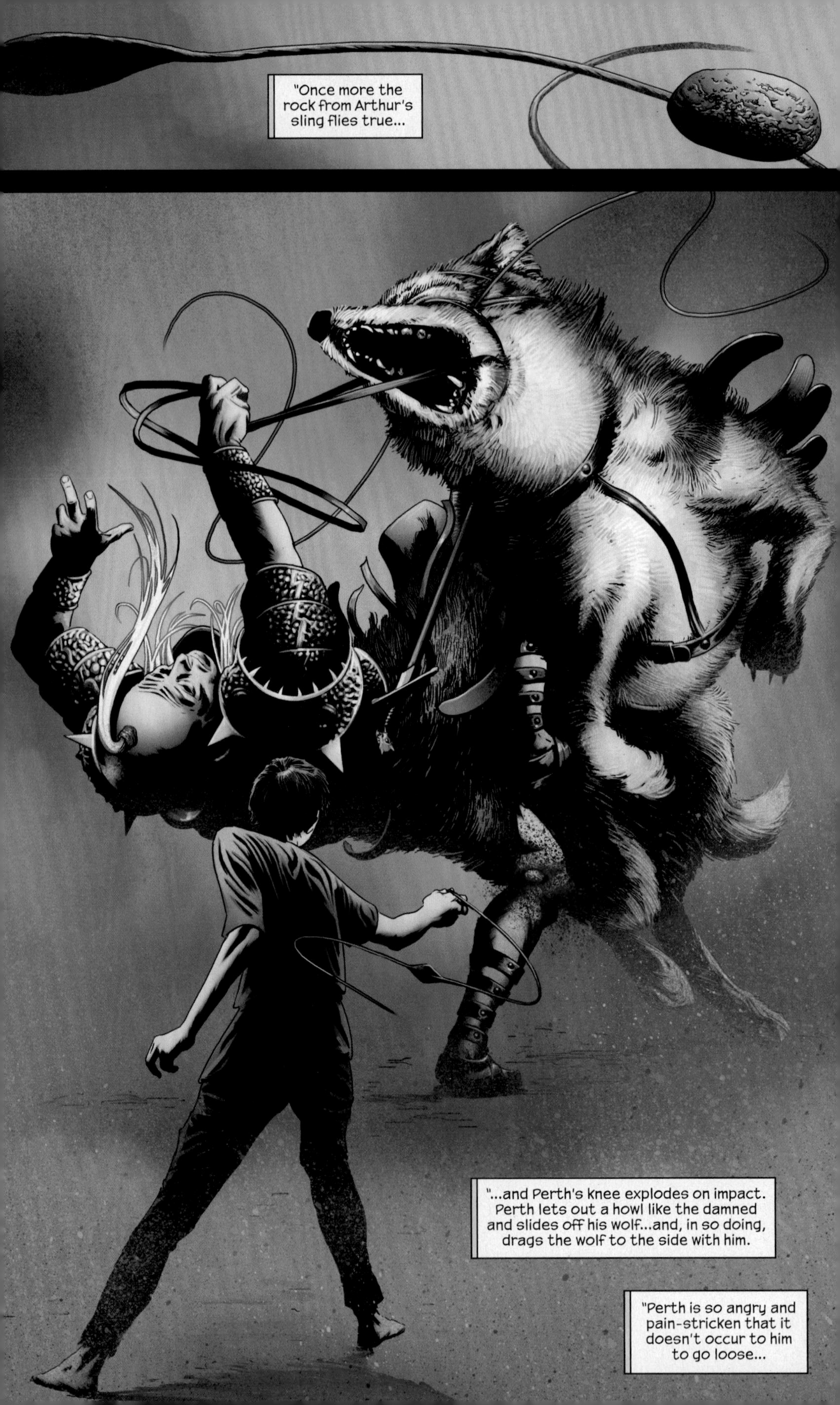
"Once more the rock from Arthur's sling flies true...
"...and Perth's knee explodes on impact. Perth lets out a howl like the damned and slides off his wolf...and, in so doing, drags the wolf to the side with him.
"Perth is so angry and pain-stricken that it doesn't occur to him to go loose...

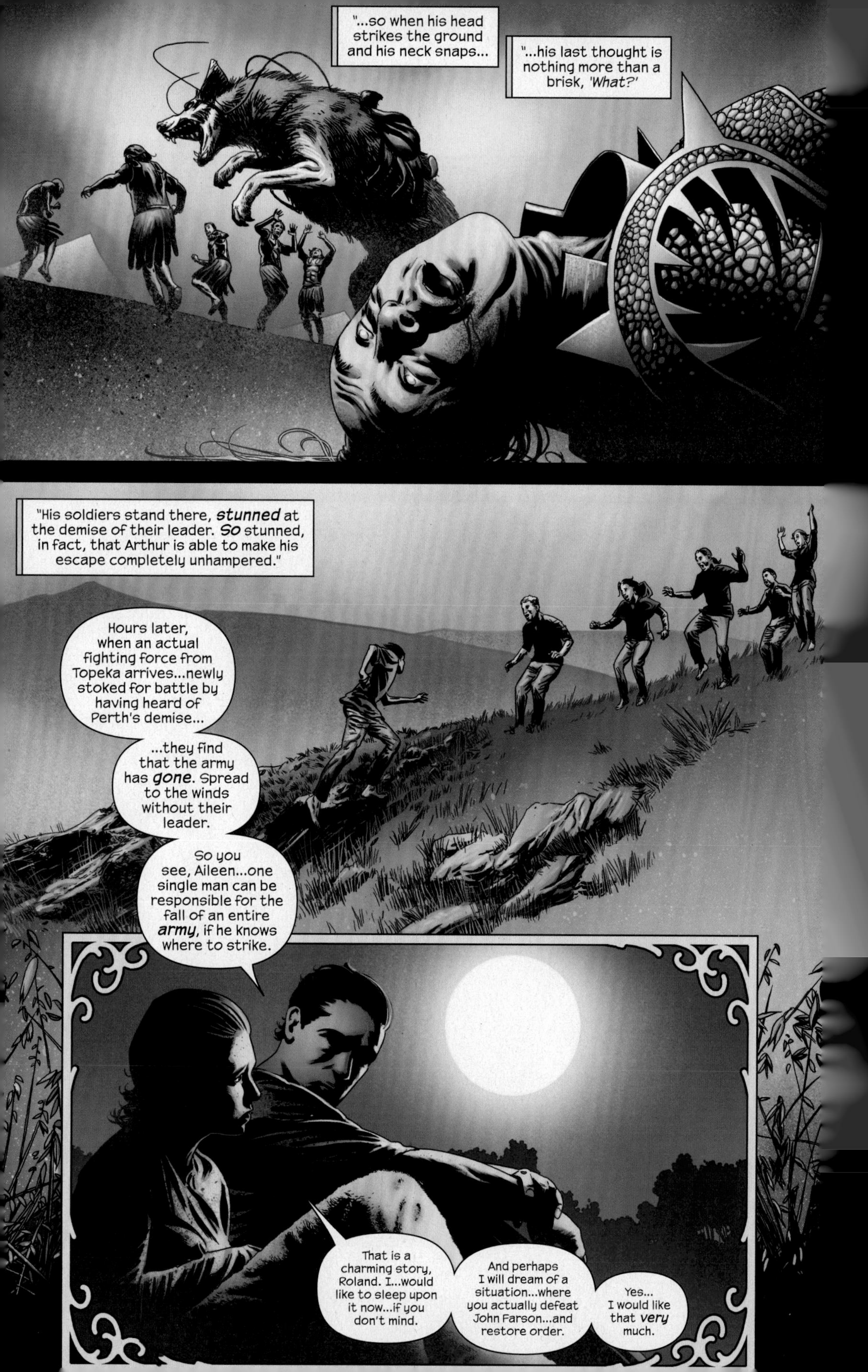
"...so when his head strikes the ground and his neck snaps...
"...his last thought is nothing more than a brisk, *'What?'*
"His soldiers stand there, ***stunned*** at the demise of their leader. ***So*** stunned, in fact, that Arthur is able to make his escape completely unhampered."
Hours later, when an actual fighting force from Topeka arrives...newly stoked for battle by having heard of Perth's demise...
...they find that the army has ***gone***. Spread to the winds without their leader.
So you see, Aileen...one single man can be responsible for the fall of an entire ***army***, if he knows where to strike.
That is a charming story, Roland. I...would like to sleep upon it now...if you don't mind.
And perhaps I will dream of a situation...where you actually defeat John Farson...and restore order.
Yes... I would like that ***very*** much.

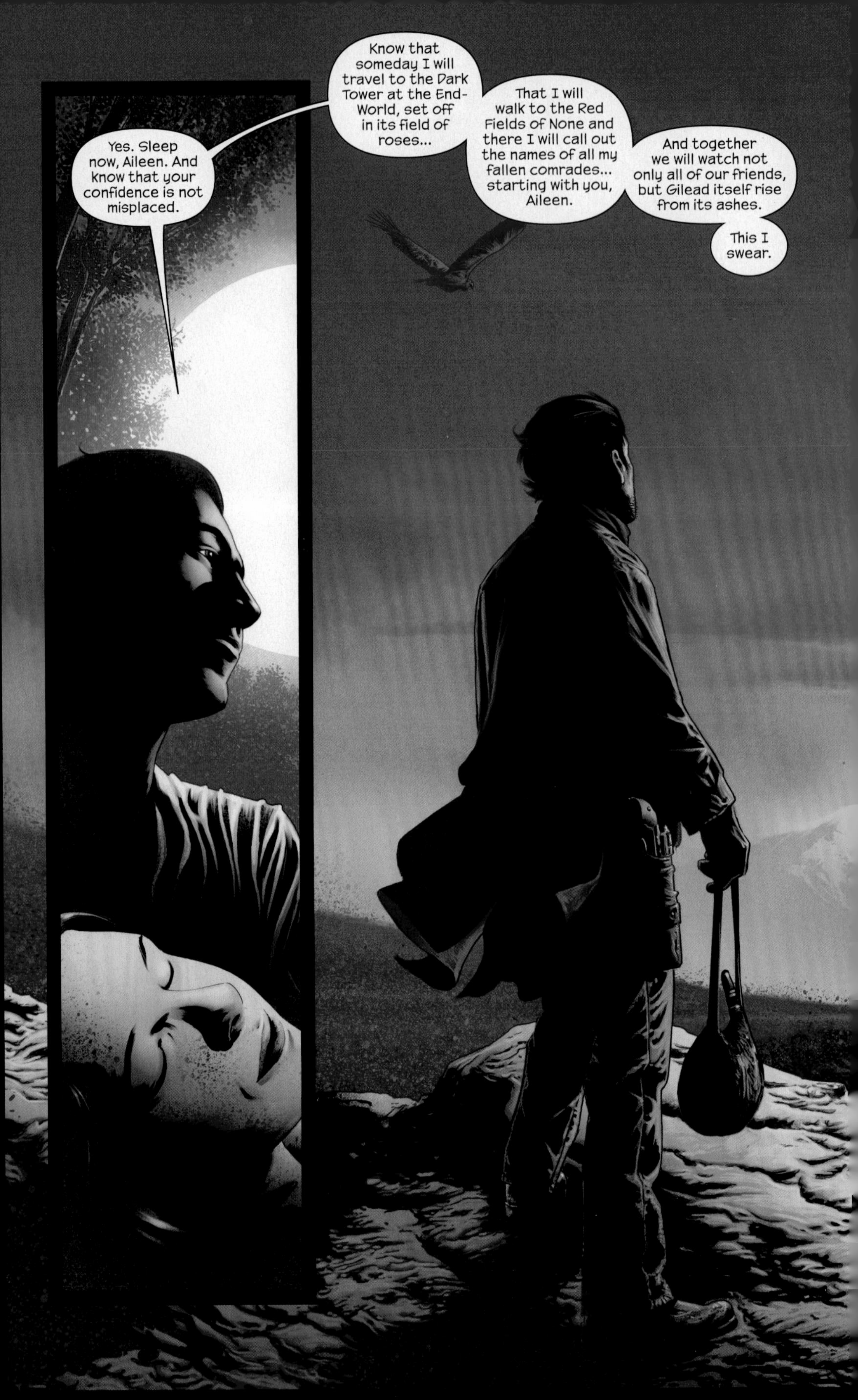
Yes. Sleep now, Aileen. And know that your confidence is not misplaced.
Know that someday I will travel to the Dark Tower at the End-World, set off in its field of roses...
That I will walk to the Red Fields of None and there I will call out the names of all my fallen comrades... starting with you, Aileen.
And together we will watch not only all of our friends, but Gilead itself rise from its ashes.
This I swear.

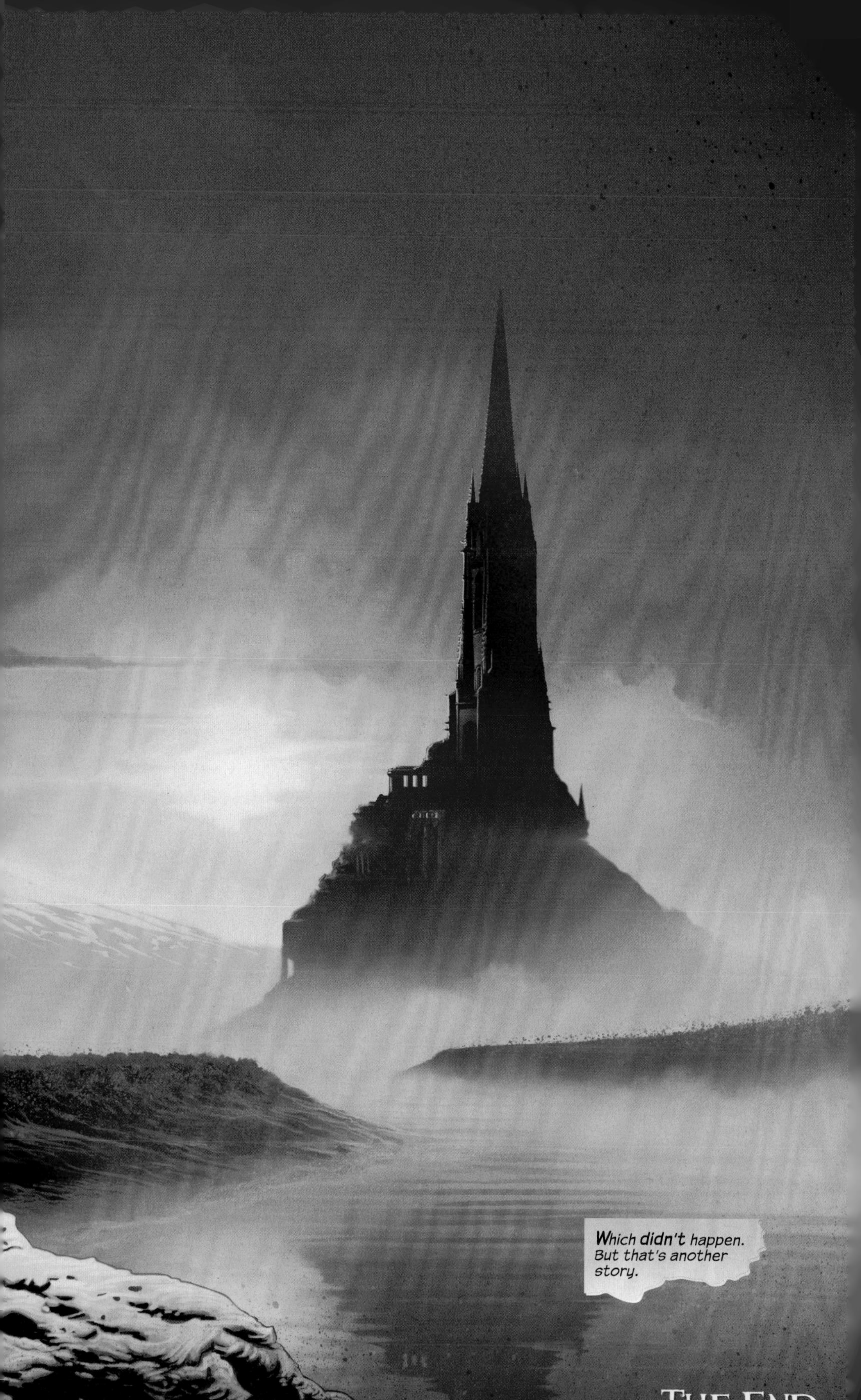
Which didn't happen. But that's another story.
THE END...

The Dark Tower: The Gunslinger — Sheemie's Tale #1 **Cover by Richard Isanove**

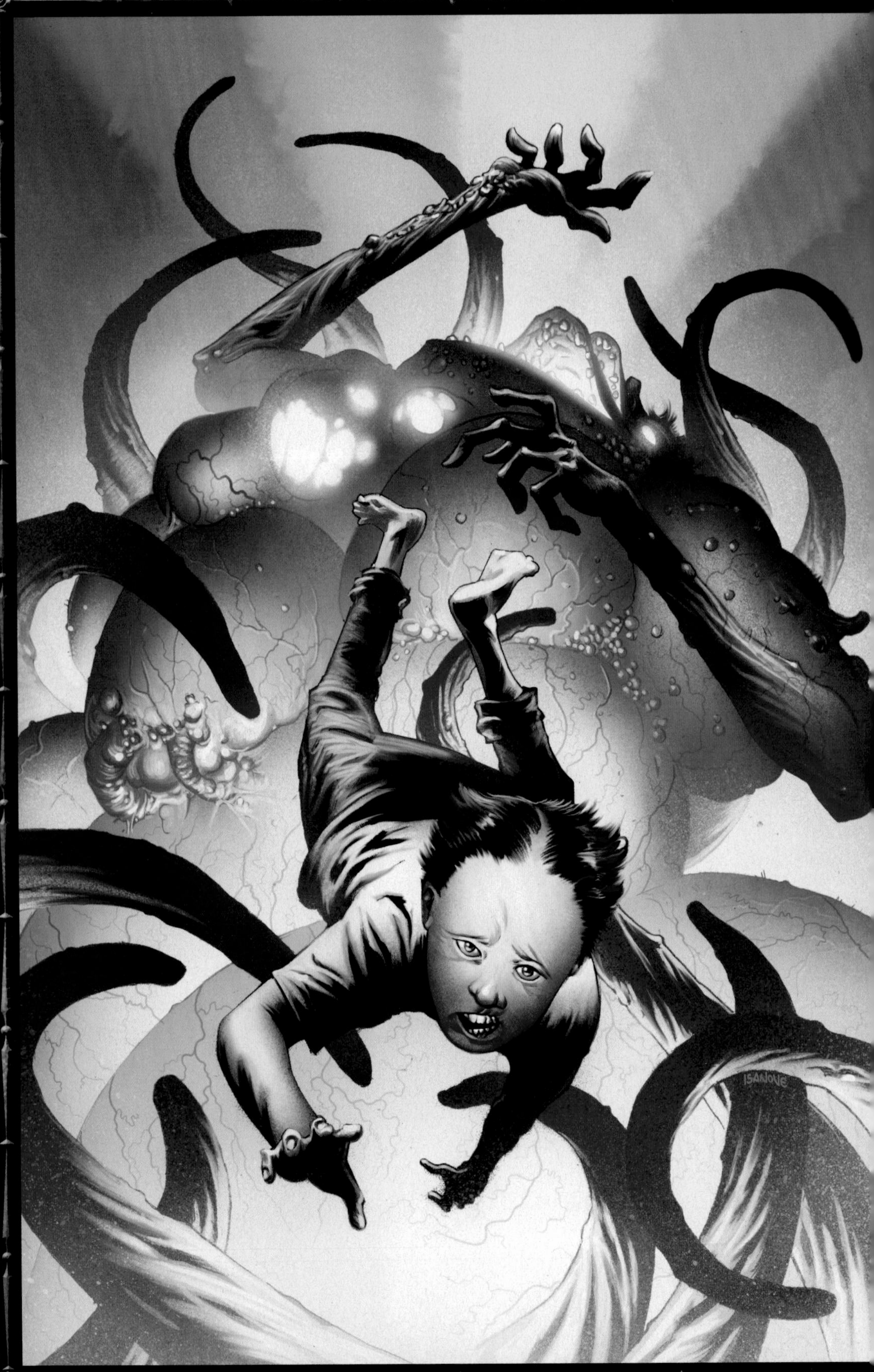

The Dark Tower: The Gunslinger — Sheemie's Tale #2 **Cover by Richard Isanove**

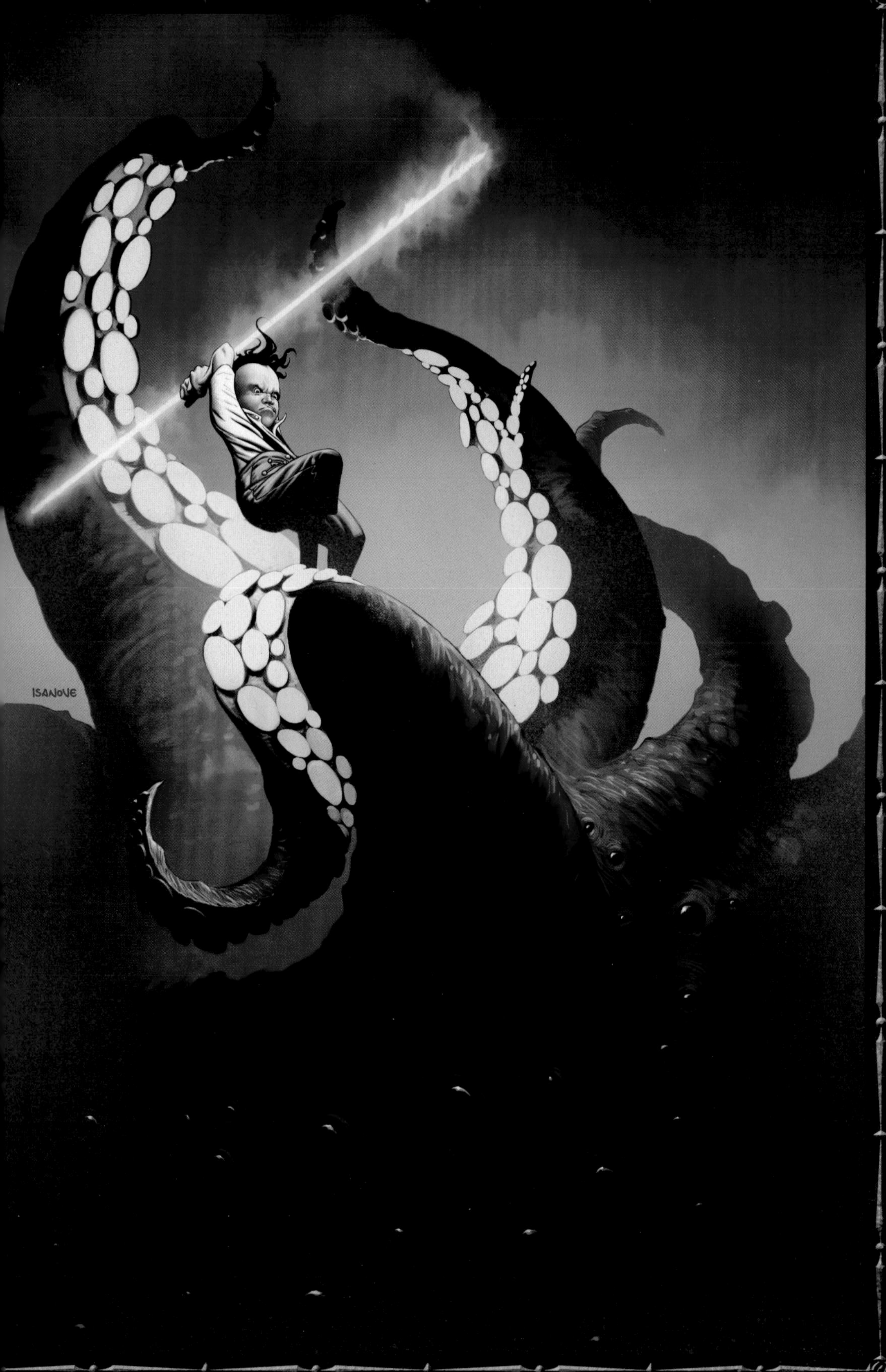
ISANOVE

The Dark Tower: The Gunslinger — Evil Ground #1 **Cover by Richard Isanove**

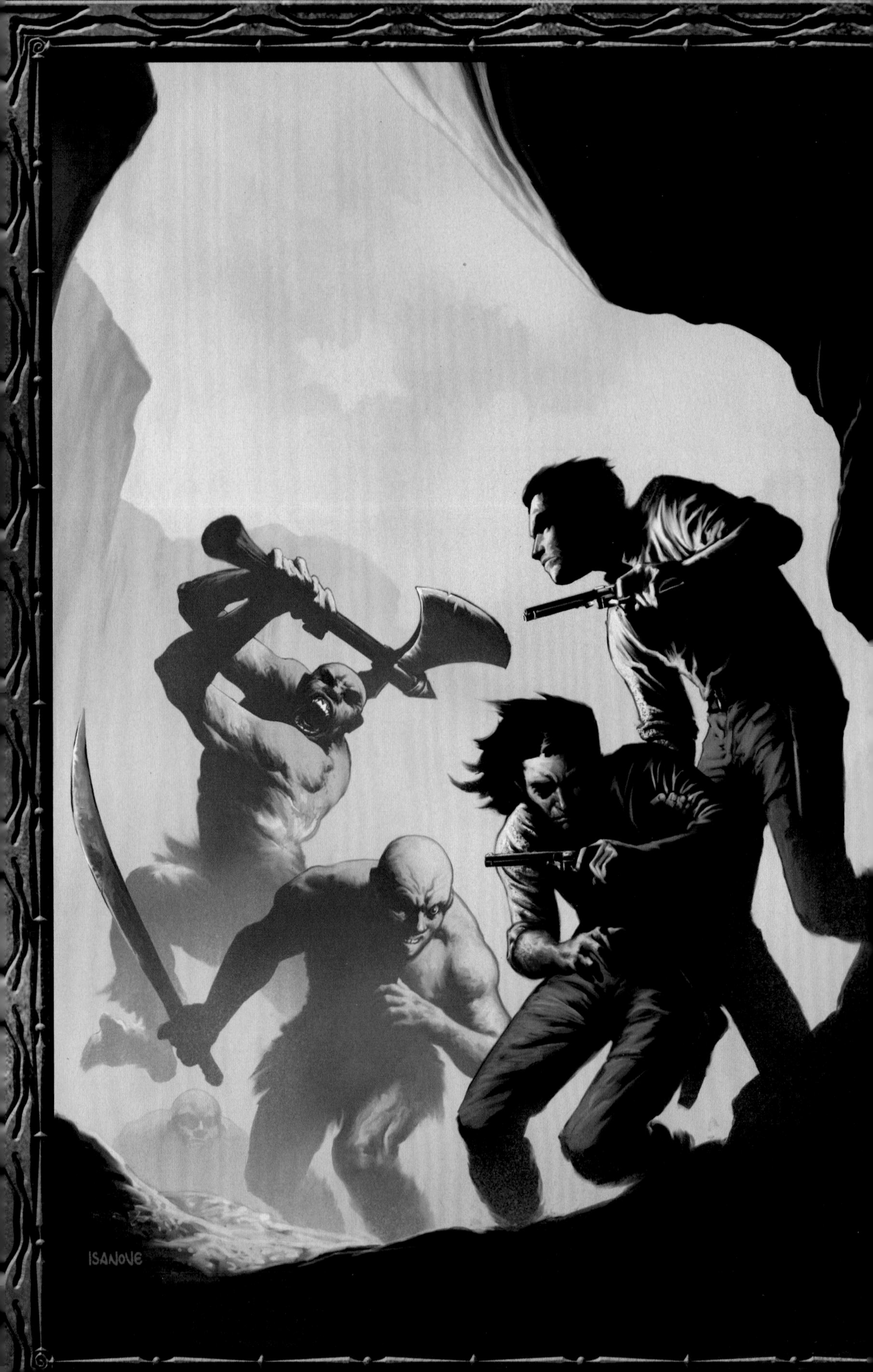
ISANOVE

The Dark Tower: The Gunslinger — Evil Ground #2 **Cover by Richard Isanove**

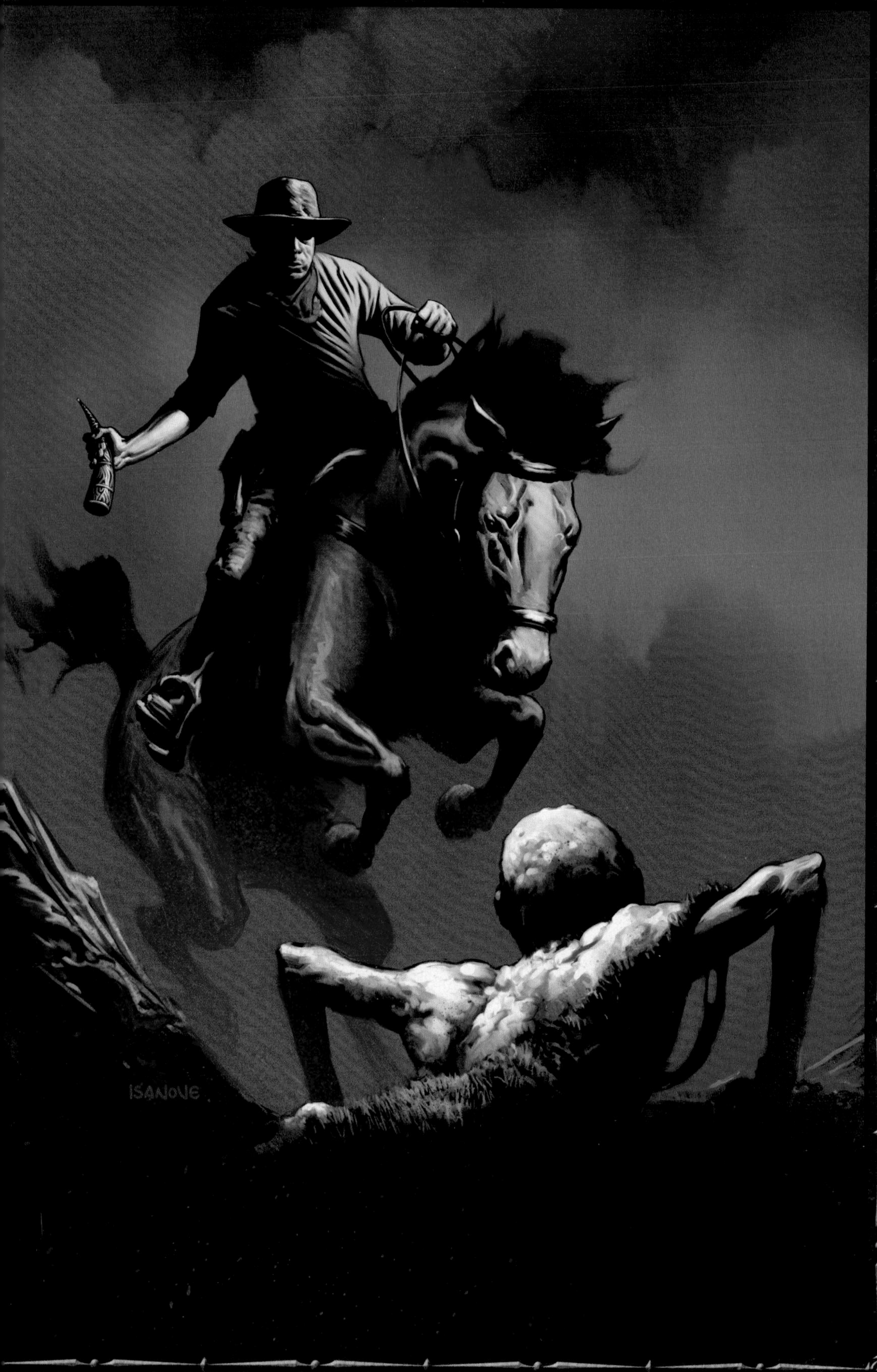
ISANOVE

The Dark Tower: The Gunslinger — So Fell Lord Perth #1 **Cover by Richard Isanove**

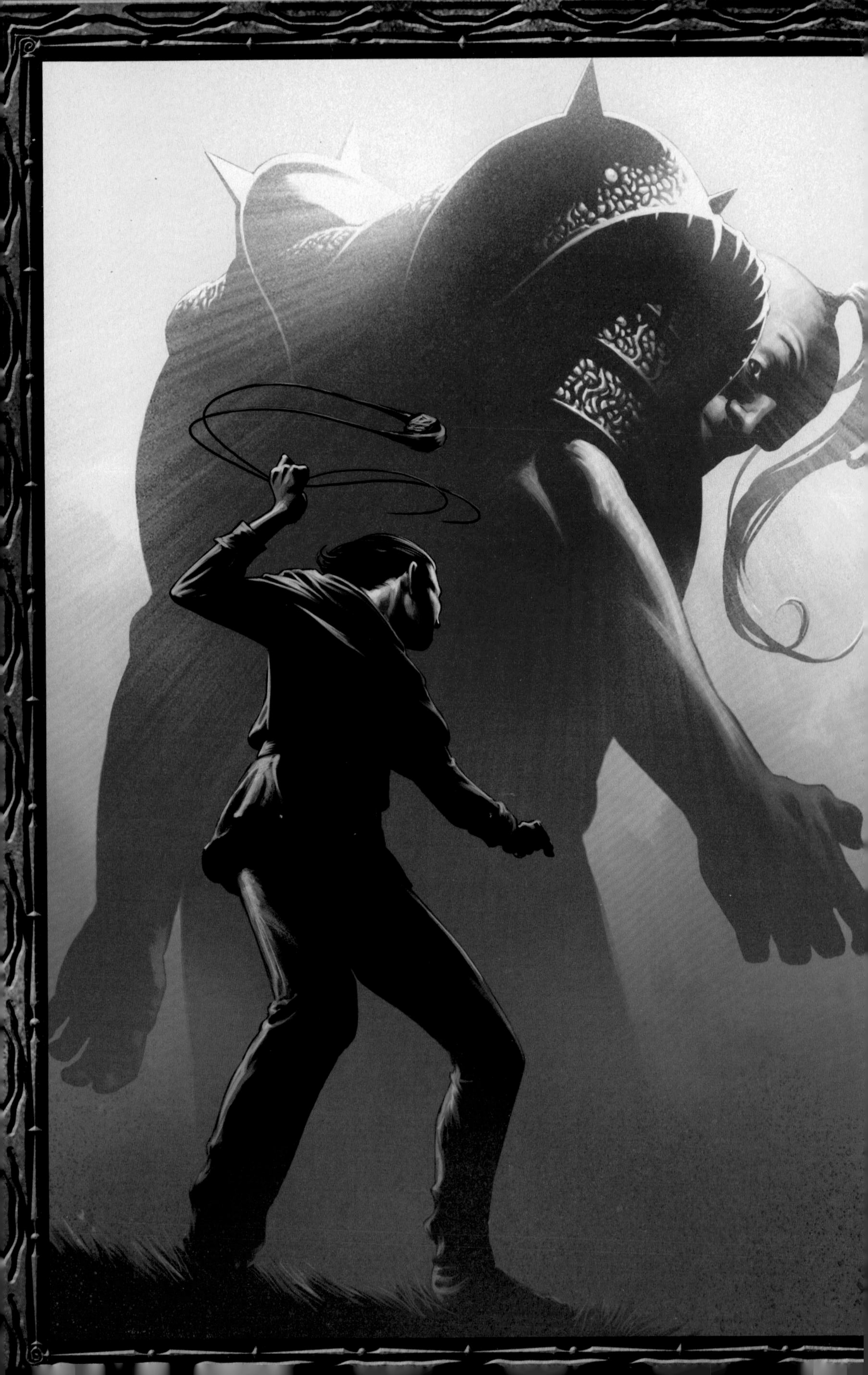